A HISTORY OF ACTFL

IN CELEBRATION OF ITS 50TH ANNIVERSARY

ACTFL

50 YEARS

MOVING FORWARD, GIVING BACK

ROBERT M. TERRY

ACTFL AMERICAN COUNCIL ON THE
TEACHING OF FOREIGN LANGUAGES

Commissioned by the American Council on the Teaching of Foreign Languages © 2016

ACTFL MISSION STATEMENT

Providing vision, leadership, and support for quality teaching and learning of languages.

ACTFL VISION STATEMENT

Believing that language and communication are at the heart of the human experience, that the U.S. must nurture and develop indigenous, immigrant, and world language resources, and that the U.S. must educate students to be linguistically and culturally prepared to function as world citizens, ACTFL is uniquely positioned to lead this endeavor by

- Meeting the needs of language professionals

- Ensuring a dynamic and responsive organization

- Working proactively through advocacy and outreach

- Working to ensure that the language-teaching profession reflects the racial, ethnic and linguistic diversity of U.S. society

- Promoting research that impacts the development of professional programs and enhances the quality of language teaching and learning.

TABLE OF CONTENTS

PREFACE

In early 2013, Marty Abbott, Executive Director of ACTFL, asked me if I would write a history of the organization as a part of its fiftieth anniversary celebration. I excitedly agreed to write this book. Then it immediately struck me that, during my formal education, history had been the bane of my academic studies. I had never been able to see the proverbial forest, because I was so interested in the trees, shrubs, and bushes that surrounded me. I knew the dates of the Yalta Conference, who had been there (FDR, Churchill, Stalin), and where they had met, but never quite grasped just why they had been meeting.

Later, in graduate school, I became interested in history… well, that history that was relevant to what I was studying: the medieval period, nineteenth-century France. And now, in my retirement from over 45 years of teaching, I find myself a part of history, a history in which I have been an active participant, the history of an organization that has grown from a mid-1960s thought, a desire, a project called Xanadu, a small dependent offshoot of the Modern Language Association to a very large, dynamic organization that has had a monumental impact on world language studies as a leader, innovator, advocate, missionary, researcher, analyst, mentor.

Getting under way with this book was quite an experience. Arriving at ACTFL headquarters in Alexandria, VA, one day in June 2013, I was confronted with a mountain of boxes that had been stored off-site ever since the transplanting of headquarters from Yonkers, NY, to Alexandria. For two days, I sorted through box after box of file folders, books, knick-knacks, fliers, brochures, journals, professional samples of textbooks, audiocassettes, tapes, filmstrips, movies, and grant proposals. Culling materials that would help me in this daunting task, I reduced the heaps to more manageable piles of… "stuff," which was then transported back to my office, where eventually it evolved into a mini-mountain of boxes, files, folders, and… "stuff."

To make work flow more smoothly, I scanned numerous documents that were handwritten, mimeographed, dittoed (remember those purple fingers and that smell?), and typed or printed. Carrying out OCR (optical character recognition) made the materials legible and more accessible. Copious note-taking and page after page of highlighted printed matter started to come together in a reasonably chronological sequence. Then, the inevitable stumbling blocks loomed: *Where can I find a photo of Emma Birkmaier? Who wrote this document…and when? Can I find a picture of ACTFL's first headquarters? How can I fill in the gaps in the photo gallery of past presidents? Is this person still alive?*

The sleuthing and detective work to answer these questions and many others was exciting. Google and Wikipedia were good beginning points. Search after search of school and college libraries and websites started to pay off. I wrote many letters to historical societies, research librarians, archivists, and friends. All who responded were most gracious and helpful, either furnishing me with what I was looking for or putting me on a more fruitful track. It is quite a task to thank each person who helped me through a list of names, but I have recognized them throughout the book.

Writing a history requires many judgment calls: Is this important or not? Should I include this or not? Have I given enough information or not? Do readers need to know this or not? Let's face it: everything cannot be said or included. If I am guilty, I am guilty of saying too little rather than too much. I can assure you, however, that you will know far more about ACTFL than you did before you began to read this book.

On April 25, 2014, Marty Abbott sent me the following message about the history book: "Ed [Scebold] would be really happy that you are the one doing this!!!" That was all I needed to hear. Ed Scebold and I were very good friends, and our friendship went back to the early 1970s. We often worked, traveled, roomed, ate, and laughed together. It was his dream to see ACTFL become a major force in the field of world languages. He also wanted ACTFL to have its own "home"—a headquarters building. His death in September 2001 was unexpected and devastating.

ACTFL has survived, has prospered, and is thriving. Ed would truly be happy.

Robert M. Terry
April 15, 2016

Students in a foreign language laboratory at Syracuse University follow lessons through headphones, 1966. ACTFL was established that year to further expand and professionalize the teaching of foreign languages, which had been growing since the early 1950s.

CHAPTER 1

THE 1960s

The Problem and the Challenge

In August 13, 1963, Kenneth W. Mildenberger, Director of the Division of College and University Assistance at the Department of Health, Education, and Welfare, delivered the summer commencement speech at Middlebury College in Vermont. He lamented the lack of "private enterprise" in foreign language training and teaching, mentioning the "seemingly bountiful Federal funds" that were available for summer language study. He pointed out the impact on American education the National Defense Education Act (NDEA) had had since 1958. With this sudden influx of federal funds and the numerous NDEA activities, Mildenberger pointed out that the statistics about these activities should awe those present as much as they did him. Yet, he spoke of a specter that those in Washington were constantly eying uneasily:

"What we fear is that the private sector in your profession, out of awe and satisfaction, will be uncritical and will, by silence, desert its proper role of policy leadership."

In Washington, an advisory committee of eminent scholars and educational administrators was set up to advise the Commissioner of Education on language matters. Stephen A. Freeman of Middlebury College was called upon to given the independent, candid, and scrupulous professional direction that was needed for guidance with the NDEA program.

But Mildenberger was still bothered by the "immense stillness of the profession." The Modern Language Association's (MLA) Foreign Language Program of the 1950s had apparently settled all of the questions of the language field. All that was needed, then, was for government funds to implement the foreign language program policies; then American education would be fully served.

He then asked, "What has happened to the private sector and its leadership in policy-making?" The Foreign Language Program of MLA had begun in 1952 and, insofar as its

Kenneth W. Mildenberger

original objectives were concerned, ended in 1958 with six years of support from the Rockefeller Foundation. This Foreign Language Program was an amazing educational phenomenon—it began when modern foreign language study in the American educational system was at rock-bottom. The Program mobilized professional leadership, made foreign language in the elementary school (FLES) a national issue, and developed basic policies concerning language instruction in secondary schools. Leaders in the language profession were constantly consulted. The Program assembled the facts about the critical meaning of language instruction to our national interest and communicated them to the world of professional education, to the general public, and to Congress. In fact, in 1958, the United States Commissioner of Education affirmed that, had it not been for the MLA Foreign Language Program, foreign languages might not even have been a part of the NDEA.

Indeed, the Foreign Language Program examined the needs for modern foreign languages in American society, developed the profession's policies regarding the means by which these needs could be met, and made a start at implementing such policies. Consequently, the Foreign Language Program was so successful that its original objectives had been consummated, and now it had taken its place in history … past history.

The NDEA program's bounty had altered the state of affairs in the modern foreign language field, and it was now time for a new taking of stock. What was needed now was a comprehensive reassessment of where we had come from and where we should be going in the next decade…indeed, in the next 25 years. This new major investigation of modern foreign language study at all levels of American education had to begin soon…very soon.

Such an investigation was both the duty and privilege of the private sector, not to be initiated by or even paid for by the federal government, according to Mildenberger. The private sector had to fashion such an investigation, and its leadership had to have the vision, wisdom, scholarship, and stamina to face this professional task. He warned, "Unless the language profession seizes the initiative in this immediately, other forces will necessarily move into the void"— the kind of enterprise and independence Middlebury College was demonstrating on that Vermont hillside.

Alea iacta est [The die is cast] — Action

On November 9, 1963, the Advisory Committee of the Foreign Language Program of MLA examined the direction it thought the Program should take in the period ahead. Increased emphasis had to be devoted to two areas for which funds were available: the preparation of foreign language teachers and the development of materials for teaching "culture" courses. The Advisory Committee also recommended that the Foreign Language Program devote immediate attention to an evaluation of past accomplishments and future needs of the language development titles of NDEA. In addition, if funding could be arranged, staff work provided, and commissions established, the Program should devote attention to:

1. the improvement of conditions and controls for study abroad by teachers and future teachers;
2. international education cooperation;
3. teaching English as a Second Language (ESL) to non-English-speaking Americans, and conserving the foreign language resources of Americans whose native language was not English;
4. programmed instruction; and
5. small group projects on areas such as useful descriptive grammars of the commonly taught languages, agreement on advanced levels of language courses, the types of courses taken as third or fourth languages, and a competent

authoritative paperback instructing adults how to go about learning a foreign language on their own.

The Foreign Language Program Advisory Committee made a statement of qualifications for a first-time full-time college teacher of modern foreign languages:

1. Competence in the major foreign language.
2. Ability to plan and conduct first- and second-year courses in that language.
3. Knowledge about current methods of language instruction.
4. Ability to convey some knowledge of the culture of the people studied.
5. Ability to present effectively in the foreign language the literary masterpieces studied in lower-division courses.

The MLA Foreign Language Program was still acting on behalf of the profession. No other members or organizations in the private sector had stepped forth to share and/or assume the charge that had been leveled to the profession.

On October 12, 1965, after returning to MLA from his service in the U.S. Office of Education, Mildenberger set forth plans for a program for expediting curricular reform in modern foreign languages: the Xanadu Project. On November 12-13, the project's first draft was brought to the Foreign Language Program Advisory Committee for their reaction and thoughts. Citing the progress of foreign language instruction in North Carolina and several other states, Mildenberger mentioned the preoccupation of professional vigor with "churning expansion" that had overshadowed examination of some fundamental problems: "The sudden flowering of modern foreign language study in recent years may wither unless a sound integrated national effort is made to interpret and consolidate advances while identifying the key critical areas requiring further research and experimentation." He warned that this happy progress might be "a tragic exercise in futility" unless consummate efforts were made to: (1) assimilate everything that had been learned about the modern foreign language curriculum in schools, and (2) make these findings available "in an immediately usable form" to American school systems seeking to improve their language curricula.

Whose responsibility was the planning of such curricular development? Local officials and faculty? State departments of education? Consultants from institutes of higher education? Supplementary educational centers supported with federal funds from Title III or the Elementary and Secondary Education Act of 1965? Wherever the responsibility might lie, nothing satisfactory could be done because one fundamental consideration had not yet received serious attention: "the absence of fuller definition of levels of learning, or terminal goals, in the various stages of the foreign language curriculum."

Mildenberger proposed a plan that, over three years, would seek to mobilize all relevant resources into the development of a program to meet the urgent situation. He advocated a plan for orderly, productive curricular reform in foreign language teaching that must be adaptable to newer formulations and clarifications of national needs, to different and changing local conditions, to the goals of instruction in both schools and colleges, and to the special problems posed by different languages and different learners. This plan had to also include effective instruments for its own evolution in light of new knowledge, which implied a developing research base. For such a plan to succeed, collaboration among the most productive of university scholars and most forward-looking teachers and administrators was essential. Such collaboration would suggest short-range changes and an evolving research base grounded on the problems of the learner observed while going through the learning process and the research insights whose results could be tested in the schools.

Mildenberger's proposal set out to accomplish these outcomes:

1. Preparation of a set of tool publications for investigating and improving a school system's modern foreign language curriculum; these tools were designated as:
   a. the curriculum rationale;
   b. curriculum planning guides for French, German, and Spanish that were not autonomously prescriptive; and
   c. a documentation bank, in which all relevant bibliography would be recorded and annotated and all conference and consultant recommendations reproduced.
2. Identification of many areas in which research and experimentation were needed.
3. Initiation of a newsletter for disseminating information, inviting comments and criticism, and cultivating the potential for research in areas with gaps.
4. Implementation of a comprehensive plan for using the tool publications in reviewing and developing language curricula.

Now that a plan was in place, how would it be carried out? Who were the key players who would realize it? Would the "private sector" step up and accept its challenge?

The Idea of ACTFL

On October 14, 1966, the Executive Council of MLA issued a policy statement on the creation of the American Council on the Teaching of Foreign Languages. To maintain and further the remarkable rise of interest in both the study and teaching of foreign languages from the early 1950s to 1966, the MLA took the responsibility for beginning such an organization and for giving it continued support. The MLA's membership was 24,000 in 1966, having quadrupled in 20 years, and it could call upon impressive professional resources that could nurture an organization for foreign language teaching. The MLA's own Foreign Language Program, begun in 1952, had sought to make foreign language instruction an effective component in American education.

Yet the MLA did not consider the battle won. Now it was time to create an individual-membership organization "in which all persons and groups interested in the quality of foreign language teaching might participate directly." This organization would be called the American Council on the Teaching of Foreign Languages (ACTFL). "It will provide an institutional center for the new professionalism that has developed since 1952 among foreign language teachers and supervisors in public and private education on all levels and in college faculty responsible for the preparation of teachers."

The Executive Council of the MLA established the Foreign Language Program Advisory Committee with appropriate additions to its membership to form the Committee on Organization for ACTFL and set up guidelines for organizing this new group of foreign language professionals.

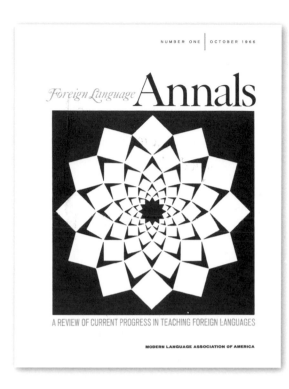

EDITORIAL COMMENT

Quite frankly, this is an experimental publication, and we hope you will forgive the rough edges in this modest beginning. We are seeking to develop a new kind of medium for reaching members of the language-teaching profession at all levels of education (and everyone else with an interest in foreign language instruction) with news and information of immediate significance to all. (Right now, the most important news is the initiation of the MLA/ERIC Clearinghouse on the Teaching of Foreign Languages, described elsewhere in this issue.)

We do not intend the title of this publication to seem pretentious. *Foreign Language Annals* is, as the sub-heading explains, a review of current progress in foreign language teaching—a chronicle of useful current information about the profession of foreign language teaching. The three holes punched in this copy symbolize the nature of this continuing venture; a ring-back binder will help store issues conveniently and prevent their loss in a drawer or among a pile of miscellaneous papers.

You may wonder how issue Number One has come into your hands. The mailing list consisted of (1) recipients of state foreign language newsletters (insofar as their editors were able to assist us), (2) all foreign language teachers who belong to the MLA and are resident in the United States, and (3) various other special mailing lists. The MLA financed the publication of 50,000 copies. All of these have been distributed, so if a foreign language colleague failed to receive a copy and is concerned, tell him to send us his mailing address and state simply that he did not receive issue Number One; we'll put him on the list. If by chance you received an extra copy, please pass it on to a neglected colleague. And if you have any ideas for making *Foreign Language Annals* more useful, please let us know; we especially appreciate thoughtful letters, critical or complimentary, which do not call for personal reply.

Finally, let's be very honest with you. The MLA cannot continue to prepare and dispatch 50,000 gratis copies of this publication for very long. We plan two or three issues this academic year, at no cost to recipients. If after that it appears desirable to continue, we'll have to ask for a modest subscription fee from those who are interested.

Kenneth W. Mildenberger
Director of Programs, MLA

Mildenberger, in an address to the Foreign Language Program General Session of the Annual Meeting of the MLA on December 29, 1966, spoke of "Prospects for a Unified Profession":

By "unified profession" I mean a national community of teachers of any and all foreign languages at all levels of education genuinely and actively concerned with common pedagogical and professional problems, as well as with scholarly interests… Only an organized and unified profession will be able to contend with, and indeed utilize, the powerful pressures that are closing in around us.

He enumerated some of the pressing problems that demanded national attention:

- FLES
- Articulation
- Sequence of language learning
- Certification
- The adequate preparation of new school teachers
- The adequate preparation of new college teachers
- The role of culture in the language classroom
- The psychology of language learning
- Study abroad
- Flexible scheduling
- Junior high schools
- The role of language instruction in the rapidly expanding junior college
- Bilingualism in American society
- Educational television
- Self-instruction

Foreign Language Annals, the MLA newsletter — Number 1 (October 1966)

Editorial Comment from *Foreign Language Annals,* Volume I, Number 1 (October 1967), inside front cover

In October 1966, the first issue of *Foreign Language Annals* (the MLA newsletter, not the future ACTFL professional journal) was sent out to more than 60,000 teachers (see p. 5). Its subhead called it "a review of current progress in teaching foreign languages." This was the newsletter Mildenberger discussed in the Xanadu Project in 1965, and he was editor of this newsletter while serving as Director of Programs at MLA. In his address at the MLA in December, he said this was the first time so many foreign language teachers—from graduate school to elementary school—shared the same information simultaneously.

Mildenberger believed this new organization, ACTFL, would provide an institutional center for the new professionalism that had developed since 1952, with the establishment of the MLA Foreign Language Program among foreign language teachers and supervisors in public and private education on all levels and among college faculty responsible for teacher preparation (*Modern Language Journal* (March 1967) Vol. LI, No. 3, pp. 169-173). He concluded his 1966 MLA address with this hope: "ACTFL is now an empty vessel, waiting to be filled with sound ideas, hard work, and progress. I pray that it will not turn out to be just a ceremonial association" (*Modern Language Journal* (March 1967) Vol. LI, No. 3, p. 173).

One cannot help but notice the mention of the establishment of the MLA/ERIC Clearinghouse on the Teaching of Foreign Languages, one of the tool publications Mildenberger had mentioned in the Xanadu Project. This clearinghouse "collects research and related information dealing with the teaching of the modern foreign languages commonly offered in American education — i.e., French, German, Italian, Russian, Spanish — and Latin and Classical Greek."

Work had begun on ACTFL. In its October 14, 1966, meeting, the MLA Executive Council authorized the establishment of ACTFL and invited the National Federation of Modern Language Teachers Associations (NFMLTA) to be a co-founder. At the NFMLTA's Executive Committee meeting in December 1966, a resolution was unanimously passed accepting this invitation, putting its *Modern Language Journal* at ACTFL's disposal as soon as appropriate, and representing each AAT that was at that time a constituent member of the Federation (AATF, AATG, AATI, AATSP, and AATSEEL) by one delegate on the ACTFL Board of Directors.

Later that day, the Committee on Organization for ACTFL approved the resolution as set forth by the Federation. A deadline of June 30, 1967, was set for the vote by constituent NFMLTA members in hope that, upon ratification by two-thirds of the eleven constituent associations, the *Modern Language Journal* would be legally transferred to ACTFL before September 1, 1967, and would be published after that date as an official organ of ACTFL.

Regrettably, in the six months between the NFMLTA resolution and the deadline date, the NFMLTA Executive Committee was unable to agree upon a satisfactory means for implementing the transfer of the *Modern Language Journal* to ACTFL. The proposal that each constituent AAT be authorized a delegate on the ACTFL Board of Directors was accepted by the Committee on Organization, and formal invitations to that effect were issued by the acting ACTFL Executive Secretary, F. André Paquette.

The second issue of the *Foreign Language Annals* newsletter was mailed out to more than 85,000 teachers in April 1967. At that time, Mildenberger explained in his second editorial that the MLA Executive Council had authorized the establishment of ACTFL, that the NFMLTA had voted to be a co-founder of ACTFL, and that, upon ratification of the resolution, ACTFL's members would receive the *Modern Language Journal* and *Foreign Language Annals*, "an occasional newsletter of significant current announcements." He ended his editorial with the statement, "The success of ACTFL will depend upon maximum participation. It offers teachers of all languages — modern and classical — at all levels of instruction, who are concerned about pedagogical and professional affairs, the opportunity to unite for progress. Isn't it worth a try?" (*Foreign Language Annals*, Number 2 (April 1967), p. 2)

Inserted in the center of this Number 2 issue of *Foreign Language Annals* was a message from John Hurt Fisher, Executive Secretary of the Modern Language Association, in which he explained the process underway to establish ACTFL, discussed the benefits of joining it, mentioned the proposed ACTFL publications, announced the first annual meeting in Chicago in December 1967 as well as the proposed professional activities, and included a membership form, with the annual dues listed as $4. Also included were the Policy Statement on the Creation of ACTFL and the MLA Executive Committee Guidelines for Organizing ACTFL.

MLA EXECUTIVE COUNCIL GUIDELINES FOR ORGANIZING ACTFL

1. The MLA secretariat is authorized to initiate immediately necessary steps to organize a new association with individual membership open to persons engaged in the teaching or supervision of any foreign language at any level of education and to all others interested in the improvement of such teaching.

2. The new organization shall be called the *American Council on the Teaching of Foreign Languages (ACTFL)*. ACTFL will seek to become a unifying focus for efforts to advance pedagogical and professional aspects of the teaching of all foreign languages at all levels.

3. The present membership of the MLA Foreign Language Program Advisory Committee, with appropriate additional individuals, shall be constituted the Committee on Organization for ACTFL, with the term of office of the present members to extend through 31 December 1968, or until such time as a constitutional governing body of ACTFL shall succeed it. Until that time, the Committee on Organization shall perform the regular functions of the MLA Foreign Language Program Advisory Committee and also have authority to direct the work of ACTFL. If the Committee on Organization in its development of an ACTFL constitution determines that any significant modifications of these guidelines are advisable, the Committee shall present such modifications to the MLA Executive Council for approval.

4. Until such time as it may wish to incorporate as a separate nonprofit organization, ACTFL shall be considered part of the MLA, under the MLA charter, as a nonprofit organization.

5. The MLA shall provide the necessary funds for ACTFL staff and developmental activities, and income to ACTFL shall accrue to the MLA treasury. The MLA Treasurer shall be Treasurer of ACTFL until such time as ACTFL may wish to incorporate as a separate organization.

6. Until an elected Executive Committee of ACTFL exists and meets to take appropriate action, the MLA Executive Council shall appoint the ACTFL Executive Secretary and the Editor of the ACTFL periodical(s) and other publications. [At its 13-14 October 1966 meeting the MLA Executive Council appointed F. André Paquette Executive Secretary and Kenneth Mildenberger Editor.]

7. The policy making and administration of ACTFL will reside in three bodies: an Advisory Assembly, a Board of Directors, and an Executive Committee.

8. The Advisory Assembly will be made up of delegates from regional and national organizations of teachers of foreign languages which become affiliated with ACTFL. The Committee on Organization will review applications for such affiliation until an elected ACTFL Executive Committee is operative. Annual dues for affiliated organizations will be $25.00. Delegates to the Advisory Assembly and all individuals on the governing bodies of affiliated organizations must hold ACTFL membership. The Advisory Assembly will meet annually to discuss current issues concerned with foreign language teaching and to make appropriate recommendations to the ACTFL Board of Directors. The President-Elect of ACTFL will preside at meetings of the Advisory Assembly.

9. The Board of Directors will be responsible for the general management of ACTFL and will consist of representatives of all state foreign language associations which become constituent units of ACTFL. In order to qualify for constituent status, a state association must meet the following conditions: membership must be open to teachers of all languages at all levels of instruction from both public and private institutions; it must not impose requirement of membership in any national organization upon its own members; all members of its governing body and its representative(s) on the ACTFL Board of Directors must be members of ACTFL. The Committee on Organization will review applications of state associations until an elected ACTFL Executive Committee is operative. There will be no annual dues for constituent state associations. Each constituent state association shall be entitled to one voting representative on the Board of Directors. However, when the number of ACTFL members resident in a state exceeds 1,000, the constituent association for that state will be entitled to an additional voting Board representative, whether or not all the ACTFL members are also members of the constituent state association; and for each 1,000 additional ACTFL members in a state, the constituent state association will be entitled to another voting representative on the Board. The President of ACTFL will preside at annual meetings of the Board of Directors. The Directors will discuss the affairs of ACTFL and make recommendations for implementation by the Executive Committee. Annually, the Board of Directors will elect a nominating committee to choose from the membership of ACTFL a President, a President-Elect, and a Vice President for ACTFL.

10. The Executive Committee will administer the affairs of ACTFL and oversee its policies and finances. It will appoint the Executive Secretary, Editor, and other major officials, and conduct the business of ACTFL between meetings of the Board of Directors. The membership of the Executive Committee will be the President, President-Elect, Vice President, and seven members elected for staggered terms of three years by mail ballot from the ACTFL membership at large, from a slate prepared by the Executive Committee, with provision for nomination by petition (but until ACTFL is financially self-supporting, three of the seven shall be appointed by the MLA Executive Council). The Executive Secretary, Treasurer, and Editor of ACTFL publications will be, *ex officio*, nonvoting members of the Executive Committee.

11. ACTFL will accept individual membership dues, Advisory Assembly dues, and institutional subscriptions effective September 1967, and an ACTFL publication shall be issued initially in September 1967, with at least six numbers projected during academic year 1967-68.

From *Foreign Language Annals*, Volume I, Number 2 (April 1967), p. 5.

Foreign Language Annals and ACTFL Affairs

Finally, in October 1967, the first issue of the journal *Foreign Language Annals (FLA)* appeared, published by the American Council on the Teaching of Foreign Languages, with its dark yellow-and-gray cover. In his editorial, Ken Mildenberger, Interim Editor, spoke of his 15-year struggle to improve and strengthen the role of foreign language education in American education. He talked of his and others' continual frustration over "the absence of a comprehensive official medium which could communicate regularly the unfolding chronicle of information which gives meaning to the concept of a profession of foreign language teachers" (*FLA*, Vol. I, No. 1 (October 1967), p. 3.) He recognized that every language teacher must support the national association dedicated to the language taught…but that each teacher should also identify actively with a larger national profession, "the profession of foreign language teaching, which ACTFL and *Foreign Language Annals* now seek to serve."

He then talked of the threat to the very existence of foreign language teaching, citing the president of a state university who, in 1966, declared publicly (after calling for required typing courses in the public schools):

I am convinced that the whole business of foreign language has, in recent years, been greatly overemphasized. … If we weren't so benighted in the colleges, moreover, requiring languages for admissions, we could largely forget about foreign language in the high school.

Mildenberger's solution? "Only a strong and unified profession can respond effectively. The membership of you and your colleagues in ACTFL will help build a powerful voice of your profession." Such a rallying cry begged to be heeded. ACTFL was born.

Foreign Language Annals, Volume I, Number 1 (October 1967).

Its first annual meeting was held jointly with the MLA on December 27–29, 1967, at the Sheraton-Blackstone Hotel in Chicago. Registration for the conference was $2 for ACTFL members and $6 for those who registered and joined ACTFL at the meeting. A detailed program that included sessions for FLES teachers, secondary teachers, junior college and undergraduate college teachers would appear in the December issue of *FLA*. Everyone was to find useful professional discussions at this meeting — editors of state foreign language newsletters, local foreign language supervisors, trainers of school

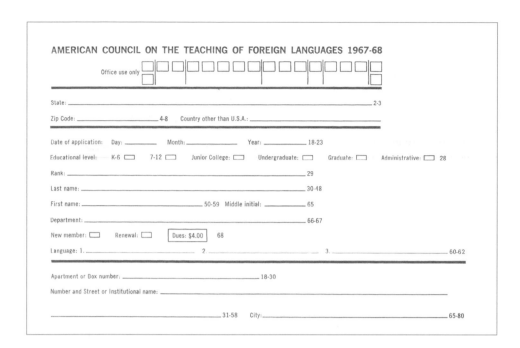

AMERICAN COUNCIL ON THE TEACHING OF FOREIGN LANGUAGES 1967-68

Office use only

State: _____ 2-3

Zip Code: _____ 4-8   Country other than U.S.A.: _____

Date of application: Day: _____   Month: _____   Year: _____ 18-23

Educational level: K-6 ☐   7-12 ☐   Junior College: ☐   Undergraduate: ☐   Graduate: ☐   Administrative: ☐ 28

Rank: _____ 29

Last name: _____ 30-48

First name: _____ 50-59 Middle initial: _____ 65

Department: _____ 66-67

New member: ☐   Renewal: ☐   Dues: $4.00   68

Language: 1. _____ 2. _____ 3. _____ 60-62

Apartment or Box number: _____ 18-30

Number and Street or Institutional name: _____

_____ 31-58   City: _____ 65-80

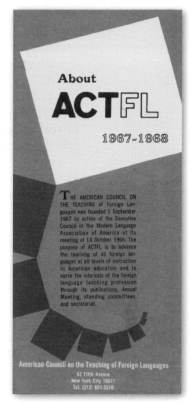

Above left: ACTFL Membership Form (1967–68), from *Foreign Language Annals*, No. 2 (April 1967), p. 3 insert.

Above right: First ACTFL brochure (1967–68)

and college teachers, specialists in the teaching of linguistics and culture. Sessions would be devoted to teaching individual languages, both modern and classical.

In fact, if we look at some of the session titles, we can see that several topics discussed at today's ACTFL annual meetings have an incredible resemblance to those from the past:

- "ACTFL Can Serve the Foreign Language Classroom Teacher"
- "Teaching World History in German"
- "Maintaining Interest Throughout the FLES Years"
- "How to Teach Culture in a Language Program"
- "Effective Grading of Foreign Language Essays"
- "Foreign Language Learning in the Year 2000"
- "Foreign Language Supervision and Leadership Techniques"
- "Rating Speaking in a Foreign Language"

The ACTFL Board of Directors would hold its first meeting in Chicago in December to set ACTFL's broad policy. ACTFL constituent organizations were to name members of the Board of Directors; the affiliate organizations would be represented in the Advisory Assembly. These Advisory Assembly members would make recommendations to the Board of Directors and the Committee on Organization, which would serve as the Executive Committee until one was elected.

Emma M. Birkmaier
First ACTFL President, 1968

UNIVERSITY OF MINNESOTA–TWIN CITIES

F. André Paquette
First ACTFL Executive Secretary

In his report at ACTFL's first Annual Meeting on December 29, 1967, André Paquette said that, as of December 22 (less than four months after ACTFL's official founding), it had more than 4,200 members in the United States, more than 100 college and school library subscribers to *FLA*, and more than 100 members who paid more than one year's dues. More than 130 others joined ACTFL at that first Annual Meeting.

The Committee on Organization, which met five times between November 1966 and November 1967, functioned as both the organizing group and an executive committee. The Committee chose a President and Vice President for the 1968 calendar year, and the Board of Directors endorsed its recommendations for these positions. The Committee also nominated fourteen members for election to four positions on ACTFL's first Executive Council. The MLA Executive Committee, as provided in the Guidelines, appointed three additional members to the ACTFL Executive Council.

The permanent ACTFL Bibliography Committee was established, along with six interim ones: FLES, Study Abroad, Research, Strengthening State Organizations, Teaching Literature and Culture, Professional Preparation.

ACTFL's headquarters were at 62 Fifth Avenue, New York. The council was supported by $50,000 from the MLA General Budget for the year ending September 1, 1967. Next year's budget would logically be larger, with support coming from individual dues, affiliate dues, advertising in *FLA*, and other minor sources, as well as from the MLA. Organizing Committee members' responsibilities would be transferred to the ACTFL Executive Committee as of January 1, 1968.

ACTFL Under Way

ACTFL's newly established Executive Committee held its first meeting on February 4-5, 1968. At this productive meeting,

- A rotation and staggering of terms of members of the Executive Committee was determined.
- A Constitution Committee was set up with the charge of writing the first ACTFL constitution.
- The ACTFL Executive Secretary was appointed to serve as Editor of *FLA*.
- The term of office of the Executive Secretary was set at no fewer than four years, beginning in the fall of 1968. Interim Executive Secretary Paquette was invited to accept this permanent appointment.
- The Editorial Board of *FLA* was established.
- It was determined that the 1969 and 1970 Annual Meetings would be held at Thanksgiving time.
- Three new committees were set up: Bilingualism, Foreign Language for the Non-College Bound, and Local Supervisory Services.

ACTFL Charter State Constituents (as of March 1967)

Alaska Foreign Language Association
Arkansas Foreign Language Teachers Association
California Council of Foreign Language Teachers Associations
Connecticut Council of Language Teachers
Florida Foreign Language Association
Classical and Modern Foreign Language Association of Georgia
Hawaii Association of Language Teachers
Idaho Foreign Language Teachers Association
Kansas Modern Language Association
Maryland Modern Language Association
Massachusetts Foreign Language Association
Michigan Foreign Language Association
Minnesota Council of Teachers of Foreign Languages
Mississippi Modern Language Association
Modern Language Association of Missouri
Nebraska Modern Language Association
New Hampshire Association for the Teaching of Foreign Languages
New Jersey Modern Language Teachers' Association
Oklahoma Foreign Language Teachers Association
Oregon Department of Foreign Languages, OEA
Pennsylvania State Modern Language Association
South Carolina Foreign Language Department, SCEA
Texas Foreign Language Association
Utah Foreign Language Association
Vermont Modern Language Teachers' Association
Washington Association of Foreign Language Teachers

Charter National & Regional Affiliates (as of March 1967)

American Association of Teachers of Arabic
American Association of Teachers of Italian
American Association of Teachers of Slavic and East European Languages
American Classical League
American Association of Teachers of Spanish and Portuguese
American Philological Association
Association of Teachers of English as a Second Language (NAFSA)
Association of Teachers of Japanese
Chinese Language Teachers Association
Classical Association of the Atlantic States
Classical Association of New England
Classical Association of the Middle West and South
Classical Association of the Pacific States, Central Section
Classical Association of the Pacific States, Northern Section
Department of Foreign Languages, NEA
Middle States Association of Modern Language Teachers
National Association of Language Laboratory Directors
National Association of Professors of Hebrew
Northeast Conference on the Teaching of Foreign Languages
Pacific Northwest Conference on Foreign Languages
Rocky Mountain Modern Language Association
Société des Professeurs Français en Amérique
South Atlantic Modern Language Association
South Central Modern Language Association
Southern Conference on Language Teaching
Teachers of English to Speakers of Other Languages

From Foreign Language Annals, Vol. I, No. 1 (October 1967), pp. 9-10.

Leo Benardo
ACTFL President 1969

At its February 4-5, 1968, meeting, the ACTFL Executive Committee issued its first policy statement: "Criteria for Evaluating Foreign Study Programs for High School Students." The statement, written by Stephen A. Freeman, Director of the Language Schools at Middlebury College, was first adopted by the National Council of State Supervisors of Foreign Languages (NCSSFL) in 1966 and then by ACTFL in 1968 with prior agreement of NCSSFL. The Executive Committee certainly recognized the value of foreign travel and study, but was alarmed by the rapid proliferation of so-called "study" programs, offered by numerous private, commercial and "non-profit" organizations, that took advantage of the tremendous popularity of foreign travel and study. ACTFL believed it was not feasible for a specific organization to "accredit" acceptable programs, but found it imperative to assist those interested in evaluating a given program's quality and suitability for a given purpose. The criteria for this evaluation were based on: (1) sponsorship, (2) recruitment and selection of students, (3) selection of the group leader, (4) study, (5) living abroad, (6) financial viability, and (7) *Caveat emptor* (*FLA*, (May 1969), Vol. I, No. 4, pp. 288-290).

On March 22-23, 1968, the Executive Committee again met. One of its major actions was to accept the procedures for preparation of an ACTFL constitution. The writing committee was: President Emma Birkmaier, Chair of the Constitution Committee; Kenneth Mildenberger and Stowell Goding from the Board of Directors; Gerald Else from the Advisory Assembly; and Mildred Boyer from the Committee on Organization for ACTFL. André Paquette was named Executive Secretary of ACTFL and Editor of *FLA* for five-year term beginning September 1, 1968.

At ACTFL's October 18-19, 1968, Executive Committee meeting, five membership/subscription categories were set up:

1. Regular membership: $4 — including subscription to *FLA*
2. Sustaining membership: $25 — including subscription and listing in *FLA*
3. Library subscriptions: $8 — *FLA* subscription only
4. Comprehensive membership: $20 — including *FLA* and selected publications
5. Comprehensive subscription: $24 — including *FLA* and selected publications

Professor Jack Stein's Executive Committee term had ended, and Jean Carduner was elected to replace him. Frank M. Grittner was appointed to a three-year term by the MLA Executive Council to replace Barbara Ort, who had served a one-year term.

Before the 1968 Annual Meeting, ACTFL sponsored an invitational working FLES conference on November 8-9 in Minneapolis on the theme of "New Dimensions in the Teaching of Foreign Languages in the Elementary School." The symposium was attended by some 75 people: commissioned writers of the five papers presented, scholars in foreign language teaching, FLES teachers, selected FLES coordinators, members of ACTFL's FLES Committee, and representatives of national associations interested in American elementary school education.

The ACTFL Annual Meeting was again jointly held with MLA at New York's Park Sheraton Hotel on December 27-19, 1968. Topics discussed there continued to be a distant echo of today's concerns:

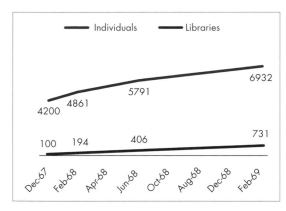

Membership data from December 1967 – February 1969

- Foreign Language Learning as a Social Force
- Bilingual Education for Americans
- Structure and Vocabulary Control Text-writing
- Culture with a Small 'c'
- Demonstration of Teaching Materials for Japanese
- Foreign Language Learning and Computers
- Using the Native Speaker in the High School

Individual membership in ACTFL was increasing. Nonetheless, 1969 President Leo Benardo launched a two-year Membership Drive with the goal of 15,000 members by December 31, 1969, with the Executive Committee's approval. This drive was to strengthen state organizations and ACTFL simultaneously. ACTFL was to make Assistance Payments to its constituents based on a two-part formula: for each new membership from that state during 1969, ACTFL would pay $0.40; for each membership renewal in 1969, $0.20.

Under the editorship of Emma Birkmaier, ACTFL initiated sponsorship of an *Annual Review of Research* to be published by Encyclopaedia Britannica. She said: "The *Review* is intended to serve educators, and especially classroom teachers and curriculum specialists in the field of foreign education…. The *Review* will also prove useful to researchers and professors of education….

We intend the *Review* as a guide for the orientation of newcomers to the field, as well as a report of new works for the refreshment of experts." The 1968 *Annual Review* was sold for $10 to ACTFL members and libraries and $15 to the general public.

In the May 1969 issue of *FLA* (Vol. 2, Number 4), the 1969 Annual Meeting was announced for November 28-30. The theme was "The Teacher as an Architect of Learning," and the meeting was held at the Roosevelt Hotel, New Orleans, LA. This was ACTFL's first meeting on its own, no longer a joint annual meeting with MLA during the week after Christmas. More than 50 major publishers exhibited materials and equipment. Two three-day workshops preceded the Annual Meeting: a FLES symposium ("Managing Change") and a Secondary symposium ("Individualizing Instruction").

Two Years Old

By the end of 1969, after two years of existence, ACTFL's membership had almost doubled — from 4,000 to 7,221. Its constitution had now reached draft form and was being reviewed. Many ACTFL constituents were extremely active; others were virtually dormant. Efforts at producing a *Handbook on Strengthening State Organizations* had not been productive. The biggest problem ACTFL had encountered was communication. It had no permanent officer; terms of office varied; some Board members had difficulty getting to the Annual Meeting, among other problems. President Benardo's membership drive was working, but numbers could have been better. Only Alabama and Louisiana had met their suggested state goals for 1969. *FLA* was doing quite well in both content and advertising revenue. Thirteen focus reports had been published, and another twenty had been commissioned.

Thirty-six ACTFL-GRAMS had been sent to selected foreign language leaders in 1969. Executive Secretary André Paquette believed

ACTFL Program Cover (1969)

ACTFL should extend the facilities of the Materials Center, originally established by the MLA, to make available for inexpensive distribution classroom instructional materials not ordinarily available through commercial channels. ACTFL had several projects under way; two focused on study abroad through strong collaboration with the Council on International Educational Exchange (CIEE), the National Association of Secondary School Principals (NASSP), the National Association of Independent Schools (NAIS), and regional accrediting associations. ACTFL, in co-sponsorship with the Indiana Language Program, had organized FLES Symposium I (1968), "The Student's World is the World: New Dimensions in the Teaching of FLES." FLES Symposium II and Secondary Symposia I and II were introduced at the 1969 Annual Meeting. Plans were under way

for the 1970 Annual Meeting and preconference workshops to be held in Los Angeles at the Biltmore Hotel.

ACTFL's headquarters staff now numbered six full-time, four part-time, with four support offices. The organization's relationship with MLA continued in a positive direction: the ACTFL Executive Secretary continued to serve as Secretary for Foreign Languages for the MLA, which was a useful liaison with ERIC, the new Foreign Language Program Advisory Committee, the newly formed Association of Departments of Foreign Languages (ADFL), and the MLA administration. The MLA's direct and indirect financial support was helping ACTFL to become a viable, forceful organization. Nonetheless, it was believed that ACTFL should plan on decreased financial support as MLA redefined its interests in response to its memberships' appeals.

Lester McKim was elected as the 1970 ACTFL President, and Lowell Dunham (University of Oklahoma) became President-elect. McKim presided over the November 1969 Executive Committee meeting at the Annual Meeting, at which Paquette announced that a second draft of the ACTFL constitution was being presented to and discussed by the Board of Directors.

So, as the 1960s ended, ACTFL had taken shape as a dynamic force in foreign language teaching and learning, but inevitable growing pains and concerns remained: how to satisfy constituents and their myriad desires, increase membership, work cooperatively with a wide range of organizations that had their own interests at heart, expand the reach of ACTFL beyond the borders of the United States, forge a document— a constitution—that would fully address the mission and the intent of the organization, and be a leader among leaders. The 1970s would see ACTFL continue to grow, to come to grips with these and new concerns, and to prove that this new organization was not a ceremonial association, but a vessel that was slowly beginning to fill with sound ideas, hard work, and progress.

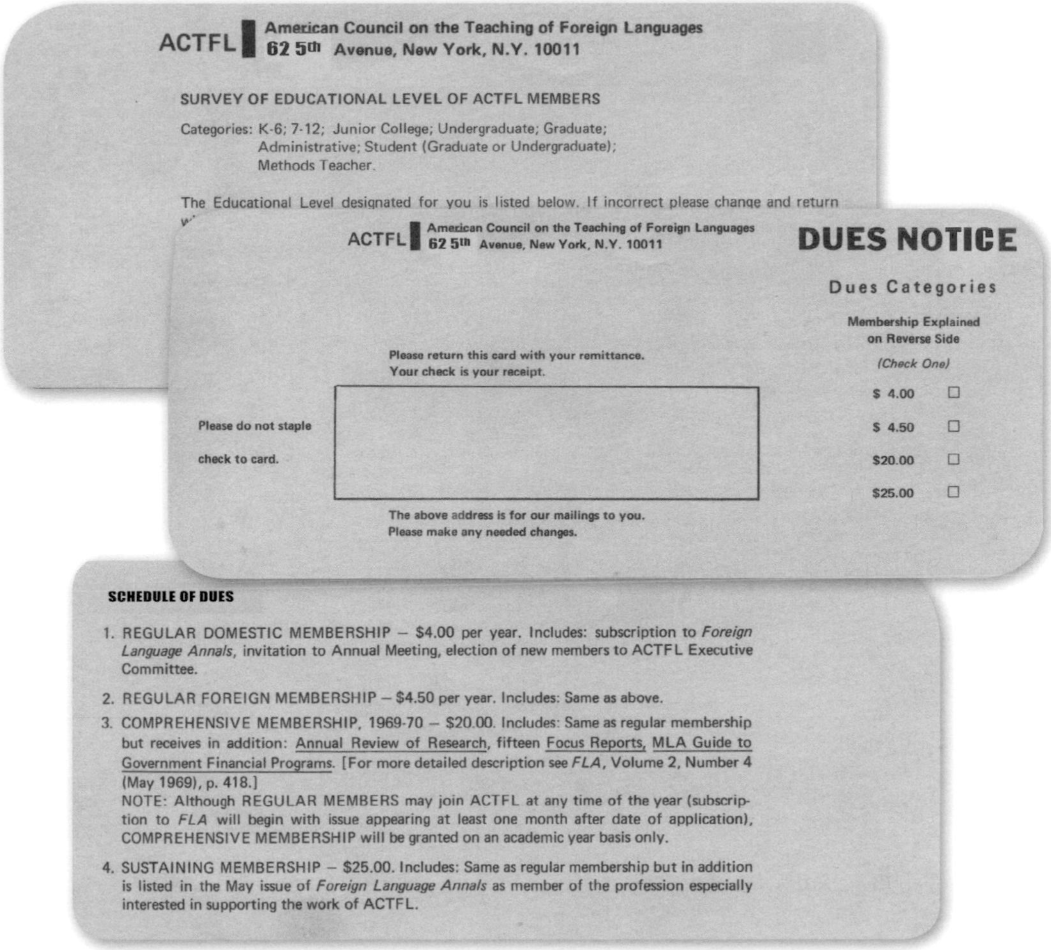

ACTFL | American Council on the Teaching of Foreign Languages
62 5th Avenue, New York, N.Y. 10011

SURVEY OF EDUCATIONAL LEVEL OF ACTFL MEMBERS

Categories: K-6; 7-12; Junior College; Undergraduate; Graduate;
Administrative; Student (Graduate or Undergraduate);
Methods Teacher.

The Educational Level designated for you is listed below. If incorrect please change and return

ACTFL | American Council on the Teaching of Foreign Languages
62 5th Avenue, New York, N.Y. 10011

DUES NOTICE

Dues Categories

Membership Explained
on Reverse Side

(Check One)

$ 4.00 ☐

$ 4.50 ☐

$20.00 ☐

$25.00 ☐

Please return this card with your remittance.
Your check is your receipt.

Please do not staple
check to card.

The above address is for our mailings to you.
Please make any needed changes.

SCHEDULE OF DUES

1. REGULAR DOMESTIC MEMBERSHIP — $4.00 per year. Includes: subscription to *Foreign Language Annals*, invitation to Annual Meeting, election of new members to ACTFL Executive Committee.

2. REGULAR FOREIGN MEMBERSHIP — $4.50 per year. Includes: Same as above.

3. COMPREHENSIVE MEMBERSHIP, 1969-70 — $20.00. Includes: Same as regular membership but receives in addition: Annual Review of Research, fifteen Focus Reports, MLA Guide to Government Financial Programs. [For more detailed description see *FLA*, Volume 2, Number 4 (May 1969), p. 418.]
NOTE: Although REGULAR MEMBERS may join ACTFL at any time of the year (subscription to *FLA* will begin with issue appearing at least one month after date of application), COMPREHENSIVE MEMBERSHIP will be granted on an academic year basis only.

4. SUSTAINING MEMBERSHIP — $25.00. Includes: Same as regular membership but in addition is listed in the May issue of *Foreign Language Annals* as member of the profession especially interested in supporting the work of ACTFL.

ACTFL dues notice (1969–70)

President Jimmy Carter at work in the Oval Office, 1978. On April 21st of that year, Carter created the Presidential Commission on Foreign Language and International Studies to promote foreign language education and enhance awareness of foreign cultures.

CHAPTER 2

THE 1970s

Growth and Independence

Effective 1 July 1970, F. Andre Paquette, Executive Secretary of the American Council on the Teaching of Foreign Languages since the creation of the organization in 1967, has resigned this position to become Director of the Summer Language Schools of Middlebury College, succeeding Dr. Stephen A. Freeman. (ADFL Bulletin, Vol. 1, No. 4 (May) 1970)

As a result of Paquette's pending resignation, the ACTFL Executive Committee appointed a Committee to Select the Second Executive Secretary, comprised of Leo Benardo, 1969 President of ACTFL; Lester McKim, 1970 President of ACTFL; and Freeman Twaddell, MLA Executive Council member and ACTFL Committee on Organization member. The ACTFL Executive Committee passed this resolution: "The ACTFL Executive Committee requested the MLA Executive Council to agree to the appointment of Edward Scebold as ACTFL Executive Secretary [and Editor of *Foreign Language Annals*] for a four-year term beginning 1 July 1970." Scebold was confirmed as MLA Staff Associate and was Executive Secretary-elect of ACTFL from June 1, 1970, until his term as Executive Secretary for fiscal years 1970-74 began on July 1, 1970.

Raised on his family's farm in Missouri Valley, IA, Scebold began his career in foreign language education as a junior high school Spanish teacher in Shawnee Mission, Kansas. He was state foreign language consultant to the Nebraska Department of Education prior to coming to ACTFL.

He came to his job as the head of an organization that had no constitution, that was supported and housed by the MLA, that was growing very rapidly, and that, like so many other professional organizations, was beginning to suffer from increasing expenses and decreasing income. In 1970, the MLA Executive Council passed a resolution:

C. Edward Scebold
ACTFL Executive Secretary/Director
1970 – 2001

Lester W. McKim
ACTFL President 1970

Lowell Dunham
ACTFL President 1971

...the MLA requests the ACTFL Executive Committee, and instructs the MLA administrative staff, to plan for regularly diminishing direct financial support of ACTFL activities over the next five years, leading to the complete cessation of direction financial support by MLA for ACTFL by the (fiscal year) 1975-76 MLA budget. At that time, the financial situation of ACTFL may be reviewed and a schedule be developed for its gradually assuming its own overhead expenses.

Nonetheless, ACTFL was moving ahead under the leadership of Lester McKim (WA), 1970 President. Membership had increased to 9,249 as a result of the membership drive begun in the late 1960s by President Leo Benardo.

In cooperation with the Council on International Educational Exchange (CIEE), ACTFL set up a model study abroad program for high school students at the Lycée de Grand Air in Arachon, France. This program, under the directorship of Edward Bourque, featured a six-week immersion program; most of the faculty were native French speakers. It was attended by 39 American high school students, 16 French *lycée* students, and 7 French group leaders from the University of Bordeaux. Following the success of this pilot program, ACTFL decided to expand it to include two centers in France and one in Colombia in 1971.

ACTFL was also preparing to launch a new publication, *Accent on ACTFL*, a bulletin that would publicize news, practical articles, local projects, and activities that had implications for the profession. This new bulletin relied on close cooperation with state newsletter editors.

A draft of the ACTFL Constitution was mailed to all members in the early fall of 1970, along with ballots for the election of 1971 officers. The results were announced at the Annual Meeting at the Biltmore Hotel in Los Angeles (November 26-29, 1970). The new constitution was approved by the membership, took effect on January 1, 1971, and was published in *FLA*, Vol. 4, Number 3 (March 1971), pp. 243–247 [see Appendix A].

At the 1970 Annual Meeting, Lowell Dunham (OK), President-elect for 1971, presided over the Advisory Assembly, at which Kenneth Mildenberger, ACTFL Treasurer, distributed copies of the ACTFL Budget:

ACTFL BUDGET: FIRST FOUR YEARS

	1967–68		1968–69		1969–70		1970-71
	Estimated	Actual	Estimated	Actual	Estimated	Actual	Estimated
(1) Income	49,025	52, 122	65,410	58,394	107,030	127, 364	151,400
(2) Expenses	104,760	124,348	117,387	110,370	157,220	207,921	202,580
(3) Deficit*	(55,735)	(72,266)	(51,977)	(51, 976)	(50,190)	(80,557)	(51,180)
(4) Indirect*	—	—	—	—	—	—	—

*Deficit and indirect costs (space, furniture and equipment, utilities, etc.) paid by Modern Language Association.
Budget year is from 1 September to 31 August.

From Foreign Language Annals (Vol. Four, Number Three (March 1971), p. 261.

Now, with a deficit budget and with MLA reducing its subsidy, the ACTFL Executive Committee was charged with recommending action to reduce the deficit; no further expenditures could be authorized.

In 1971, ACTFL began to operate under a membership-approved constitution. Membership continued to increase—from 8,729 in late 1970 to 9,306 in early 1971. The Executive Committee voted to continue the Membership Drive begun by Leo Benardo and the Constituent Assistance Payments of $0.40 for each new member and $0.20 for each renewing member through 1971.

That February, the Executive Council appointed a Financial Committee to reconsider the ACTFL budget as necessary. Raising the registration fee for the Annual Meeting to $8 was discussed, but the Financial Committee finally reduced it to $6. Also discussed was raising the membership dues to $10 in the next year or so. (At the Annual Meeting in Chicago, the Constituent Assembly voted that increase.) A further move to cut costs prompted instituting two temporary emergency measures: discontinuing both the State Constituent Payments for fiscal 1971-72 and the policy of awarding complimentary comprehensive and regular membership for 1971-72. Coincidentally, as of October 1, 1971, ACTFL had 9,284 individual domestic and foreign members, and library subscriptions had increased to 1,312 (total memberships and subscriptions were 10,596).

MEMBERSHIP GROWTH

Date	Domestic	Foreign	Library	Total	Increase
1 February 1968	4750	111	194	5055	
1 February 1969	6932	142	731	7805	54%
1 February 1970	8145	195	1065	9465	21%
1 February 1971	9086	220	1144	10450	10%

From Foreign Language Annals, Vol. Five, Number Three (March 1972), p. 285.

Plans were made for the 1971 Annual Meeting in Chicago on November 25-28, themed "Pluralism in Foreign Language Education: Opportunities and Innovations." At this meeting, it was announced that Gail Hutchinson (GA) had been elected Vice-President and President-elect for 1972.

During 1971, Encyclopaedia Britannica began to phase out its entire Review operation and terminated its contract with ACTFL for production of the *Britannica Review of Foreign Language Education* (*BRFLE*), which was now in its third volume. Under the editorship of Emma Birkmaier (Vol. 1) and Dale L. Lange (Vols. 2 and 3), the *BRFLE* had proved to be a worthwhile project. Volume 1 (1968), *Foreign Language Education: An Overview*, had two major themes: the content and organization of foreign language learning, and the theory and practice of foreign language teaching and learning. The inaugural volume sold 3,000 copies. The theme of Vol. 2 (1970) was "Individualized Instruction," the then-current focus of language instruction. This volume sold 2,500 copies. In 1971, Vol. 3 appeared, with the theme "Pluralism in

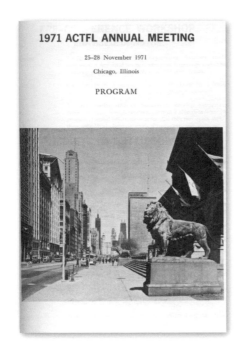
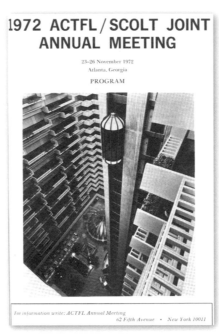

Programs from ACTFL Annual Meetings
1971 – 1973

Foreign Language Education." Negotiations were under way with several publishers to continue publication of this annual review volume.

ACTFL's other publications, *FLA* and the new bulletin, *Accent on ACTFL,* were successfully filling a much-needed gap in pertinent and current information for foreign language instruction. The number of manuscripts submitted to *FLA* had increased enough to ensure sufficient in-house material to complete the next two volumes. *Accent on ACTFL* was in its second volume. Contributions were increasing. This new bulletin was created to fill the gaps between issues of *FLA* by supplying current newsworthy articles that were not appropriate for a journal such as *FLA*.

The second ACTFL/CIEE Study Abroad Program in Arachon, France, saw 65 students participating in the summer of 1971 under the directorship of Edward and Jane Bourque. Plans had originally called for programs in Arachon and Toulon, France, and a center in Bogotá, Colombia, but applications were insufficient due to the economic state of the U.S. in general. In 1972, it was planned to add a center in Cádiz, Spain.

The 1971 Annual Meeting was held November 25-28 at the Conrad Hilton Hotel in Chicago. On November 22-24 at the same hotel, two preconference workshops on behavioral objectives and teaching culture preceded the annual meeting. Concurrent with the workshops was a Conference on Child Language, sponsored by the international Association of Applied Linguistics and its Commission on Child Language (Stockholm), the Center for Applied Linguistics (CAL), and ACTFL. The subject of this conference was "The learning of two or more languages or dialects by young children, especially between the ages of 3 and 8, with particular attention to the social setting."

Financial, Membership, and Other Concerns

In early 1972, ACTFL Executive Secretary Scebold sent out the letter below to the organization membership (see p. 21). The current economic situation had called for annual dues increases from $8 to $10 for domestic membership (including Canada and Mexico) and from $10 to $12 for foreign membership. A new category—student membership verified by a faculty member's signature—was added for $6 annually for a maximum of three years. The comprehensive membership was discontinued for the 1972-1973 period. Scebold pointed out that MLA had been covering ACTFL's deficit each year and that its financial support was to end in 1975, as a result of a resolution the MLA Executive Council passed on May 22-23, 1971. Supplementing this resolution was the subvention of $100,000 from MLA, which signaled "terminal direct support of the continued development" of ACTFL. Direct support of ACTFL by the MLA was terminated in May 1971, but four equal payments from the subvention would occur over the next four fiscal years.

The study abroad program was having its problems as well. Due to a lack of interest in the program in Spain, that program was canceled, while, surprisingly, the third year's program in Arachon, France, had 47 students enrolled. In addition, starting in 1973 the CIEE was to withdraw its support of ACTFL's study abroad programs, and ACTFL would have to operate them independently. As a result, a motion was passed: if the study abroad programs could not be sustained on a self-supporting basis, they should be discontinued at the earliest moment.

Additionally, the membership base had to be increased to 15,000 members — a challenging 50% increase. As of February 1, 1972, domestic membership stood at 9,300 and foreign membership at 263. As of October 10, 1972, individual domestic and foreign membership had dropped to 8,264, the result of dropping unpaid renewals from the membership rolls. In reaction, ACTFL produced a brochure, "Why Join ACTFL," to spur a significant membership increase (see p. 23). Brochures were available to all with a simple request to the membership office at ACTFL headquarters. With support of the membership, ACTFL planned to continue, and even expand, its commitment to the profession.

Publications in 1972

Two new regular features were added to *FLA* in 1972: "Individualized Instruction," with Ronald Gougher and John Bockman as Contributing Editors; and "Foreign Language Teacher Education," with Dale Lange as Contributing Editor.

Volume 4 of the *Review of Foreign Language Education* series, published by National Textbook Company, would be available at the 1972 Atlanta meeting. This volume and earlier ones would now appear in paperback. Volume 4's theme was "Foreign Language Education: A Reappraisal." Dale Lange resigned as editor of the series upon completion of Vol. 4, and Gilbert Jarvis of The Ohio State University took over as Editor beginning with Vol. 5, whose theme was "Foreign Language Education: Responding to New Realities."

Gail Hutchinson Eubanks
ACTFL President 1972

ACTFL | *American Council on the Teaching of Foreign Languages*
62 Fifth Avenue · New York 10011 · Telephone 212 · 691-3210

Dear ACTFL Member:

It is time to renew your membership in ACTFL, and we ask that you please return the enclosed dues notice with your renewal payment. You will note that for 1972-73 there have been changes in the membership categories and dues rates. The first and most obvious change is the increase in regular domestic and foreign membership dues. Regular domestic membership (including Canada and Mexico) has been increased to $10.00 and foreign membership increased to $12.00.

Several changes have been made in the membership categories, with the addition of the Student Membership category and the temporary abolition of the Comprehensive Membership category. Student members will have the same rights and privileges as regular members, and may retain their student membership rate for three years; a professor's signature must accompany the request for student membership. It is our hope that Comprehensive Membership will be reinstituted in 1973-74, if the supply of significant publications warrants it. As in other areas, ACTFL operations have been subject to the high rate of inflation of the past several years. Costs of materials, communication, printing, and general overhead have all been on the rise, and we, as a membership organization, have been forced to meet these costs primarily through both increasing our membership and membership dues. Alternate sources of income, such as advertising in Foreign Language Annals and charges for exhibits and registration at the Annual Meeting, have helped meet some of the costs in the past and it is our hope that the Annual Meeting, for one, will soon become a self-supporting activity. Certainly we will continue to explore possibilities in this area.

At present ACTFL is running a considerable deficit. In 1971-72, sixty percent of each member's dues ($3.60 or $36,000 total) went toward the printing and mailing of Foreign Language Annals and Accent on ACTFL. The remaining forty percent ($2.40 or $24,000 total) went toward the costs of running the national office, maintaining the membership files, supporting the Annual Meeting, preparing new publications, supporting the work of the regional and state language teachers' associations, paying the salaries of the publication staff, and initiating new projects. Very simply, $24,000 is not enough money to support that level of activity.

The Modern Language Association has covered ACTFL's deficit each year, but MLA financial support will end in 1975. Obviously ACTFL must begin immediately to increase its income to meet the costs of current programs and future plans. Our first step has been to raise the membership dues.

The second step must be to increase our membership base. ACTFL needs 15,000 members to be self-supporting; in other words, we need to increase our membership by 50%, by 5,000 people. Difficult--yes; but with your cooperation and hard work, it is not all impossible. Each must work to make ACTFL better known and understood; we must persuade others to join. This is not just another membership campaign. The results of our work over the next two years will determine whether or not ACTFL is to become a viable force in foreign language education in America. I believe that a national organization of all foreign language teachers, with a clear commitment to pedagogy and classroom teachers, is vital to the profession.

-2-

What will be the nature of ACTFL's commitment to the future? In 1972-73, Accent on ACTFL will be expanded under the very capable editorship of Miss Ruth Keaton, formerly the State Supervisor for Foreign Languages in Georgia and editor of the Georgia Foreign Language Beacon. We are certain that Accent on ACTFL will become a first-rate national bulletin.

ACTFL will continue to support the Series on Foreign Language Education, which will be introduced in both paperback and hardback editions for Volume 4. Foreign Language Annals will continue as a journal devoted to providing relevant articles on subjects relating directly to the classroom teacher, supervisor, and methods instructor.

ACTFL is committed to preparing, with many of its state and national affiliates, evidence of the need and importance of foreign language study, and we are investigating the possibilities for a national public relations program for the foreign language teaching profession.

ACTFL will continue to support and promote better classroom teaching through encouragement of innovative methods, curricula, and materials at the Annual Meeting and through publication of relevant articles, pamphlets, and other materials for teachers and administrators.

Further exploration must be done with the potential of offering additional state and local workshops ... in fact, the list of possible future projects is as endless as the number of challenges which face the foreign language teaching profession.

Finally, I would like to emphasize once again the need for your strong support in the current membership campaign. ACTFL is its members, and we need the participation and help of a great many people if it is to become a strong, more active, and self-sufficient organization. I believe that ACTFL is a very necessary organization and that its operations will become even more significant as it grows and develops. One thing is certain; it depends in a very vital way on you and your support.

Sincerely yours,

C. Edward Scebold
Executive Secretary

CES:he

Affiliates and the birth of JNCL

On October 1-2, 1971, the first meeting of representatives of ACTFL Affiliate organizations was held at ACTFL headquarters in New York. As a result, the organizational work undertaken by the AAT Joint Committee led to an article in *Accent on ACTFL* in November 1972, which opened as follows: "As a result of the cooperative planning of several national foreign language associations, The Joint National Committee for Languages [JNCL]has been launched."* The group wrote the following statement of purpose for the JNCL:

The National Officers of AATF, AATG, AATI, AATSEEL, AATSP and ACTFL, mindful of the importance of foreign languages in our society and of the pressing need for close collaboration between the various language associations, hereby announce the establishment ofapermanent joint committee which shall meet at least twice a year, composed of a maximum of three representatives of each association, who shall be: the President, the Executive Secretary (or Secretary-Treasurer) and one other to be designated by the association. ACTFL, because of its structure, shall have the option of appointing two delegates to represent other language groups.

The Joint National Committee shall have as its main purpose the implementation of a continuing movement in favor of learning foreign languages in the United States, as well as the sponsorship of special projects to improve and enhance the teaching of these languages.
(*Foreign Language Annals*, Vol. 6, Number 3, March 1973, pp. 292-293)

---

* However, according to J. David Edwards, the first director of JNCL, the organization was officially founded in 1976 at a meeting in Arizona, with the Washington, DC, office created in 1979.

Why Join ACTFL?

American Council on the Teaching of Foreign Languages
62 Fifth Avenue
New York, N.Y. 10011

ACTFL's services to its members include . . .

a journal, *Foreign Language Annals*
a newsletter, *Accent on ACTFL*
an Annual Meeting
Pre-Convention Workshops
Materials Center
Annual Bibliography
Review of Foreign Language Education Series
Information Services

ACTFL is the *major professional organization* in the United States devoted exclusively to foreign language teaching.

ACTFL speaks for *classroom teachers* as represented in the Constituent Assembly by 48 State FL organizations.

ACTFL speaks for *language associations*, 36 of which are represented in the Affiliate Assembly.

ACTFL's *Foreign Language Annals* is the outstanding professional FL teachers' journal. It is published in October, December, March, and May and includes professional articles and information covering all aspects of the profession of interest to teachers and supervisors on all levels and an Annual Bibliography on Foreign Language Pedagogy.

ACTFL's Newsletter, *Accent on ACTFL*, keeps teachers and administrators aware of current news and notes in the profession and ACTFL activities. ACTFL hopes its Newsletter will serve as an ex-

change of teacher ideas for more effective classroom teaching.

ACTFL's *Annual Meeting* is the only national meeting devoted exclusively to foreign language education. It is held in a different part of the country each year so that more teachers may participate in a national meeting.

ACTFL's *Review of Foreign Language Education* has been recognized as an essential resource for FL teachers.

ACTFL's *Focus Reports* [in cooperation with the ERIC Clearinghouse on Languages and Linguistics] provide information on a wide variety of topics related to FL education.

ACTFL's *Workshops* bring FL educators together to study and discuss current trends and innovative ideas.

ACTFL's *Materials Center* [in cooperation with MLA] makes available at low cost publications of interest to FL teachers.

Membership in ACTFL . . . is open to all who are interested in the teaching of foreign languages.
Membership includes—four issues of *Foreign Language Annals*, four issues of *Accent on ACTFL*, invitation to the Annual Meeting, election of new members to the ACTFL Executive Council, professional information services.
Two types of membership are available:
Regular Membership—annual dues for domestic (including Canada and Mexico) are $10.00; foreign dues are $12.00.
Student Membership—annual dues are $6.00. Open to students pursuing a degree program. An individual joining ACTFL as a student member is entitled to retain the student membership at $6.00 per year for three years. Student members have the same benefits and privileges as regular members. Applications for student membership must be accompanied by a professor's signature.

American Council on the Teaching of Foreign Languages (ACTFL)
Membership Application and Change of Address Form

"Why Join ACTFL" — Membership Recruitment Brochure, 1972

The work of JNCL (originally TJNCL) in 1972–1973 focused the concerns of the various professional groups involved. Two of its major contributions were: (1) establishment of communication among those involved with foreign languages at the national level, and (2) launching pilot projects to promote an improved public image for foreign languages in order to test preliminary ideas.

Growing Pains

With ACTFL now operating under its first Constitution, the Executive Council wanted to change its own makeup. At its February 25-25, 1972, meeting, the following motion was passed:

The immediate past president of ACTFL should serve as a regular voting member of the Executive Council for at least one year after the term expires. The Executive Secretary was instructed to take the necessary action to accomplish the change in the Constitution.

Therefore, an amendment to Article v.1.b. was proposed. A special ballot appeared in the November 1972 issue of *Accent on ACTFL*, with ballots due back from the membership by December 29, 1972.

At the February 1973 Executive Council meeting, it was announced that Kenneth Mildenberger, Treasurer of MLA, had resigned his position. Scebold was to work with the Executive Secretary of MLA to set up steps to appoint an ACTFL Treasurer. Also, the Executive Council instructed Scebold to initiate a secret ballot that would go to all ACTFL members, asking them to vote on the incorporation of ACTFL as a separate nonprofit organization, as provided in the ACTFL Constitution Bylaws. The vote was announced in early 1974: Yes, 1,019; No, 28.

Simultaneously, negotiations were going on between the National Federation of Modern Language Teachers Associations (NFMLTA)

and ACTFL concerning combining issues of *The Modern Language Journal* and *FLA* and the possible merger of NFMLTA and ACTFL. Joint and concurrent meetings of ACTFL and its affiliated associations were also proposed. The 1974 Annual Meeting in Denver, was, in fact, the first joint meeting co-sponsored by ACTFL, the American Association of Teachers of French (AATF), and the American Association of Teachers of Spanish and Portuguese (AATSP).

Discussions continued about The Joint National Committee for Languages. Several projects had been initiated but provoked frustration, because it was commonly believed that the Committee had not yet begun to function effectively. Recommendations were made about the need for ACTFL to coordinate the Committee's work, because JNCL's purposes were considered central to the reasons for ACTFL's existence.

MLA Executive Secretary William D. Schaefer reported on the organization's Foreign Language Program for the 1970s. A proposal was made to the National Endowment for the Humanities (NEH) for a multi-faceted, multilevel program for the promotion and improvement of language learning in the coming years. It was hoped that ACTFL and the AATs would join with MLA in proposing this. A document, "A National Foreign Language Program for the 1970's" was drafted in the spring of 1973 and presented to the NEH, as well as to numerous other private foundations, government funding agencies, and interested individuals, both within and outside the foreign language teaching profession. The Steering Committee's first priority was public awareness which provided direction for the efforts of ACTFL, MLA, and ADFL with JNCL's cooperation. The document was also a focal point for numerous other projects in the developmental stage.

The seventh Annual Meeting, held November 22-25 in Boston, was the first meeting organized with the assistance of the newly created ACTFL Annual Meeting Committee. At this meeting, it was decided that the Executive Council be restructured by adding four committees: Steering (President, President-elect, Immediate Past President), Annual Meeting, Membership, and Publications.

Jermaine Arendt, University of Minnesota, was ACTFL President in 1973, a year that marked the beginning of several significant changes in the Executive Council's structure and function. First, the Immediate Past President became a member of the Executive Council for a one-calendar-year term. Executive Council was divided into specific committees that would assist ACTFL headquarters staff in planning activities of the organization. As ACTFL was growing, there became a need for an operations manual, a series of guidelines for the organization.

The October 1973 issue of *FLA* (Vol. 7, Number 1, pp. 72-77) published guidelines for:

- Executive Council Members and Officers
- Code of Ethics
- President
- President-elect
- Immediate Past President
- Steering Committee

- Membership Committee
- Annual Meeting Committee
- Directions of ACTFL
- Preconference Workshops
- Concurrent and Joint Meetings
- Editorial Procedures and ACTFL Publications

Jermaine Arendt
ACTFL President 1973

In February 1973, the "Act for ACTFL" membership campaign was launched through *Accent on ACTFL*, in cooperation with the State Membership Chairmen and State Constituent organizations. The basic idea was to stimulate present ACTFL members to enroll new ones. By November 1973, 420 new members had been added as a result of this campaign. ACTFL's membership rose to 9,812 (domestic and foreign), and including subscriptions, the total membership was 11,330.

Volume 5 of the *Review of Foreign Language Education Series* was available in Boston at the Annual Meeting. Volume 6 was being planned, under the editorship of Gilbert Jarvis, with the theme "Communication in Foreign Language Education." ACTFL also published proceedings from the 1972 joint meeting with the Southern Conference on Language Teaching (SCOLT), *Dimension: Languages '72*.

The 1973 Study Abroad Program in Arachon, France, had to be canceled due to low enrollment and the American dollar's fluctuating rate of exchange. Because a considerable deficit was incurred in organizing the program and no income was received, the program's reinstatement would be unlikely in the near future.

In 1974, Carl Dellaccio, Tacoma (WA) Public Schools, became ACTFL President. The Executive Council voted to reelect Scebold as Executive Secretary effective June 1, 1974, for a one-year term, with a provision that his employment could be terminated if financial conditions of the organization made it necessary.

During 1972-1973, ACTFL had been subcontracting with the Far West Laboratory for Educational Research and Development in San Francisco, conducting a survey of innovative foreign language programs at the elementary and secondary school levels

Carl Dellaccio
ACTFL President 1974

Florence Steiner
ACTFL President-Elect 1975

Foreign Language Annals:
October 1973

in the country. Financed by a contract with the U.S. Office of Education, the survey resulted in a publication, *Options and Perspectives: A Sourcebook of Innovative Foreign Language Programs in Action, K–12*, published for ACTFL by MLA.

Florence Steiner became President-elect in 1975. During the November 1973 Executive Council meetings, budgetary discussions arose, not only concerning merging *FLA* and *Accent on ACTFL* into a single publication, but also on a larger organizational scale. An ad hoc Committee on Redesigning the Budget was appointed to address the situation for 1974. Dues were increased from $10 to $15, effective January 1, 1975. Kenneth Mildenberger was appointed ACTFL Interim Treasurer, effective through November 1974. At that time, a permanent arrangement and an appropriate appointment of Treasurer would be made.

The Executive Secretary was authorized to proceed with ACTFL's incorporation as a separate non-profit organization, based on the overwhelming approval voted by the Constituent Assembly and prior membership approval by mail advisory vote.

The final number of *FLA* for Vol. 7 (December 1974) saw a change in the journal's format. The cover color changed from dark gold to a lighter ecru. Binding was changed from perfect binding, in which pages are attached with adhesive to a cover that has a flat spine, to a saddle-stitch binding, in which the pages are folded and then stapled through the fold-line.

Beginning in November 1973, ACTFL saw much dramatic change. The separation of ACTFL from MLA began. On March 14, 1974, the now-independent organization was officially incorporated as the American Council on the Teaching of Foreign Languages, Inc., under provisions of New York State law. Application for its nonprofit rating by the Internal Revenue Service was pending completion of nine months of operation independent from MLA's accounting system. Upon receipt of the IRS ruling, the Constitution and Bylaws would need immediate revision to conform the documents to the new structure of the corporation.

Sadly, Steiner, 1975 President-elect, died unexpectedly on July 21, 1974. After significant discussion by the Executive Council, it was decided that the ACTFL Constituent Assembly, which had a broad base of representation from various state associations, should vote on Steiner's replacement. Two candidates were nominated: Frank Grittner and André Paquette. The election would take place at the 1974 Annual Meeting in Denver.

The joint proposal to NEH for support of the national effort for public awareness was rejected. As a result, JNCL continued its public awareness effort by distributing a set of cassette recordings of famous personalities who spoke of the value of second language study. These tapes were used both as radio publicity spots as well as classroom materials.

Negotiations with NFMLTA for a joint publication were continuing, albeit sporadically. A committee was formed with three representatives each from NFMLTA and ACTFL to work out a contractual agreement for the publication of *The Modern Language Journal* (MLJ) in close association with ACTFL for a designated period of time. After a hiatus of several months, formal contact was renewed in August of 1974 to continue the negotiations.

In a letter to the general ACTFL membership (p. 29), Executive Secretary Scebold announced a simplification of the membership cycle from four different cycles to only one based on the calendar year. He also spoke of the move away from MLA and asked members to "make a modest investment in ACTFL's future."

Membership was increasing, with a total domestic and foreign membership of 10,119, and with domestic and foreign library subscriptions at 1,392. At this time, membership in ACTFL included:

- four issues of *Accent on ACTFL*
- four issues of *FLA*
- an invitation to the Annual Meeting and Pre-Conference Workshops
- voting privileges for the election of officers and determination of the structure and future direction of ACTFL
- professional information services
- special prices on publications produced in cooperation with National Textbook Company
- two insurance plans:
  - ACTFL Term Life Insurance Plan
  - ACTFL Hospital Money Plan

The ACTFL Publications Committee began to consider review of the total ACTFL publication program, which was approved in November 1974:

- *FLA* and *Accent on ACTFL* were to be combined into one journal, beginning in September 1975, appearing quarterly in 1976.
- The editor of this single journal would no longer be the Executive Secretary of the organization.
- When fiscally feasible, occasional thematic publications would be produced, in addition to a newsletter for selected audiences.
- The *Review* would be maintained.
- An ACTFL Materials Center would be created, if it were operable at a profit.

In 1974, Ruth Keaton, Editor of *Accent on ACTFL*, resigned her position, and Robert Gilman (NV) was named the new Editor.

The 1974 joint meeting with AATF, AATSP, and ACTFL was the first meeting of its kind—the culmination of a move started in 1972 with the creation of The Joint National Committee for Languages, which was the first national, coordinated effort by all major professional

First ad for the ACTFL Materials Center, *Foreign Language Annals*, Volume 8, Number 1 (March 1975).

Frank M. Grittner
ACTFL President 1975

Helen Warriner
ACTFL President 1976

foreign language associations. Success or failure was yet to be determined, however; future projects and activities should enable these associations to join forces in areas that directly relate progress as a profession. Simultaneously, the ACTFL Annual Meeting Committee was beginning to assess the reaction of the membership to alternate Annual Meeting dates.

At the Denver meeting, Frank Grittner was elected President, and Helen Warriner (VA) was elected 1976 President-elect.

In the October 1975 issue of *FLA*, the 1975 Annual Meeting was announced for November 27-30 at the Washington Hilton Hotel, Washington, DC. This would be the first international foreign language teachers' convention, since delegates and speakers from the Fédération Internationale des Professeurs de Langues Vivantes (FIPLV) would join ACTFL and AATG. For the first time, with the October 1975 issue of *FLA*, the full conference program was not published except in abbreviated form. The complete program would be received at the Annual Meeting. It was determined that preregistration for this meeting would be $10 while on-site registration would be $15.

Publications Committee Chair Lorraine Strasheim was appointed Chair of the Moving Contingencies Committee, which was to explore ACTFL's possible relocation to a university campus. This committee was to draw up lists of headquarters operation requirements as a basis for future decisions regarding this relocation.

Discussions with NFMLTA concerning the joint publication of journals were ongoing, but due to pending changes in ACTFL's publication policies, opportunities for further discussion were held open until those policies were finalized. The policies were adopted in the summer of 1975 and published in *FLA* (Vol. 8, No. 3, pp. 246-247).

Significant decisions were made concerning ACTFL's new status as an independent corporation: checking account resolution, ACTFL's official seal, the organization's official place of business (62 Fifth Avenue, New York City), the fiscal year (January 1–December 31), investment of funds, and the Executive Secretary's salary. Executive Secretary Scebold was renamed to his position for a three-year term, June 1, 1975–May 31, 1978.

The year 1976 saw big changes in *FLA*. The cover was changed to include color coding for each issue, and that issue's theme was announced on the cover. The graphic was the same one used for all ACTFL publications for 1976. "ACTFL Affairs," a column that included all information pertinent to the organization, was removed. Photos and artwork were included in the journal. Its style and format changed. "A Message from the President" was a new feature. *Accent on ACTFL* was terminated as a separate publication in November 1975. All editorial work was now handled in-house, a new full-time staff position was added to the headquarters staff, and Warren C. Born was hired as Acting Editor of *FLA*.

President Warriner, in her first letter to the membership, addressed ACTFL's more pressing issues. Concerning the potential move, she explained:

"Some members are under the impression that the ACTFL Headquarters will change location in the near future. We have rent-free space from MLA at the present address until 1 September 1976. For the next year, we would pay half of the rent—$400 per month. After

ACTFL | *American Council on the Teaching of Foreign Languages*
62 Fifth Avenue · New York 10011

February 1974

Dear ACTFL Member:

1974 is a very significant year for ACTFL--*and we need your help as we become independent and plan for the future.*

In the past months, ACTFL has begun to move from its status as a part of the Modern Language Association to that of a separate non-profit organization. The membership approved incorporation through an advisory ballot in the fall of 1973, and, at the Annual Meeting in Boston, the Constituent Assembly and Executive Council authorized the Executive Secretary to take the steps necessary for incorporation.

These initiatives coincide with measures taken to transfer from MLA to ACTFL the management and expense of certain internal services. ACTFL has already assumed full responsibility for editing and producing its own publications. With incorporation, ACTFL will establish its own accounting system. ACTFL will continue to receive financial support from MLA for certain indirect costs (e.g., office space and related overhead) through 1975, when it will assume such expenses on a schedule established by the MLA Executive Council in 1971. By 1980 ACTFL will be carrying all costs of its operation.

To accommodate these important changes, *ACTFL's present system of four membership cycles per year is being revised into a single membership cycle based on the calendar year.* In addition, the ACTFL fiscal year has been changed to coincide with the calendar year, and economy measures have been instituted to hold the line on expenses, including sizeable reductions in salary and printing budgets. In order to maintain the full range of ACTFL services, some functions normally performed by headquarters staff will be carried on with the assistance of Executive Council members and the voluntary efforts of other individual members.

We need your cooperation to make these changes. First, since your present membership cycle does not coincide with a calendar year schedule, we ask that you assist us by making a dues payment of $2.50, $5.00, or $7.50 to put your membership on a paid-up basis through December 1974. A special dues form and an explanation of your present membership cycle and the amount needed to pay your membership through December 1974 are enclosed. *This will in no way affect the number or timing of copies of ACTFL publications which you will receive in 1974.*

Second, of great importance to the association, *we ask that you make a modest investment in ACTFL's future.* Until now, ACTFL has drawn upon MLA cash reserves to pay for services to members that were delivered in advance of dues payment. MLA funds will no longer be available, and ACTFL must now establish a minimum reserve. An average contribution of $10.00 per member will enable ACTFL to build a reserve fund of approximately $30,000 and will also provide sufficient additional income to restore staff and printing budgets. ACTFL must cover the reduction in 1974 income which will result from conversion to a single membership cycle and consequent partial billing in the transition year of 1974.

As an ACTFL member, you believe in the concept of a unified foreign language profession. *Your contribution should reflect the degree to which you are able to support this belief and commitment.* While we suggest $10.00 per member, *any amount will be important to ACTFL.* The viability of ACTFL depends on the individual involvement of each member, as we seek to strengthen our profession.

Sincerely yours,

C. Edward Scebold
Executive Secretary

Foreign Language Annals,
October 1976

Foreign Language Annals, Volume 8, Number 3 (October 1975), p. 248.

1 September 1977, we would pay full rent ($800 per month) to stay at 62 Fifth Avenue. A committee of Council members is investigating alternatives available to us; many types of sites are being considered. The decision will be made by Executive Council during 1976, according to a number of criteria, such as space, availability of supportive services necessary for a professional organization, accessibility, potential for permanency, and other factors. An announcement of decision will be made to the membership at the earliest opportunity" (*FLA*, Vol. 9, Number 1 (February 1976), p. 48).

It was later decided to keep ACTFL headquarters in the New York metropolitan area.

In his report for 1975, Executive Secretary Scebold mentioned progress in a number of areas that would lead to greater service to the membership and said these changes could be announced at a time when the association's fiscal outlook continued to improve. The association did receive nonprofit status from the IRS on June 4, 1975, which called for an immediate revision of the Bylaws to conform to its new legal status. ACTFL would operate under the Articles of Incorporation, replacing the Constitution the membership had adopted in 1970. Input into the new Articles was requested from the membership and those represented by the numerous ACTFL affiliates. An ad hoc committee was set up to examine the nominating procedures for selection of the President of ACTFL, procedures the Executive Council accepted. The current President was to appoint a nominating committee of five ACTFL members; each organization represented in the Advisory Assembly could submit one candidate for President-elect and two names for the Executive Council; only two names for President-elect would go on the ballot.

Scebold wrote of the greater contact and cooperation among larger foreign language associations in the country, indicating that the JNCL's creation had brought to the national level a mutual degree of concern and support that formerly existed at only the state and local levels. Its creation opened channels of communication and led to cooperation in launching projects that did not encroach on the "turf" of any single association. JNCL had offered a proposal to consolidate that organization and its activities into the official ACTFL structure, but Scebold said there was no strong consensus for such a move.

He also reported that, as a result of ACTFL Moving Contingencies Committee studies, consensus was reached that the tentative relocation date would be January 1, 1977.

Negotiations with NFMLTA were at a standstill. The ACTFL Executive Council had stated "...that one of the major problems which emerged in the course of the discussions was that of attempting to find grounds for discussing cooperative endeavors between a publisher and a membership organization."

A new drive for increasing membership was brewing. A brochure was sent out using the new 1976 publication graphic. As of November 1, 1975, ACTFL had 9,878 total members and subscribers; 450 new members were added by January 1, 1976, as a result of the new campaign. Student membership was limited to only one year.

The "retired membership" category was added at student membership prices. Membership now included six issues of *FLA*, which now included *Accent on ACTFL*.

The *ACTFL Review of Foreign Language Education Series* underwent a change: it was now to be called the *ACTFL Foreign Language Education Series*. Volume 8 of the series was being planned, with the theme "Choosing Among the Options: An Integrative Approach." The *ACTFL Bibliography* was discontinued, pending the commitment of extramural funding for the project. The ACTFL Materials Center was doing well; sales to date in 1975 were $6,000.

ACTFL's financial situation, however, was not on a strong, solid footing. The organization's accountant pointed out that joint meetings were not feasible from the standpoint of the financial impact on ACTFL. To help bolster ACTFL, a reserve fund was created, announced by President Warriner in the December 1976 issue of *FLA* (see p. 32).

"We are growing up!"
—Lowell Dunham, ACTFL Past President 1971

In his first "A Message from the President" in *FLA*, Vol. 10, Number 1 (February 1977), Howard B. Altman repeated his message from a session he had presented at the 1976 Annual Meeting:

As we look at ACTFL's first ten years, we have reason to be proud of our accomplishments in some areas. We are the largest national, nongovernmental, multilingual association of foreign language teachers in the world today!... Through our journals, our occasional publications, our bibliography, our Series on Foreign Language Education, and more recently our Materials Center, we have provided classroom teachers and researchers with concise, up-to-date information about the issues in teaching and learning foreign languages."

Membership brochure, 1976

A SPECIAL ANNOUNCEMENT TO THE ACTFL MEMBERSHIP

It is my pleasure to announce to you that the ACTFL Executive Council has established a Reserve Fund for ACTFL. I would also like to explain why we took this action:

1. Most professional associations and service organizations have special membership categories or funds designed to generate income beyond that produced by basic membership fees. ACTFL hopes to build a sufficient reserve so that funds will be available for special projects which may be required to respond to specific professional needs.

2. Every organization needs a cushion against which it can draw, should an emergency occur. To choose a specific, hypothetical example, a national emergency could result in the cancellation of an annual meeting. Such a development could destroy the balance of expenses and income, even with the best of planning. In addition, there is the concern of maintaining adequate cash flow during the summer months. Expenses continue, but income almost ceases. A reserve fund is essential at that time.

3. As a young organization, ACTFL is relatively small with approximately 10,000 total members. If we had, for example, 30,000 members, we could provide the same services and publications for little more money. In other words, the larger the membership, the lower the per member costs. As a small organization, ACTFL is forced to struggle to make ends meet while providing good services to members.

4. During 1977, ACTFL will most certainly move from its present location. We must acquire furniture and office equipment and incur additional costs which are not usually a part of the budget.

As you can see, there are immediate needs as well as long-range goals for the Reserve Fund.

Members are encouraged to contribute any amount, large or small, that they may wish above the basic membership fee. For the foreseeable future, this money will be placed in the Reserve Fund to be drawn from only for emergencies or during the low cash-flow period. The money will be replaced in the Reserve Fund unless emergency circumstances prevent it. Short-term investments will be made to generate additional income from the fund. If, in the future, this fund becomes larger than necessary for the purposes described above, the Executive Council and professional leadership of ACTFL anticipate that a portion of it would be applied to special, significant projects.

On your dues card there is a new category, "Trust Fund." We hope that you will check that block each year and increase the amount of your check to the degree you desire. If you have already sent your membership dues, a supplementary check will be gratefully received. (The use of "Trust" does not have legal significance.)

Let me assure you that this is not a one-shot campaign or emergency drive. It is a permanent means by which the believers in ACTFL may make their support evident.

Helen P. Warriner
1976 President of ACTFL

But, he points out,

"We have been less successful in unifying our profession or in influencing the formation of policies which affect us. In this respect, we language teachers remain today much as we were ten years ago: a fragmented body of individuals, each pulling for his or her special language, classroom behaviors, and methodological preferences. There is no unified voice for foreign language teachers in the United States. And yet nothing may prove to be more important for us in the decade ahead!" (p. 96).

The year 1977 marked the beginning of ACTFL's second decade, and saw significant changes. All ties with the parent organization, MLA, were severed; dependence on MLA for ACTFL's day-to-day operation ceased. By the end of January, ACTFL had moved from MLA headquarters to a new location in Manhattan: 2 Park Avenue. President Altman's letter in *FLA*, Vol. 10, Number 3 (May 1977) followed up the earlier announcement, and discussed the move:

ACTFL's Moved!
New Address: 2 Park Avenue, New York, NY 10016
New Telephone: (212) 689-8021

Two Park Avenue may sound like a fancy address for a struggling not-for-profit corporation like ACTFL, but I can assure you, as I write this message from ACTFL headquarters, that

the rental costs of our new headquarters reflect the minimum amount ACTFL could pay to obtain adequate facilities from which to provide the growing number of services which our members demand. New headquarters furniture had to be purchased, since almost everything at 62 Fifth Avenue belonged to the MLA. Most of the new furniture was purchased second-hand, from companies such as "AAA Rock Bottom Buy and Sell" (honest—that's the name!). Our moving company did not have the reputation of Allied Van Lines, but "Nice Jewish Boy with a Truck" did the job for us at considerably less cost (I'm really not making up these names!). The combination of careful planning, fortuitous furniture purchases, and a make-do-with-what-we've-got attitude resulted in a savings of thousands of dollars. Incidentally, our new headquarters is both attractive and comfortable. (p. 288)

Howard B. Altman
ACTFL President 1977

ACTFL's former constituents (delegates representing various state organizations) and affiliates (regional conferences and national associations) became known as "the Assembly" when the organization's Bylaws and Constitution were being rewritten.

Membership had gradually increased from 1968 to 1973, but 1974 to 1977 had seen a small but steady decline, despite focused membership campaigns.

The 1977 Annual Meeting in San Francisco, CA, was to be the first conference since 1973 that was not a joint meeting with other national or international organizations.

Despite the failure of the proposal to merge JNCL with ACTFL, ACTFL remained an active participant in JNCL activities. Ed Scebold was named Treasurer of JNCL.

In October 1976, ACTFL was selected to participate in a series of career education mini-conferences sponsored by the Office of Career Education, U.S. Office of Education. Meetings were held throughout 1977.

Part of ACTFL's adjustment to its new independent status involved guidelines, which began to appear as follows:

- Guidelines for Nominations: President-elect and Executive Council Positions
- Role of the ACTFL Executive Council Committee
- Policy Statement on Collaboration

ACTFL was experiencing a good year financially. In fact, it seemed poised to end the year with a surplus of income over expenses. With its new independence, the organization immediately began to seek extramural funding, and received one grant in fiscal 1977, had another pending, and planned additional proposals for early 1978.

All aspects of ACTFL's project and activities were opened to scrutiny—the membership had been offered numerous opportunities to criticize, evaluate, and suggest improvements for the new independent organization.

The new Bylaws to the Constitution, rewritten as a result of independence, were passed by the Assembly at the Annual Business Meeting in New Orleans.

President Altman appointed the Public Relations Committee, one of whose first charges was to create a packet of materials that could be widely distributed to help celebrate Foreign Language Week.

Point of Interest

The title of Executive Secretary was changed to Executive Director (and later Executive Director and Treasurer). This change in title appeared for the first time in the minutes of the Executive Council Meeting of February 12-15, 1977.

FLA, Vol. 10, No. 4 (September 1977), p. 427

June K. Phillips was named Editor of Vol. 9 of the *ACTFL Foreign Language Education Series*. She also agreed to be Editor for Vol. 10, the theme of which was "Building on Experience—Building for Success." Sales through the Materials Center exceeded $30,000 as of November 1, 1977.

At the Executive Council meeting on November 23-24, 1977, ACTFL voted to support JNCL activities with direct financial contributions to the degree feasible in terms of the current ACTFL budget. Also, a revision of the dues structure for membership was adopted to go into effect in 1979:

- Student members (1-year eligibility) $9
- Retired members $9
- Regular Members (first two years) $15
- Regular Members
  (salary under $10,000) $20
- Regular Members
  (salary $10,000-$20,000) $25
- Regular Members
  (salary over $20,000) $30
- Joint Membership $35

It was announced that the 1979 Annual Meeting would be with SCOLT in Atlanta on November 22-24, 1979, and that the 1980 meeting would be in Boston, but taking place before Thanksgiving at the membership's request: November 21-23, 1980, with workshops the following week.

Thanks to the generosity of the Illinois Foreign Language Teachers Association (IFLTA) and various ACTFL members, two awards were established to honor the memory of two leaders in the foreign language profession, Florence Steiner and Paul Pimsleur. Two Florence Steiner Awards for Leadership in Foreign Language Education would be presented, one to a public or private school foreign language teacher (K-12), the other to a person in either postsecondary foreign language education or foreign language

administration. The Pimsleur Award was for research in foreign language education. Both awards were to be presented for the first time at the 1977 Annual Meeting in San Francisco. The first Steiner Award recipients were Robert Ludwig of the Schenectady (NY) City Schools and Wilga Rivers of Harvard University. The first Pimsleur Award recipient was Robert Politzer of Stanford University.

In his final letter to the membership (*FLA*, Vol. 10, No. 6 (December 1977)), President Altman made an announcement which, in retrospect, we know was of primary importance for the foreign language profession: President Jimmy Carter had agreed to set up a Presidential Commission to deal with foreign language and culture study in the United States (p. 656). The impetus for this commission had come from Congress, especially from Congressman Paul Simon of Illinois.

The President's Commission on Foreign Language and International Studies

Indeed, the Commission on Foreign Language and International Studies was set up by President Jimmy Carter by Executive Order 12054 on April 21, 1978. But prior to the establishment of this commission, ACTFL had assumed an active role in the discussions and the planning. Subsequent to the meetings of August 17, 1977, President-elect Lorraine Strasheim and Executive Director Scebold prepared and forwarded a statement to Congressman Paul Simon and Commissioner of Education, Ernest L. Boyer. Then, after Scebold attended a special briefing regarding the Commission, with the advice and consent of the ACTFL Steering Committee, a jointly-prepared statement from ACTFL and the MLA was prepared and forwarded to Graeme Baxter, Assistant Commissioner for Executive Operations, Office of Education (See Appendix B).

Lorraine A. Strasheim
ACTFL President 1978

In the second half of 1978, a dynamic public awareness effort by all associated with foreign language education began, as a result of the President's Commission on Foreign Language and International Studies. Ed Scebold opened his Annual Report of 1978 with: "This annual report is a call to action!" As a result of the first meeting on October 26-28, 1978, at the headquarters of the Organization of American States in Washington, DC, he cautioned: "Our response— or lack of one [to the Commission]—may have serious bearing on the final report by the Commission; thus the role of foreign languages in education, and federal priorities and funding which relate to foreign languages at the national level may be significantly affected over the next decade" (*FLA*, Vol. 12, No. 1 (February 1979), p. 12). He called for focus on the upcoming meetings of the Commission, as well as regional meetings, throughout 1979. Commission Chairman James A. Perkins discussed the areas of the Commission's focus:

- International education in elementary and secondary schools.
- International education in undergraduate studies at college and university levels.
- Foreign language:
  — for learning about other countries and cultures;
  — for developing competency.
- Advanced training and research.
- International exchanges of teaching staff and students.
- Interest of the business, international trade and finance community in foreign languages and international study.

"An ACTFL Resolution" 1978; "Resolutions on Language In American Education" 1978

The meeting also saw recurring emphasis on the need to initiate a program to increase enrollments in foreign languages, particularly at the school level, and the need for language and area studies experts to meet the national and international needs of the U.S., at all levels of labor, business, industry, and government. But primary concern was on perceptions of various Commission members regarding the relationship between foreign language and international education.

"An ACTFL Position Paper: Foreign Language and International Education in the Twenty-First Century" was issued by ACTFL Executive Director Richard Brod at the request of James Perkins and submitted to the members of the Commission. This position paper appeared in *FLA*, Vol. 12, No. 1 (February 1979), pp. 27-28.

The "plan of attack" focused on various levels of involvement on numerous fronts. The work of the MLA/ACLS Task Forces were to be widely disseminated within the profession and endorsed by many of the influential foreign language associations at the state, regional and national levels. These Task Forces had examined five areas of concern:

1. Institutional language policy;
2. The commonly taught languages;
3. The less commonly taught languages;
4. Public awareness;
5. Government relations.

"An ACTFL Resolution," written and signed by members of the Executive Council, was mailed to President Carter, Vice President Mondale, Education Secretary Califano, and all members of Congress in November 1978. ACTFL received many positive responses.

To synthesize a statement of purpose and future objectives for the foreign language teaching profession, Brod and S. Frederick Starr drafted a resolution (see p. 36). These Resolutions were endorsed by a number of associations and formally presented to the President's Commission when it met in January 1979.

Other documents were prepared and submitted to the President's Commission:

- Recommendations to the President's Commission, submitted jointly by ACTFL and the National Council for the Social Studies (*FLA*, Vol. 12, No. 5 (October 1979), pp. 383-386.
- "Priorities for Action," compiled from discussions at regional hearings of the President's Commission, by ACTFL, MLA, the Center for Applied Linguistics (CAL), and endorsed by JNCL (*FLA*, Vol. 12, No. 5 (October 1979), pp. 387-391).

Amid this flurry of activity, ACTFL continued to serve its membership and the profession. The 1976 Bylaws were thoroughly reviewed. Membership increased slightly in 1978 to a total of 9,019 members and subscriptions. The ACTFL Materials Center was proving to be a self-sustaining unit of the total ACTFL operation. Two grants were received in 1978:

1. Inservice Training in Career Education: Incorporating the Career Concept in Foreign Language Programs, funded by the Office of Career Education, U.S. Office of Education; and
2. "National Survey of Foreign Language Teaching in Secondary Schools," funded by the Division of International Education, U.S. Office of Education.

Finally, the organization now had a ten-year lease on its new headquarters at 2 Park Avenue (see p. 39). Its only financial ties to MLA were for the purchase of computer services for the maintenance of the ACTFL membership and subscription files.

On March 22, 1979, Kenneth Mildenberger, former Editor of *FLA*, Treasurer of ACTFL, Deputy Director of MLA, and the driving force behind the founding of ACTFL, died at the age of 57.

At the May 1978 Executive Council meeting, it was decided that the membership would vote on one of two dues plans: (1) a fixed structure, or (2) a graduated dues structure proposed in 1977 (see p. 34). It was announced that the 1979 President-elect and 1980 President was Dale L. Lange (MN). In the September 1978 issue of *FLA* (Vol. 11, No. 4 , p. 445), a note on ACTFL's new Restricted Funds appeared:

ACTFL presently has four different restricted funds designed to serve special purposes. Contributions to any or all of these funds are welcome at any time; make checks payable to ACTFL and enclose a note indicating for which fund the contribution is intended, or use the form below.

(1) The ACTFL Commitment Fund. This fund is intended to meet short-term needs and long-range goals. It is used to assist in maintaining a stable cash-flow situation or to meet immediate needs; as this fund becomes larger, it will be used to generate additional income and can be utilized for special projects of significance to the profession. (For further details, see FLA, 9 [1976], 562.)

(2) The Florence Steiner Award Fund. This fund was established through the generosity of the Illinois Foreign Language Teachers Association and is used to make possible two annual awards for leadership in foreign language education, one to a public or private school foreign language teacher foreign language education or foreign language

Jane M. Bourque
ACTFL President 1979

administration. The first Steiner Awards were made in 1977. (For further information on the 1978 Steiner Awards, see FLA, 11 [1978], 270.)

(3) The Paul Pimsleur Award Fund. The generosity of various ACTFL members enabled the establishment of this fund. The annual Pimsleur Award is based on a published or publishable contribution to research in foreign or second language education. The first award was made in 1977. (For further details, see FLA, 10 [1977], 413.)

(4) The Nelson Brooks Award Fund. The ACTFL Executive Council approved the establishment of this fund at its May 1978 meeting; the fund was made possible through the generosity of the Connecticut Council of Language Teachers in providing the initial contribution. The award will honor a member of the profession who has made an outstanding contribution to the teaching of culture.
(*Foreign Language Annals*, Volume 11, Number 4, September 1978, p. 445)

In her "Message from the President" in *FLA,* Vol. 12, No. 5 (October 1979), President Bourque announced a campaign to raise money for a media-related national public awareness program, the LENGUA project (Language Education Now for Global Understanding and Awareness). Its goal was to raise the $100,000 needed to secure the National Advertising Council's services for the public awareness program needed to raise the consciousness of parents so they would *demand* more foreign language instruction and be willing to pay for it. Bourque cautioned, however: "The demand for *more* language instruction will be accompanied, no doubt, by a call for *better* language instruction. After all, the lack of appreciation for foreign languages in this country is due not only to the fact that we are a society of monolinguals and ethnocentrics (an overemphasized generalization), but to the testimony of many Americans that they have had poor language experiences" (p. 413). A public awareness campaign was a wonderful opportunity for dialogue between language teachers and other members of the community on these issues. With that, ACTFL set up a Public Awareness Network to spur the LENGUA project and its goals.

LENGUA Brochure
August 1979

LENGUA

In order to initiate a national fundraising project in support of the public awareness effort, ACTFL has created Project LENGUA — Language Education Now for Global Understanding and Awareness.

ACTFL has designated $10,000 to launch this fundraising effort. We seek your support in helping us achieve the goal of $100,000 to launch the first national, media-related phase of the project.

In 1975 the Helsinki Agreement was signed by 35 nations, including the United States. These 35 nations agreed that the study of foreign languages and civilizations must be encouraged as a means of strengthening international cooperation.

In 1978 the President's Commission on Foreign Language and International Studies was created to recommend means for directing public attention to the importance of foreign language and international studies for the improvement of communications and understanding with other nations in an increasingly interdependent world.

During the course of the deliberations of the Commission, a recurrent theme has been the need for greater public awareness and appreciation of the value of foreign language and culture studies on the part of United States citizens.

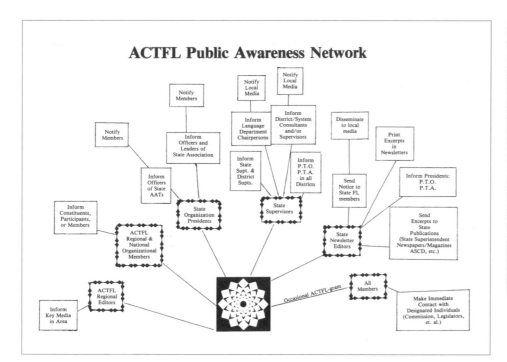

ACTFL Public Awareness Network

Lease for 2 Park Avenue New York, NY

On October 15, 1979, the President's Commission issued its report to the President, "Strength through Wisdom: A Critique of U.S. Capability." Chairman Perkins, in his letter to the President accompanying the report, said it was presented "with a great sense of urgency. We have discovered and documented weaknesses in the area of our inquiry which, in our view, pose threats to America's security and economic viability…. The Commission's report explains why competence in foreign languages and international understanding is important to all Americans; it identifies the points of greatest weakness; and it presents carefully considered recommendations for remedial action" (*The Modern Language Journal,* Vol. 64, No. 1 (Spring, 1980), p. 9).

Perkins said, "Leadership is paralyzed without a well-informed public that embraces all citizens."

Now, ACTFL had a charge, and its LENGUA project was an integral part and essential beginning point. ACTFL's 1980 President Dale Lange (MN) and President-elect Thomas H. Geno (VT) together assumed the helm of an organization that could have a powerful impact on the future of foreign languages in the U.S.

Retrospective on ACTFL in the 1970s

In my opinion some of the most significant events in the history of ACTFL took place during the 1970s. I refer here to the pulling away from dependence upon MLA and becoming a separate not-for-profit organization serving educators whose functions covered the field from elementary school through graduate school. Also of significance was the fact that classical as well as modern languages were included in the membership. At the time, many thought that ACTFL should somehow take over the Modern Language Journal instead of starting a new, competing publication. This did not work out; we started Foreign Language Annals, and it seems that there was plenty of demand for a second pedagogical journal in the area of foreign language education.

With ACTFL's creation we now, for the first time, had a foreign language organization which helped break down the "Balkanization" of language professionals and to promote communication across language lines. This has led to a stronger profession in terms of higher visibility, more power as a political entity, and a better vehicle for dealing with pedagogical matters.

Frank M. Grittner
ACTFL President 1975

ACTFL Memories: 1977

When I reflect back upon my year as president of ACTFL, my fondest memories are of planning and working with a very dedicated executive council and headquarters staff. ACTFL was still a very young organization, a bit troubled by aspects of its relationship with its "founding mother" — the MLA — and chronically concerned about whether dues revenues and annual meeting fees — which, for all practical purposes, were ACTFL's only sources of income in those days — would suffice to pay the bills of running the organization and publishing Foreign Language Annals. The calculation of an estimated budget for the following year was always a triumph of hope over anxiety.

1977 was also the year in which ACTFL became more heavily involved in externally sponsored research. Research monies today are a significant part of ACTFL's budget and allow ACTFL to exercise a leadership role in such areas as proficiency testing. I remember many days of that year in which Ed Scebold and I worked on grant proposals, not knowing (thanks to our own relative inexperience) whether we were wasting our time or not. I am proud that I was able to serve as a catalyst for this involvement in research.

Howard B. Altman
University of Louisville

CONSTITUTION AND BYLAWS OF THE AMERICAN COUNCIL ON THE TEACHING OF FOREIGN LANGUAGES CONSTITUTION

I. Name

The name of the organization shall be The American Council on the Teaching of Foreign Languages, hereinafter referred to as ACTFL.

II. Purpose

The purpose of ACTFL shall be to promote and improve the teaching of all foreign languages, literatures, and cultures in American education, to provide educational services to the members of ACTFL, to publish appropriate journals and other publications, and to conduct an annual convention and other meetings. ACTFL is a not-for-profit organization.

III. Membership

1. Individual membership in ACTFL is open to any person engaged in the teaching of any foreign language, literature, or culture at any level of education, and to all others interested in the improvement of such teaching. The dues and privileges of individual membership are described in the Bylaws.

2. Constituent membership in ACTFL is open to associations of foreign language teachers which represent states or similar political subdivisions. Requirements and privileges of constituent membership are described in Article IV.2, Article V.2, Article VIII, and the Bylaws.

3. Affiliate membership in ACTFL is open to regional and national associations of teachers of foreign languages, literatures, and cultures. The dues, requirements, and privileges of affiliate membership are described in Article V.3 and the Bylaws.

IV. Officers

1. The officers of ACTFL shall be the President, the President-elect, the Executive Secretary, and the Treasurer.

2. *The President and President-elect*

a. The Constituent Assembly shall annually nominate a slate of at least two members for the position of President-Elect. Election shall be by secret ballot sent by mail to all individual members of ACTFL. Blank spaces shall be provided for additional nominations. Of the names on the ballot, the one receiving the highest number of votes shall be declared President- Elect.

b. The President-elect shall hold office for a term of one calendar year, and at the end of this term he shall become President for one calendar year.

c. If any President or President-elect or other member of the Executive Council is unable or unwilling to serve, the Executive Council shall appoint an individual member of ACTFL to serve his term.

d. The President is Chairman and Presiding Officer of the Executive Council, which is the policy-making body of ACTFL. He shall be Chairman of meetings of the Constituent Assembly. He is empowered to appoint committees to fulfill and carry out the aims and programs of ACTFL, but all such appointments are subject to majority approval of the Executive Council.

e. The President-elect shall serve as Chairman at meetings of the Executive Council in the absence of the President. He shall serve as Chairman at meetings of the Affiliate Assembly, and he shall serve as Chairman of the Constituent Assembly in the absence of the President.

3. *The Executive Secretary and Treasurer*

a. The Executive Secretary shall be appointed for a specified term by the Executive Council. He shall administer the business of ACTFL subject to the instructions and review of the Executive Council. He shall be Editor of the official journal of ACTFL, and he shall arrange the program of the annual meeting of ACTFL. He is authorized, within the limits of the approved annual budget, to appoint staff members necessary to carry out his responsibilities. He shall report at the annual meeting of ACTFL on the activities of ACTFL during the past year. He shall tabulate all ballots and report the results.

b. The Treasurer shall be appointed by the Executive Council for a specified term. He shall be responsible for the handling of all financial affairs of ACTFL and shall maintain records in keeping with generally accepted principles of accounting. The financial records shall be subjected annually to a public audit, and the Treasurer shall submit a report of the financial record and the auditor's report to the Constituent Assembly at its annual meeting and shall publish these reports annually in the official journal. He shall be bonded in a sum commensurate with his responsibilities. He shall each year prepare for presentation to the Executive Council, for its approval, rejection, or amendment, a budget of expenditures for the ensuing official year. For budgetary and other administrative purposes, the official year shall be determined by the Executive Council.

V. Administration

1. *The Executive Council*

a. Policy making for ACTFL shall be the responsibility of the Executive Council, which shall be known as the Board of Directors of the Corporation, and which shall meet at least twice a year, at the call of the President, with at least forty days advance written notice.

b. The Executive Council shall consist of the President, the President-elect, the Executive Secretary, the Treasurer, and seven members elected for staggered terms of three calendar years by secret ballot sent to all individual members of ACTFL. The Executive Council shall, as terms expire, make at least two nominations for each of six of these seven posts. Any member of ACTFL may initiate a petition, signed by twenty-five members in good standing, proposing the name of an additional candidate. The petition shall be forwarded to the Executive Secretary no later than the first of April of the year in which the election is to be held. With it shall go a detailed biography of the additional candidate for one of these six posts. Of the names on the ballot for each of these posts, the one receiving the highest number of votes shall be declared member of the Executive Council. All candidates for the Executive Council shall be members of ACTFL. The Affiliate Assembly shall make nominations for the seventh member of the Executive Council.

c. The Executive Secretary and Treasurer shall be, ex officio, nonvoting members of the Executive Council. The President shall vote in the case of a tie vote.

d. A quorum of the Executive Council shall be five of the voting members.

2. *The Constituent Assembly*

a. The Constituent Assembly shall review the actions of ACTFL at the annual meeting of ACTFL. The time and place of the annual Constituent Assembly meeting shall be set by the Executive Council and published in the official journal. The President, the Executive Secretary, and the Treasurer will provide detailed reports on the past year's activities and the plans for the future. The Constituent Assembly shall offer comments and recommendations which the Executive Council must consider at its next meeting.

b. The Constituent Assembly shall consist of representatives of state foreign language associations (and representatives of such associations for similar political subdivisions) which are constituent units of ACTFL. In order to qualify as a constituent, an association must meet the following conditions: (1) its member ship must be open to all teachers of all languages at all levels of instruction from both public and private institutions; (2) it must not impose requirement of membership in any national organization upon its own members; (3) any official representative to the Constituent Assembly must be an individual member of ACTFL. The Executive Council has the power to determine the definition of "state," to accept or reject applications of organizations, and to suspend or revoke constituency status for cause. There will be no annual dues for constituent organizations.

c. Each constituent organization shall be entitled to one voting representative to the Constituent Assembly. The representative shall be named by the association according to its own procedures, and his identity shall be re ported to the Executive Secretary of ACTFL no later than sixty days before the annual meeting of the Constituent Assembly in order to qualify for participation. When the number of ACTFL members in a state exceeds 1,000, the relevant organization shall be entitled to an additional voting representative to the Constituent Assembly, whether or not all of the ACTFL members are also members of the constituent organization; and for each 1,000 additional members of ACTFL in a state, an additional representative shall be authorized.

d. A quorum of the Constituent Assembly shall be one-third of the representatives authorized from state organizations currently approved by the Executive Council.

3. *The Affiliate Assembly*

a. The Affiliate Assembly shall meet at the annual meeting of ACTFL to discuss special interests and current issues concerning the teaching of foreign languages, literatures, and cultures and to make appropriate recommendations to the Constituent Assembly and the Executive Council. The time and place of the annual Affiliate Assembly meeting shall be set by the Executive Council and published in the official journal.

b. The Affiliate Assembly shall consist of single delegates from regional and national organizations of teachers of foreign languages, literatures, and cultures which are affiliated with ACTFL. The Executive Council has the power to accept or reject applications of such organizations, and to suspend or revoke affiliate status for cause. Official representatives to the Affiliate Assembly must hold individual ACTFL membership. Each affiliate will name its representative according to its own procedures, and his identity shall be reported to the Executive Secretary of ACTFL no later than sixty days before the annual meeting of the Affiliate Assembly in order to qualify for participation.

c. The Affiliate Assembly shall every third year be responsible for the nomination of at least two ACTFL members to stand for election to the seventh post on the Executive Council. Election shall be by secret ballot sent by mail to all individual members of ACTFL. Blank spaces shall be provided for additional nominations. Of the names on the ballot for this office, the one receiving the highest number of votes shall be declared member of the Executive Council.

d. A quorum of the Affiliate Assembly shall be one-third of the representatives of organizations currently approved by the Executive Council.

VI. Meetings

1. ACTFL shall hold an annual meeting at such time and place as the Executive Council shall determine. The Executive Council may cancel the annual meeting in an emergency, but only with the concurrence of a majority mail vote of current representatives to the Constituent Assembly who respond to a ballot.

VII. Amendment of the Constitution

1. Amendments to be proposed must have approval of at least two-thirds of the Executive Council.

2. The Executive Secretary shall publish such approved proposed amendments in the official journal of ACTFL at least one month prior to the time when a mail ballot is to be distributed to the individual membership.

3. Adoption of an amendment or of a new constitution shall be voted on by mail ballot sent to all individual members of ACTFL at least one month after, and not later than two months after, its publication. The Executive Secretary shall receive and tabulate the ballots and report the results to the membership. For an amendment to be adopted, a majority of the returned ballots must approve it.

VIII. Bylaws

Bylaws may be adopted or changed at any annual meeting of the Constituent Assembly by a majority vote, providing a quorum is present and providing such proposed adoptions and changes have been published in the official journal of ACTFL at least one month prior to the meeting with the approval of a majority of the Executive Council.

IX. Dissolution

ACTFL may be dissolved only at a special meeting called for that purpose, and in the manner described by the laws of the State of New York. Subject to compliance with the applicable provisions of such laws, upon any such dissolution of ACTFL, no member shall be entitled to any distribution or division of its remaining property or its proceeds, and the balance of all money and other property received by ACTFL from any source including its operations, after the payment of all debts and obligations of ACTFL of whatsoever kind and nature, shall be used or distributed, subject to the order of the Supreme Court of the State of New York as provided by law exclusively for purposes within those set forth in Article II of this Constitution and within the intendment of Section 501 (c) (3) of the Internal Revenue Code of 1954 [26 U.S.C.A., Section 501 (c) (3)], as the same may be amended from time to time.

BYLAWS

1. Dues

a. Annual individual membership dues are $6.00 ($6.50 for members living outside the United States).

b. Annual Regular Library subscription to the official ACTFL journal is $10.00.

c. The Executive Council shall be authorized to offer an annual Comprehensive Individual Membership and an annual Comprehensive Library Subscription, to include automatic receipt of certain other publications, currently produced or distributed by ACTFL, in addition to the official journal. The cost of this comprehensive arrangement shall be set annually by the Executive Council, depending upon the anticipated volume of additional publications.

d. The affiliated member organizations shall pay annual dues of $25.00, on or before 30 September.

e. The Executive Council shall be authorized to arrange for the time and terms for the collection of dues and library subscriptions.

2. Privileges of Individual Membership

All individual members of ACTFL shall receive the official journal, be entitled to attend the annual meeting after payment of a registration fee set by the Executive Council, vote on ACTFL affairs as set out in the Constitution and Bylaws, and have access to such special services as the Executive Council may authorize.

3. Official Journal

The official ACTFL journal shall be *Foreign Language Annals*.

4. Nominating Committees

a. The Constituent Assembly shall annually appoint a Nominating Committee from among its own members to propose names of possible candidates for the office of President-elect.

b. The Affiliate Assembly shall triennially appoint a Nominating Committee from among its own members to propose names of possible candidates for the post of one member of the Executive Council.

5. Relationship to the Modern Language Association of America

a. ACTFL shall be considered part of the Modern Language Association of America (hereinafter referred to as MLA) under the MLA charter as a nonprofit organization, and the MLA shall contribute financial support to ACTFL to the extent authorized by the MLA Executive Council. The Executive Council of ACTFL may initiate a secret advisory mail ballot to the individual members of ACTFL on the question of incorporation as a separate nonprofit organization no sooner than one month after publication of its intention and recommendations in the official journal. The Executive Secretary shall receive and tabulate the ballots and report the results to the Executive Council, the Constituent Assembly, and the Affiliate Assembly. If a majority of the returned ballots are for separate incorporation, the Constituent Assembly at its next annual meeting may take appropriate steps to implement this advisory ballot.

b. While ACTFL is part of MLA and MLA provides financial assistance to ACTFL, the following conditions shall substitute for relevant provisions of the Constitution of ACTFL: (1) the MLA Treasurer shall also be Treasurer of ACTFL; (2) three of the six members of the ACTFL Executive Council who normally would be nominated by the ACTFL Executive Council (see Constitution, V.l.b.) shall instead be nominated by the MLA Executive Council. At least two members shall be nominated for each such office. Elections shall be by secret ballot sent by mail to all individual members of ACTFL. Blank spaces shall be provided for additional nominations. Of the names on the ballot, the one receiving the highest number of votes shall be declared member of the ACTFL Executive Council.

(*Foreign Language Annals*, Vol. 4, No. 3 (March 1971), pp. 243-247)

RECOMMENDATIONS CONCERNING THE PROPOSED PRESIDENTIAL COMMISSION ON LANGUAGE AND AREA STUDIES

INTRODUCTION

In 1954, William Riley Parker, former Executive Secretary and President of the Modern Language Association, issued a statement entitled *The National Interest and Foreign Languages* (Washington, D.C: Department of State Publication 7324) at the request of the U. S. National Commission for UNESCO. This statement formulated a major portion of the rationale for the inclusion of second language education in the National Defense Education Act (NDEA) which was signed into law by President Eisenhower on 2 September 1958. The National Defense Education Act demonstrated the impact of international pressures upon national policies. That this impact is as valid today as it was in 1954 is reflected in the 1975 Helsinki Agreement, which encourages "the study of foreign languages and civilizations as an important means of expanding (international) communications... and cooperation."

In view of this fact, and pursuant to the discussions held in Washington, D.C. on 26 August 1977, the American Council on the Teaching of Foreign Languages, Inc. and the Modern Language Association are pleased to have an opportunity to offer recommendations for the proposed Presidential Commission on language and area studies. These recommendations relate to the areas of (1) objectives and strategies and (2) administration of the proposed Commission.

OBJECTIVES AND STRATEGIES

A. The proposed Presidential Commission should call national attention to the significance of second languages and cultures in the context of American life.

Specifically, a comprehensive statement of the impact of second languages and cultures on the national interest of the United States should be formulated. In this statement an attempt should be made to define national needs for competence in specific languages, in both public communication and commerce.

An accompanying plan for communicating this statement to the various sectors of the American public should suggest priorities for action, as well as the role of each of the following agencies:

1. professional associations of foreign language educators
2. educational institutions
3. business and industry
4. government: federal, state, and local
5. print and non-print media

B. The proposed Presidential Commission should call national attention to the significance and role of second language and culture study in the context of American education.

Specifically, the Commission should:

1. develop procedures for communicating the research findings which suggest a positive correlation between second language learning and general educational achievement. This seems particularly significant in light of the recent national publicity surrounding the findings of the panel, chaired by Willard Wirtz, which examined the on-going fourteen-year decline in scores on the Scholastic Aptitude Test
2. assert the general educational value of the study of second languages and cultures in the contexts of the humanities and of international education
3. urge the formulation and adoption of a national language policy which will provide guidance to educational institutions at all levels in the establishment and implementation of programs in second languages and cultures to persevere through the attainment of functional proficiency, which is not a reality in the majority of educational programs today.

ADMINISTRATION

Schedule for the Commission. We support the recommendation that the proposed Commission function for six months, with the understanding that this six-month period not commence until such time as the Commission is fully constituted.

Meetings of the Commission. If the Commission is planning to hold public hearings, we urge that some be held outside Washington, D.C.

Staff. As staff director for the commission, we are pleased to nominate Dr. Rose Lee Hayden, Director of the International Education Project of the American Council on Education. As alternate we propose Dr. Richard T. Thompson, Chief of the International Studies Branch, Division of International Education, U.S.O.E.

(*Foreign Language Annals*, Vol. 11, No. 2 (April 1978), pp. 233-234.)

HERITAGE NEWS SERVICE/TOM BRUNE

Students undergo tests for foreign language listening comprehension. In the 80s, ACTFL began working on proficiency testing and training, developed the *ACTFL Provisional Proficiency Guidelines,* and later worked on guidelines specific to different languages. This work was the precursor to the later *ACTFL Proficiency Guidelines* for speaking, writing, listening and reading.

CHAPTER 3

THE 1980s

ACTFL Rallies to the Call

The year 1980, just like 1979, was extremely meaningful and challenging for ACTFL, as President Lange pointed out in his first "Message from the President" in *FLA*, Vol. 13, No. 1 (February 1980), p. 9. The Report of the President's Commission on Foreign Language and International Studies remained one of ACTFL's primary focuses. In addition, two major priorities had been determined at the beginning of 1980: the establishment of a Washington Liaison Office and the development of an ACTFL Alert Network.

The Washington Liaison Office would be set up by ACTFL and the Modern Language Association (MLA), in cooperation with the Joint Committee for Languages (JNCL). It would house a lobbyist who would continually inform the profession of language legislation that had been proposed or introduced to Congress. This person would also help direct necessary action on that legislation. The lobbyist would also work with professional organizations whose interest was international education and education in the broadest sense, so that wide support for foreign language education could be established (*FLA*, Vol. 13, No. 1 (February 1980), p. 9). In fact, this office opened in Washington, staffed by Dorothy Huss of ACTFL and Leonard Schaefer as interim JNCL liaison personnel.

The Alert Network was being developed to instantaneously inform ACTFL members and leadership in all 50 states of events in Washington, particularly in 1980, regarding legislation and actions needed.

A monthly newsletter for the network was added to ACTFL's list of publications. Dorothy Huss began to set up the network in December 1979–January 1980, appointing key contacts in each state. The first test came in late January when, as a result of a follow-up meeting to the report of the President's Commission, Rep. Paul Simon (D–IL) indicated some lack of surety concerning support for his efforts on behalf of the

Dale L. Lange
ACTFL President 1980

ACTFL ALERT NETWORK

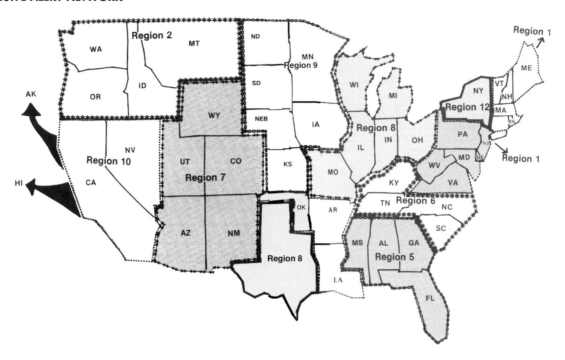

foreign language profession. On February 4, phone calls went out to regional organizers, asking them to seek support in having letters written to Simon by February 11. On that date, 450 letters had been received; by the end of the next week, over 800 letters had arrived, and Simon's aides told ACTFL, "Call off the troops!" Legislation was being framed. Paul Simon had drafted a bill on incentive funding—basically the wording from the President's Commission Report turned into legal language. Representative Leon Panetta introduced a bill for the Foreign Language and International Studies Incentive Act into the House of Representatives.

On April 15, 1980, Dr. Johanna S. R. Mendelson began her new position as permanent lobbyist and liaison officer. Funding of $60,000 had been sought from the JNCL member organizations, but that goal was not reached in 1980. While the office had been in existence for only a few months, ACTFL believed it had to direct its attention to further defining the future direction of the project, including a comprehensive plan for legislative action that would address the Priorities for Action, which ACTFL had prepared and JNCL had endorsed in 1979 (see Appendix A). Dr. Mendelson resigned her job in late August 1980 to accept a position with the Association of American University Women, and a new search was begun to choose her successor.

The network continued its success with its response to the introduction of HR 7580, the Foreign Language Assistance Act, a controversial bill for which letters were again written to Congressman Simon. By December 1980, the Alert Network had been used 15 times to communicate information and calls for action on issues such as the organization of the new U.S. Department of Education, support for legislation introduced by Simon and Panetta, and support for passage of the Higher Education Act.

Despite this strong push for implementation of its first two priorities, ACTFL continued its regular program activities. The Annual Meeting, held in Boston on November 21–23, 1980, was themed "Foreign Language Priorities for the 1980s: From Theory to Reality." The meeting's four sub-themes were closely related to the priorities stated in the "Recommendations to the President's Commission on Foreign Language and International Studies" (see Chapter 2, Appendix B): (1) Global Education, Awareness, and Involvement; (2) Research and Evaluation; (3) Teacher Education; and (4) Curriculum and Materials Development. For the first time, the Annual Meeting was held before Thanksgiving with post-conference workshops, and the number of sessions was drastically reduced so attendees could be more involved in the program. June K. Phillips was to become Editor of the *ACTFL Foreign Language Education Series,* Vol. 10 ("The New Imperative: Expanding Horizons of Foreign Language Education,") and Vol. 11 ("Our Professional Calendar: Schedule for Tomorrow"). ACTFL had three additional priorities for 1980 and beyond:

1. To reduce, if not eliminate, its debt. Two methods were tried simultaneously: membership recruitment through an outside firm, and corporate fund-raising through the efforts of corporate fund-raising consultants. By the end of December 1980, more than 550 new or renewed memberships were to be attributed to this special membership recruiting effort. Two Corporate Contributors, along with three corporate sponsors had pledged their ongoing support.

2. To organize a conference on professional priorities. This invitational conference was held in Boston on November 19-21, 1980, before the ACTFL/AATG joint Annual Meeting. The areas addressed—drawn up by ACTFL, the National Council for Social Studies, and JNCL—were: (a) teacher education; (b) curriculum and materials development; (c) research; (d) evaluation; and (e) the relationship between global education and foreign language teaching. The statements prepared during the conference were presented in Boston during the Annual Meeting in a special series of sessions.

3. To further the professional unity that had begun between the ACTFL Steering Committee and the Executive Committee of the Northeast Conference on the Teaching of Foreign Languages (NECTFL) to form a national coalition of regional conferences (Northeast, Central States, Pacific Northwest, Southern, and the yet unformed Southwest) and state associations with ACTFL. Discussions had gone from "It would be nice if there were professional unity" to specific discussions of finances, benefits, programs, publications, and other programmatic advantages to a restructuring of the relationship between ACTFL and the regional language organizations.

To illustrate how far ACTFL had come in 1980, 1978 President-elect Lorraine A. Strasheim had prepared a summary of issues that had been identified in discussions back in 1976. In light of activities in 1979 and 1980, this summary showed that ACTFL had done something about the important concerns of language educators.

One major project that had just been undertaken was a discussion and planning with the Foreign Service Institute (FSI), Educational Testing Service (ETS), MLA, and Teachers of English to Speakers of Other Languages (TESOL) of a project to define proficiency standards for the language teaching profession and the creation of testing instruments to measure outcomes. This germ of a project in 1980 was to become one of ACTFL's major undertakings—and accomplishments.

Priorities

The 1981 Annual Meeting theme was "National Imperatives for an International Vision: Implementing the ACTFL Priorities"—the very priorities that had come from the National

A SYNTHESIS OF THE 1976 ISSUES

I. In order to build greater professional cohesion; to provide for ongoing exchange and problem-solving; and to assure ACTFL's focus on the real problems of real teachers

ACTFL should provide forums on a regular basis for a variety of teacher groups

- to identify prime curricular concerns;
- to work toward more successful articulation;
- to assess public relations and program needs;
- to identify needed research; and
- to consider group-specific issues.

The groups, including teachers of all languages in each, are:

- teachers in early childhood education, teachers of the gifted, and FLES;
- junior high and middle school teachers;
- secondary-school foreign language teachers;
- junior and community college personnel; and
- college and university teachers of foreign languages.

II. In order to:

- attract more students to and hold them in foreign language programs;
- solve the problems of presenting too much too rapidly for student mastery;
- address the problems of articulation;
- meet the needs and interests of learners of different ages, a diversity of learning styles, and a variety of needs and interests;
- help teachers cope with the professional "overchoice" in teaching foci and options;
- stimulate inservice training; and
- build professional pride:

ACTFL should promote, perhaps through "working" preconferences, clear and minimal definitions for every level and every type of foreign language offering, of a working rationale;

- goals and objectives;
- subject matter;
- learning options;
- teaching strategies;
- testing and measurement; and
- program evaluation.

Documents of this kind, once they have been prepared or identified, with guidelines for adaptation to the specific school's, system's, or institution's need and population, should be made available through *Foreign Language Annals* and/or the ACTFL Materials Center.

III. In order to:

- strengthen the role of foreign languages in American life;
- influence administrators and decision-makers; and
- foster intramural cooperation and interaction with colleagues in other disciplines:

ACTFL should develop a rationale for foreign language learning which encompasses learners of all ages, all levels, and all aspirations and publicize the rationale

- through the Advertising Council of America and its free public service advertisements in magazines and on television and radio;
- through audience-specific publications and articles in the professional journals of administrators, curriculum directors, guidance counselors, and colleagues in other disciplines; and
- through cooperation with other professional and educational associations and organizations.

— Lorraine A. Strasheim, 1978 President-elect

From Foreign Language Annals, *Vol. 13, No. 5 (October 1980), pp.352-353.*

Priorities Conference in Boston in 1980. These primary concerns included giving ACTFL more visibility and influence on state, regional, and the national scene—i.e., unity—along with financial solvency, which could come primarily from an increased membership base and increased financial support.

These and other challenges now fell on 1981 President Thomas H. Geno and 1982 President-elect Charles Hancock. With the sanction of the Executive Council, they immediately went to work. Two consultancy groups were brought in: Marketing General, who focused on increasing and retaining membership; and Jeffrey Lant

Associates, who focused on fund-raising and showing ACTFL what corporate and foundation monies were available. Such funding availability depended solely on ACTFL's ability to present its cause convincingly.

Implementation of the 1980 priorities had to be followed through to their logical conclusion—reaching the profession at large—so they could be discussed, refined, and adapted to meet the needs of the local, state, and regional foreign language constituents. One of the first efforts of the ACTFL Public Awareness Committee was an "Open Letter to the Profession," which appeared in *FLA*, Vol. 14, No. 2 (April 1981), pp. 138-139,

Dear Colleagues:

We, as members of the ACTFL Public Awareness Committee, would like to tell you about some of the various activities and projects that ACTFL has been involved in during the past year, and urge you to send us your reactions. Our main objective is to establish communication between you and ACTFL.

ACTFL is trying to build support for foreign language education and attempting to strengthen the association financially by seeking outside funding for activities related to language education. We have focused on five areas of interest:

1. ACTFL has established an Alert Network, a successful national communications system. The Network has provided a mechanism for keeping the profession abreast of legislative issues. Many areas related to the Network concern us:

   • How can we make the ACTFL Alert Network a two-way communication system?
   • How can we insure that the messages will reach more people?
   • How can we make the mailings reflect the concerns of individuals and organizational members?
   • Is there a better means for gathering specific information that ACTFL may request or need at a given moment?

2. ACTFL drafted and submitted first to the JNCL, and then to Congressman Paul Simon, an alternative to the proposed legislation which would have deemphasized foreign languages at the secondary level. The ACTFL alternative has been well received by Congressman Simon. One important question has arisen related to future legislative action:

   • How can we find a mechanism for better communication with individual members who need to understand the broad role of ACTFL in representing the profession as new legislation is drafted, or issues of national concern are raised?

3. ACTFL has continued to support the Washington Liaison Office of the JNCL, both financially and philosophically. The office, under the direction of J. David Edwards, provides vital information to the language profession and must continue to reflect the overall good of the profession as well as the constituents of the members of the JNCL.

   • How can we incorporate your opinions about the upcoming legislation so that the Liaison Director can service all of the constituent members?

4. In the second year of a major membership campaign and fund-raising project, ACTFL's efforts are beginning to yield good results. With the assistance of a consulting firm, ACTFL has added 1300 new members to our roster. Our fund- raising drive has generated three Corporate Sponsors: Harcourt Brace Jovanovich, Inc.; National Textbook Company; and Scott, Foresman and Company; and one Corporate Contributor, Addison-Wesley Publishing Company. In addition, we have received a grant from the W. R. Grace Foundation to conduct a proficiency goals and testing project.

   • How can our constituents assist us in our membership promotion?
   • How can our members become involved in the fund-raising endeavor which will strengthen ties with the language community and the business world?

5. In 1980, ACTFL sponsored a National Conference on Professional Priorities to focus on important issues related to curriculum and materials development, teacher education, global education, research, and evaluation. A major outgrowth of that effort is an invitational conference to focus on curriculum and materials development, which is tentatively scheduled for fall 1981. A publication of the proceedings of the National Conference on Professional Priorities will be forthcoming.

   • What recommendations can you make prior to the conference concerning new directions for curriculum design in the 1980s?

We have provided only a sample of the many activities in which ACTFL is involved. We urge you to give us your reactions to and suggestions for current ACTFL efforts. Let us know your concerns. Great strides can be made in support of foreign language education, if we all work together. We, the members of the ACTFL Public Awareness Committee, anxiously await your response.

Sincerely yours,

Renate Schulz   Charles Hancock   Ann Beusch

Thomas H. Geno
ACTFL President 1981

Charles Hancock
ACTFL President 1982

"Open Letter to the Profession,"
FLA, Vol. 14, No. 2 (April 1981),
pp. 138-139

sharing ACTFL's vital, recent successes and then asking the members, "How can we do what we do better? What can you do to help us meet your professional needs?"

By the time the April 1981 issue of *FLA* appeared, President Geno could announce that the ACTFL Public Awareness Proposal to the Exxon Foundation had been funded. Clearly, the Executive Council's decision to seek such funds had been justified; in fact, they were convinced that this was only the beginning of a series of successes. And Geno attributed these to the membership.

Furthermore, the Executive Council had been building a model of cooperative ventures with state, regional, and national organizations seeking such collaboration. This cooperative effort would help ACTFL develop the potential for which it was originally intended. As Geno said in his first "Message from the President" (*FLA*, Vol. 14, No. 1 (February 1981), p. 7):

Professional leaders must be daring and farsighted enough to assume the full responsibility of their leadership roles and go about the task—no matter what short-range caveats might exist. In terms of long-range realities—profession, political, and especially economic—we must ask ourselves, "What's good for the future of the profession?" rather than "What's good for the future of my group or your group?" If we don't unite, there will be no future!

The 1981 Denver Annual Meeting was to be the forum for discussions stemming from the "Open Letter to the Profession." ACTFL would remain committed to the initiatives launched in its recent past:

- The Professional Priorities would be treated at the annual meeting.
- Membership recruitment would be pursued vigorously.

- A formidable campaign of political activism would continue to characterize the organization as events in Washington warranted such actions.
- ACTFL's collaboration on a national level would continue as it supported JNCL and actively participated in it.
- Regional efforts in collaboration would be realized as cooperation with the regional conferences continued;
- ACTFL's state constituents would feel more a part of the efforts as the organization broadened the discussion of issues of professional importance.

In 1981, President Thomas Geno, President-elect Charles Hancock and Past President Dale L. Lange addressed the issue of unity with a document, "Prolegomena to the Future of ACTFL and the Foreign Language Profession: ACTFL as a Unifying Focus," in which they mentioned that, in the 14 years of ACTFL's existence, most of Ken Mildenberger's four points that figured in the organization's development (see Chapter 1, pp. 3-7) had been carried out, but ACTFL had not fully realized the unifying focus he had envisioned. Therefore, these three officers presented the statements to clarify the organization's position and to generate dialogue with other organizations on the structure and function of collaboration and cooperation with those bodies with ACTFL as a means of developing a future professional agenda. There were essentially two positions: (1) unity through merger, of which they disapproved; and (2) collaboration and cooperation, toward which they were striving.

They concluded their document as follows: "This prolegomena seeks to put into perspective various components of a possible plan for the future; it is based on our current vision of ACTFL's role as it was perceived at its creation. It is ACTFL's *aggiornamento* in preparing for the

ACTFL HEADQUARTERS, THE NEW YORK YEARS

First Headquarters (MLA/ACTFL)
62 Fifth Avenue, New York, NY
1967–1977

2 Park Avenue, New York, NY
1977–1981

385 Warburton Avenue
Hastings-on-Hudson, NY
1981–1983

579 Broadway
Hastings-on-Hudson, NY
1983–1988

6 Executive Plaza, Yonkers, NY
1988–2008

years ahead. We have tried sincerely to close no doors; we hope we have opened many." And only the future would be testimony to their efforts.

The first JNCL report, printed in *FLA* (Vol. 14, No. 5 (December 1981), p. 456) mentioned the Council for Languages and Other International Studies (CLOIS), a legislative/policy action organization that JNCL had created and registered, directed by Dr. J. David Edwards. Suddenly, with the publication of Vol. 14, No. 4 (September/October 1981) of *FLA*, things seemed to change. ACTFL headquarters had a new address, though the move had not been announced. *FLA* contained no Annual Report of the Executive Director or messages from the President. New *FLA* staff members were added. News about the organization appeared only in small boxes or as column-fillers in *FLA*.

On the Move

On April 15, 1981, Executive Director Scebold notified the manager of 2 Park Avenue, New York, that the organization needed to move its offices from Suite 1814 due to "financial problems which result in the necessity for a move to smaller space outside of New York City." Scebold wrote that ACTFL would like to vacate the office space by May 29, 1981. According to documents, however, the move actually occurred on Friday, June 26, 1981. Fortunately, this in-town office space was leased effective August 1, 1981, so ACTFL was not encumbered with rent on two different offices.

The one-year lease on the new headquarters space at 385 Warburton Avenue, Hastings-on-Hudson, NY, began June 1, 1981. Annual rent was $12,000 ($1,000 per month!). Beginning on June 1, 1982, ACTFL leased more space on the building's second and third floors, and rent rose to $1,150 per month.

Surprisingly, Scebold notified the landlord that, as of the end of May 1983, the lease would not be renewed, and ACTFL again moved, this

time to 579 Broadway, Hastings-on-Hudson, with a lease from June 1, 1983–May 31, 1988. The rent rose to $1,850 per month, but there was much more space: two rooms on the first floor, two each on the second and third floors, one storage room in the basement, and four parking spaces.

Proficiency

David V. Hiple became ACTFL's Project Coordinator in late 1981. His first project was proficiency testing and training, funded by a grant from the U.S. Department of Education. The first announcement of this grant and the ensuing project appeared in *FLA* (Vol. 14, No. 5 (December 1981), p. 426):

Dear Foreign Language Educator:

The American Council on the Teaching of Foreign Languages has been awarded a grant from the U. S. Department of Education to train college and university professors to administer oral proficiency interviews to their students. ACTFL is currently accepting applications from interested professors who would like to attend a training workshop.

Modeled after the Foreign Service Institute oral proficiency test, this interview is intended to accurately rank a foreign language student so that future professors and potential employers will be able to utilize a universal scoring system to pinpoint fluency in the oral skill area.

Applicants should meet the following criteria:
1. *Be a Professor of either French or Spanish,*
2. *Be able to score 4 or better on the 0-5 FSI scale.*
3. *Be able to secure release time to attend the four-day workshop tentatively scheduled to take place during the last two weeks of February 1982. (Transportation will be paid by ACTFL, but on-site expenses will be paid by the participant. ACTFL is exploring the use of academic facilities, and every attempt will be made to keep per diem costs at a minimum.)*

Preference will be given to team applications representing different language departments from the same institution. A demonstration of institutional support, and a commitment to the concept of oral proficiency testing are crucial. Local institutions presently engaged in similar activities are especially encouraged to apply and share relevant data.

Inquiries and requests for applications should be directed to the ACTFL Project Coordinator.

Sincerely,
David V. Hiple
Project Coordinator

In early 1982, "a handful of young professionals, destined to become the leaders of the foreign language teaching profession, dared to challenge the old supposition that language teaching was something the teacher delivered to the student on a plate" (*FLA*, September/October 1, 2002, p. 581). Judith Liskin-Gasparro, who co-authored the first oral proficiency manual based on the manuals used in some U.S. government agencies at the time, wrote in the introduction to her article, "The ACTFL Proficiency Guidelines: A Historical Perspective" (*Teaching for Proficiency, the Organizing Principle*, Theodore V. Higgs, Ed., Lincolnwood, IL: National Textbook Company, 1984),

In an earlier, more innocent era, one could accept the illusion that language study was a classroom activity with little or no application in the outside world. Once could create a closed system of curriculum, textbook, and tests. Success could be efficiently gauged in terms of how well the students learned the material they were taught, i.e., by their level of achievement. The question of probable success or failure with the language outside the class was seldom asked. The only accountability was internal: whether the students measured up to the expectations of the teacher. (p. 12)

In fact, the Report of the President's Commission on Foreign Language and International Studies, published in November 1979, made eight major recommendations, including establishment of language proficiency goals and guidelines, particularly in oral proficiency, that directly relate teaching and curricula to measurable outcomes. Proficiency measures would establish yardsticks of progress and competence and, perhaps more importantly, would relate directly to curriculum development. That is, oral proficiency testing and rating in a foreign language program should not be an isolated exercise, but an integral part of a program designed to build oral facility. Curricula, materials, methods, and evaluation procedures should work in concert to give students the best possible training and proficiency in a second language (from "The ACTFL Language Proficiency Projects," Update Fall 1982).

For several years ACTFL had been concerned about the creation of foreign language proficiency goals and tests to measure the attainment of these goals. ACTFL had set foreign language proficiency as one of its five crucial priorities and had conducted several projects in that area. In September 1981, ACTFL received a grant to sponsor a five-day workshop on oral proficiency interviewing and rating for thirty French and Spanish college professors, based on a modified Interagency Language Roundtable (ILR) test. This workshop was held in Houston on February 17-21, 1982, with training provided by ETS and the CIA Language School. This group of educators was precisely that "handful of young professionals, destined to become the leaders of the foreign language teaching profession" mentioned above.

These collaborations between ACTFL and ETS and between the CIA Language School and Defense Language Institute (DLI) showed great interest in bringing oral proficiency testing and rating to academia. These teams continued when

ACTFL Provisional Proficiency
Guidelines, 1982

ACTFL and ETS went to DLI to attend oral proficiency workshops to keep abreast of the latest government techniques and trends in the advancement of language proficiency measurement.

The second proficiency project, which concluded in the fall of 1982, created generic and language-specific goals for speaking, reading, writing, and culture—the *ACTFL Provisional Proficiency Guidelines*, funded by a grant from the International Research and Studies Program of the U.S. Department of Education. These provisional guidelines were developed by a committee of experts: Dr. Pardee Lowe, CIA Language School, speaking and listening; Dr. Howard Nostrand, University of Washington, culture; Dr. Alice Omaggio, University of Illinois, Champaign-Urbana, writing; and Dr. June Phillips, Indiana University of Pennsylvania, reading. Dr. Dale Lange, University of Minnesota, was coordinating consultant.

Training workshops rapidly proliferated around the country—the Illinois Foreign Language Proficiency Project Workshop (December 8-12, 1982); Project OPT, University of New Hampshire (January 1983); ACTFL-sponsored trainers' workshop in Washington, DC (February 23-27, 1983); Miami, FL (April 13-17, 1983).

The U.S. Department of Education funded additional oral proficiency interviewing and rating workshops, "Professional Development in Foreign Language Education: Oral Proficiency Testing and Training," which were continued in 1983. One workshop was for professors of German and Italian; another was for professors of French and Spanish who had received previous oral proficiency interview training from ACTFL, ETS, or one of the government language schools. In addition, the National Endowment for the Humanities awarded ACTFL a grant for "Teacher Institutes on the Application of Oral Proficiency to Foreign Language Curricula," a three-week summer institute training secondary level foreign language teachers in oral proficiency interviewing and in designing proficiency-base curricula.

ACTFL and ETS joined resources in offering two-day familiarization workshops to be presented at colleges and universities or at other locations in a diversity of languages for groups of varying sizes. In the preface to the trainer's manual *Organizing and Conducting an Oral Proficiency Assessment Workshop* (Preliminary Version) (ETS/ACTFL, 1983), Liskin-Gasparro and Hiple wrote, "We believe that the teaching and learning of languages will be enhanced by the adoption of a proficiency-based orientation to curriculum and materials."

If we examine the chart on page 57, we can clearly see (as if we did not already know about) ACTFL's positive effect on the profession—especially with the advent of proficiency in academia—which continues to this day.

The Proficiency Years

In ACTFL's late 1982 presidential elections, Robert A. Gilman (University of Nevada, Reno) was elected President for 1983. Also in 1982, the National Textbook Company Award was established by the ACTFL Executive Council to recognize foreign language educators who had made outstanding contributions in creating community interest in and awareness of the importance of foreign language education. ACTFL began a search

Robert A. Gilman
ACTFL President 1983

for editors of *FLA* and the ACTFL Materials Center.

In the May 1982 issue of *FLA* (Vol. 15, No. 3), President Hancock announced the results of the ACTFL Membership Survey conducted that February. More than 1,500 members responded, saying they were pleased with ACTFL's activities and services, while offering constructive criticisms for the Executive Council to consider. Of ACTFL's five priorities, 81% ranked public awareness highest, teacher education second, proficiency third, curriculum and materials development fourth, and research fifth. Many respondents indicated that they regularly read *FLA* as compared with the *Foreign Language Education Series* (24%) and only 10% were reading the *ACTFL Bibliography*. Over one-quarter of the membership used Materials Center publications.

The survey also asked about the timing, location and format of the Annual Meetings. In the fourth part of the survey—unity-coalition building in the language profession—68% urged strong support for holding joint meetings with interested national, regional, and state associations, and 60% strongly supported joint memberships with interested foreign language groups (p. 216).

Contributions were steadily coming in to ACTFL Restricted Funds efforts for various awards funds and the ACTFL Commitment Fund. The Corporate Sponsor Program was also growing: three corporate sponsors donated $4,000 or more annually to ACTFL, and five corporate contributors gave $500 or more each year.

Continuing the push for unity, the 1982 Annual Meeting was jointly held with ACTFL/ AATF/AATG, in conjunction with:

- American Association of Teachers of Italian (AATI)
- American Association of Teachers of Spanish and Portuguese/Metropolitan Chapter (AATSP)

ACTFL'S POSITIVE EFFECT ON THE PROFESSION

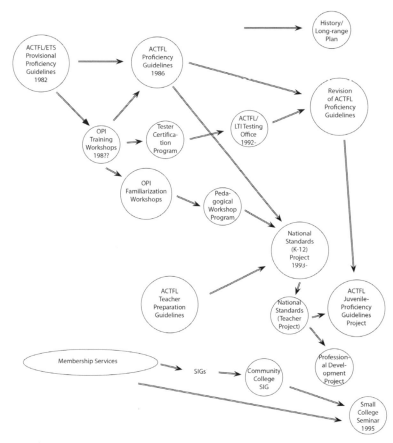

- Chinese Language Teachers Association (CLTA)
- Connecticut Council of Language Teachers (COLT)
- International Association for Learning Laboratories (IALL, formerly NALLD)
- New Jersey Foreign Language Teachers Association (NJFLTA)
- New York State Association of Foreign Language Teachers (NYSAFLT)
- Northeast Conference on the Teaching of Foreign Languages (NECTFL)
- Pennsylvania State Modern Language Association (PSMLA)

- Teachers of English to Speakers of Other Languages (TESOL).

ACTFL, in conjunction with several regional language associations, established task forces for each of its five priority areas, to build on the work begun at the 1981 Conference on Professional Priorities in Boston. Each task force was charged with defining significant issues in its area, proposing directions for the profession, and preparing a final report that would establish realistic goals. These task forces were to work during 1982 and 1983 and issue final reports in late 1983. The task forces were:

- ACTFL/Central States Task Force on Curriculum and Materials Development (Helena Anderson, Chairperson)
- ACTFL/Northeast Conference on the Teaching of Foreign Languages Task Force on Teacher Education (William E. DeLorenzo, Chairperson)
- ACTFL/Pacific Northwest Conference Task Force on Public Awareness (Les McKim, Chairperson)
- ACTFL/Southern Conference Task Force on Research (Tom Cooper, Chairperson)
- ACTFL/Southwest Task Force on Proficiency (Proposed) (Annette Lowry, Chairperson).

In 1982, ACTFL received funding from the Exxon Education Foundation to support the creation of a Public Awareness Network for Foreign Language and International Studies, designed to collect and disseminate pertinent information on these issues. A data bank was established to house periodic newsletters, clippings, articles, speeches, and similar materials, collected and sent to ACTFL by volunteers around the country.

The ACTFL Alert Network was continuing to function effectively. Twenty-six memoranda had been released to more than 500 educators, business and community leaders, and public

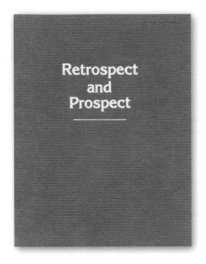

Retrospect and Prospect, published in 1982 to celebrate ACTFL's 15th anniversary

officials. The network also was supporting the Washington office of the Joint National Committee for Languages and the lobbying effort, CLOIS.

ACTFL celebrated its fifteenth anniversary in 1982 and published a brochure, *Retrospect and Prospect,* subsidized by the Exxon Foundation Grant for the Public Awareness Project. This publication highlighted ACTFL's activities and achievements since its founding and looked ahead to the future of the foreign language profession and ACTFL's role in that future. In the "Looking Ahead" section, Executive Director Scebold wrote: "Our general responsibility as educators, and our specific responsibility as language teaches, is to coalesce a plan for the 21st century."

The new Editor of *FLA* was announced, Patricia W. Cummins from West Virginia University, as well as the new ACTFL Materials Center Editor, Dorothy Gabel Liebowitz from Illinois.

In *FLA,* Vol. 16, No. 1 (February 1983), a brief paper, "Social Studies and Foreign Languages: Strengthening the Bonds Between Us," written by Anna S. Ochoa and Lorraine A. Strasheim (pp. 54-55), was published, bringing up another aspect from the Report of the 1979 President's Commission on Foreign Language and International Studies: "If the 47 million children in our schools are to function successfully as adults in the next century they must grow up with more knowledge about our people, and greater sensitivity to those peoples' attitudes and customs." In fact, the 1983 Annual Meeting in San Francisco, whose theme was "Schools in the Community: Bridges to the World," was held in cooperation with the National Council for the Social Studies (NCSS).

ACTFL received funding from the National Endowment for the Humanities (NEH) to support a three-week regional summer institute for secondary school teachers of French, German, and Spanish, which took place July 11-29, 1983, at Haverford College in Pennsylvania, and focused on proficiency-based language instruction and the ACTFL/ETS oral proficiency interview and rating system.

In the December 1983 issue of *FLA* (Vol. 16, No. 6) appeared a summary of three new proficiency grants ACTFL had received:

1. Regional Center for Language Proficiency (The Fund for the Improvement of Postsecondary Education and Exxon Education Foundation)—a project in cooperation with the University of Pennsylvania to develop a model Regional Center for Language Proficiency, a site for ongoing research projects on language proficiency and the first in what was envisioned as a national network of such Centers around the country.
2. Teacher Certification (Undergraduate International Studies Program of the Department of Education)—to establish a proficiency-based model for foreign language teacher certification in the state of Texas. Specifically, ACTFL would train faculty at higher education institutions around the state to interview and rate students on their oral proficiency in anticipation of a state-mandated oral proficiency requirement that had been proposed for implementation. This project was conducted with the cooperation of the Texas Education Agency, the Texas State Department of Education, and the Texas Foreign Language Association.
3. Proficiency Guidelines (Department of Education, International Research and Studies Branch)—to develop language proficiency guidelines for Chinese, Japanese, and Russian. In carrying out this project, ACTFL was assisted by an Advisory Committee comprised of experts in the languages to be addressed and in proficiency-based testing and teaching.

In 1984, ACTFL was still experiencing growth pains and change. One of the first issues that the new President, Helene Zimmer-Loew, New York State Education Department, Albany, NY, dealt with when it came before the Executive Council in early 1984 was changing the name of the organization by unanimous vote. Suggested new names included American Language Teachers Association (ALTA) and American Association of Language Teachers (AALT). There were two reasons cited for the recommended modifications: (1) the wish to eliminate the word "foreign" from the name of the organization since many of the languages represented by ACTFL are,

Helene Zimmer-Loew
ACTFL President 1984

indeed, the first language of a large segment of citizens; and (2) the belief that the term "association" was a more accurate description of the role and function of the organization than the term "council." In the announcement, which appeared in *FLA* (Vol. 17, No. 3) May, 1984, we were told: "As many ACTFL members will note, this is an issue which has been discussed repeatedly, and often passionately, since the creation of ACTFL" (p. 184). This was not the last time such a discussion was to go on.

The ACTFL/ETS proficiency movement was spreading and was the focus of many professional dialogs and programs. As an example, the September 1984 special issue of *FLA* (Vol. 17, No. 4), edited by June K. Phillips and Alice C. Omaggio, was based on papers commissioned for a Symposium on Receptive Language Skills held at the DLI in November 1983, conducted by ACTFL and funded by the National Cryptologic School. This event had two primary purposes: (1) to provide a forum for the exchange of ideas and research between government language training specialists and experts from within the academic community on the topic of listening and reading skills; and (2) to lay the foundation for the development of a computer-adaptive test of second-language proficiency in the receptive skills. The Symposium did achieve these purposes, while highlighting the need for increased research and development concerning its five themes:

1. the theoretical basis for teaching and testing the receptive skills;
2. the practical implications of recent research in listening;
3. the practical implication of recent research in reading;
4. the testing of listening and reading proficiency; and
5. the use of computers in teaching and testing receptive skills.

In this same issue was announced the ETS/Penn State Oral Proficiency Testing Project, funded by a three-year grant from the U.S. Department of Education's Undergraduate International Studies and Foreign Language Program, to conduct a series of workshops to train post-secondary teachers of French, German, and Spanish in oral proficiency interviewing and rating. This project helped to expand the regional network of foreign language educators committed to proficiency-based language teaching. The first workshop took place at Pennsylvania State University on November 7-11, 1984.

Another potential change brought before the Executive Council resulted from discussions among the National Executive Service Corps (NESC) and representatives from the four regional foreign language organizations (the Southwest Council on Language Teaching (SWCOLT) had not yet been formed). There were four main points presented:

1. ACTFL should increase its Executive Council membership to include a representative from each regional foreign language association (including the then-forming SWCOLT) for a normal three-year term, with reciprocal representation from the boards of each of the regional organizations.
2. The regional conferences and ACTFL should work cooperatively to facilitate conference planning.
3. ACTFL should broaden and enhance its role as a professional concerns information center.
4. The cooperating organizations should establish a common, nationally distributed newsletter that would reflect both national and regional news.

Executive Council unanimously approved "in principle" the idea of modifying membership on the ACTFL Executive Council in a manner that would assure two-way communication with the regionals. The Executive Director was encouraged to investigate acquiring a microcomputer for headquarters, an accounting person, and a membership person in order to meet the growing demands of the organization.

Beginning in 1985, enrolling in a comprehensive membership was possible. Such a membership was "a bargain at $55!" Comprehensive members received all of the direct benefits of a Regular Member:

- six issues of *FLA*;
- a 25% discount on Materials Center publications;
- a discount on fees for ACTFL institutes, seminars and workshops;

- an opportunity to participate in three group insurance plans;
- a ballot for the annual election of ACTFL officers; and
- an invitation to Annual Meetings.

In addition, a Comprehensive Member would receive

- six issues of the *Public Awareness Newsletter;*
- the annual volume of the *Foreign Language Education Series*; and
- additional publications.

And a Joint Comprehensive Membership (for two members residing at the same address) was $60.

The theme of the October 1984 issue of *FLA* (Vol. 17, No. 5) was "Proficiency in Teaching and Testing." In that issue were published the *ACTFL Provisional Proficiency Guidelines* and seven articles. The December 1984 issue (Vol. 17, No. 6) focused on materials and curriculum development.

William N. Hatfield (Purdue University, West Lafayette, IN) was the 1985 ACTFL President, and Alice C. Omaggio, University of Illinois, Champaign-Urbana, was President-elect for 1986. Volume 18, No. 1 (February 1985) of *FLA*, the last special issue for the 1984-1985 academic year, focused on teacher training and questions concerning teachers and featured a new column on computers and foreign language teaching, edited by Robert S. Hart and Nina Garrett. The contract of Patricia Cummins, Editor of *FLA,* had ended, and the position was moved back to ACTFL headquarters, with Vicki Galloway assuming editorship.

At the first Executive Council meeting of 1985 in Las Vegas, NV, President Hatfield welcomed as official members representatives from four of the five regional conferences: Frank W. Medley, Jr. (Southern Conference on Language Teaching); Phillip Campana (Central States Conference on the Teaching of Languages); Ray Verzasconi (Pacific Northwest Council on Foreign Languages); and Barbara Gonzalez Pino (Southwest Conference on Language Teaching). (The Northeast Conference on the Teaching of Foreign Languages was unable to send a representative.) To set up a rotating term for these new members, lots were drawn. After the initial terms had been completed, each regional conference would be represented for the full four years, as provided by the revised Bylaws, which addressed several issues:

William N. Hatfield
ACTFL President 1985

- The Chair of the Nominating Committee, to which five delegates to the Assembly would be appointed, was chosen from among the members.
- The Nominating Committee would nominate two persons for each ACTFL-elected position on the Executive Council and two persons to stand for election to President-elect.
- Executive Council would consist of 15 members: the Steering Committee, consisting of the President, President-elect, and the Past President; and the Executive Council at large, consisting of seven members elected by the ACTFL general membership and five members representing the five regional organizations.
- The term for Executive Council members would be four years.

- Stricter guidelines were established for the nomination procedure, with qualifications spelled out: Nominees must be ACTFL members and must have leadership ability and experience for the position for which they were nominated; nominees for President-elect should have served as a current or previous member of the Executive Council.

The 1985 Annual Meeting, held at the new Marriott Marquis Hotel on Times Square in New York, was the first joint meeting of AATF, AATG, AATI, AATSP, and ACTFL—the result of the continued efforts toward unity among various foreign language associations. Interestingly, hotel rates were exceptional (due to the newness of the hotel): $55 for a single, $65 for a double, and $75 for a triple/quad!

The keynote speaker was Edward Bateley, President of the Fédération Internationale des Professeurs de Langues Vivantes (FIPLV)—another outcome of the unity effort, this time on an international scale.

At this meeting were announced the officers of ACTFL for 1986. Jacqueline Benevento, School District of Philadelphia, was chosen President-elect.

In Vol. 19, No. 1 (February 1986) of *FLA*, ACTFL announced its new Fund for the Future, a commitment fund to help carry the organization into the next 20 years and into the 21st century.

The goal was $100,000. ACTFL sought 1,000 contributions of $100 ("**Be 1 in 1,000 for 100!**"). Contributions would support plans for the future: improved foreign language instruction through national projects, materials development, research findings dissemination, foreign language advocacy in the public and private sectors, and growth of professional unity. Contributors' names were published in *FLA* beginning in the April 1986 issue, and in the December 1986 issue we saw the number of contributors climb from 12 to 149, in addition to contributions from 14 associations and corporations.

On November 26, 1985, Emma Marie Birkmaier, the first President of ACTFL, died. The "In Memoriam" published in *FLA* (Vol. 19, No. 1 (February 1986), p. 59) concluded as follows: "Emma Birkmaier is missed by her colleagues, friends, and former students. She was a leader of people, especially of young professionals; she was a champion of women in higher education in the model she provided; she was a good person." We were grateful that she had lived long enough to see the organization for which she was so instrumental a figure grow and flourish.

A position paper and recommendations for action from the Council of Chief State School Officers, "International Dimensions of Education," appeared in *FLA* (Vol. 19, No. 3 (May 1986), pp. 243-247). In the Introduction, we read:

Emma Marie Birkmaier
1908–1985

The United States is truly an international society. Our people originate in every part of the world. Our lives are part of a global community—one joined by common economic, social, cultural, and civic concerns. Education in these United States must prepare us to participate in this global community (p. 243).

Comments made in this position paper are still relevant today:

All American students should have the opportunity to learn a language other than English. The opportunity should include study in languages other than "Western" languages, and should begin in the earliest years of elementary school with continuation through the post-secondary level. Students completing secondary school should be able to demonstrate an acceptable level of proficiency in communications, particularly speaking and listening, in a language other than English…. Study of a second language provides students not only with the ability to communicate effectively across nations and cultures, but also to understand other cultures through their languages, gain insight into the structure of language, and acquire skill for employment (p. 243).

It was announced that ACTFL had temporarily suspended the acceptance of additional items for the Materials Center, a newsletter would be introduced in the fall of 1986, and ACTFL was seeking a new Editor for it. The proposed newsletter would be published twice annually and would be mailed to all foreign language educators in the U.S.

Alice C. Omaggio
ACTFL President 1986

Membership was holding steady around 6,000; the difficulty appeared to be in keeping members rather than attracting new ones. On the other hand, ACTFL's accountant reported that increasing membership to at least 11,000 would be very helpful in meeting financial obligations for services promised.

Phillip Campana, Task Force Liaison on the Executive Council, reported that SCOLT's Task Force on Research had produced a book, *Research within Reach*, which was available for Materials Center distribution. NECTFL had completed its report on teacher education but did not recommend publishing it. PNCFL had almost concluded its report on Public Awareness, but did not want to continue with the topic. SWCOLT turned in an article on proficiency.

In Vol. 19, No. 4 (September 1986) of *FLA* were photos of the five new regional representatives on the Executive Council, including two new members: Hyde Flippo

ACTFL Regional Representatives

Campana   Flippo   Kennedy   Medley   Pino

The five new regional representatives on the Executive Council, 1986

of PNCFL and Dora Kennedy representing NECTFL. For the first time, ACTFL's 1985 financial statement was published in this issue of *FLA*, showing that the organization's assets and liabilities were concurrent with its fund balances.

Following a review of the financial outcome of recent annual meetings, and in view of ACTFL's long-range financial planning needs, it was decided at the Executive Council meeting of April 5-6, 1986, in Milwaukee to observe a five-year moratorium, during which joint meetings with other organizations would be held only on the provision that all exhibit income go to ACTFL. Furthermore, the Executive Council's Publications Committee recommended, in view of the Materials Center's financial situation over the past several years, that current commitments to publish new items would be honored but no additional manuscripts would be accepted. The Materials Center would continue to carry items purchased from other publishers, but a way to liquidate the Materials Center's inventory was sought.

In an effort to provide direction in leadership to the profession, the Public Awareness Committee of the Executive Council was overseeing the production of a manual, *Leadership for Foreign Language Organizations: A Handbook*, edited by Robert Terry, with selected authors contributing the different chapters.

At the 1986 Annual Meeting in Dallas, ACTFL Past President Frank Grittner, then with the Wisconsin Department of Public Instruction, gave a speech on the occasion of ACTFL's twentieth anniversary, "ACTFL in Retrospect: A Comment on Two Cultures." It included a brief historical overview of the organization, focusing on two concepts: a hypothesis—"two distinct and separate cultures operate within the foreign language field"—and a contrary-to-fact, conditional proposition, a "what if" clause: "What would the profession be like today if ACTFL had never been created?" He hypothesized that one of the two cultures was devoted to literary and linguistic scholarship, while the other was "involved in the art of teaching people to communicate in a foreign language" (*FLA,* Vol. 20, No. 6 (December 1987), pp. 579-581). Not surprisingly, this very same hypothesis and fact is still a matter of discussion, resurfacing fairly recently in the 2007 MLA report, *Foreign Languages and Higher Education: New Structures for a Changed World*. Grittner's speech is a wonderful compendium of teaching methods that were current in 1986, as well as a brief history of the first twenty years of ACTFL (see Appendix B).

In early 1987, ACTFL announced a new project to develop a Selected Listing of Materials (SLOM) with U.S. Department of Education funding. This listing would be a comprehensive annotated bibliography of foreign language instructional materials for grades K–12. It was to be a two-year effort, with publication expected in 1988.

The results of the 1986 election were published in Vol. 20, No. 1 (February 1987) of *FLA*: Toby Tamarkin (Manchester [CT] Community College) was to be the 1988 President.

The September 1987 issue of *FLA* announced that two professors from Manhattan College, Riverdale, NY, were beginning a study of the demographics of foreign language teachers. The questionnaire could be removed from the December 1987 issue of *FLA*, completed, and mailed to ACTFL in a prepaid mailer (see Appendix C of this chapter). The following statement explains the reasons for the study and the subjects it would cover:

There has been considerable discussion among educational policy-makers in recent years concerning the decline in modern language instruction in secondary and post secondary schools and, consequently, about the state of the profession of modern language instruction. Much of the debate about establishing a common core curriculum for college students, for instance, focuses on the role of modern languages as essential components to such common cores. Moreover, it has been asserted that the "graying of the professorate" in the traditional disciplines of the arts and sciences may lead to a serious shortage of modern language scholars and teachers in the universities and, consequently, at each level in the educational system. Given this resurgence of concern among educational policy-makers about the demand for and the supply of modern language instructors, the time is appropriate to assess the state of the profession from the perspective of the members of the profession.

Our study examines the state of the modern language profession from the perspective of its members themselves. We are undertaking an empirical examination of the demographic characteristics of modern language instructors that will provide an accurate picture of who is in the profession, how long they have been in the profession, the institutional environment in which they practice the profession, and their plans for their careers in the profession. Moreover, we are examining members' perceptions about such critical issues as the degree and quality of support of modern language instruction; the amount of satisfaction they derive from their work; the institutional characteristics that enhance or impede their performance; their assessment of the motivation and abilities of both themselves and of potential members of their profession; their optimism or pessimism about the current and future conditions of the profession; and the conditions that would prompt them to remain in, or leave, the profession of their choice.

In the September 1987 issue of *FLA* (Vol. 20, No. 4, pp. 334-335), President Benevento wrote a message to the ACTFL membership in a new feature: a center pullout section to be removed from the journal and used as informational pieces for posting or duplication and distribution. Her message included the new ACTFL Mission Statement, which the Executive Council had approved in November 1986, as well as "ACTFL in

Jacqueline Benevento
ACTFL President 1987

Action: An Interim Report," which discussed the organization's three-year project to develop new guidelines for foreign language teacher education. A first draft of these guidelines, including built-in assessment criteria, had been developed by a team of national experts and regional workshops, which were being organized for the 1987-1988 academic year to bring together faculty members in teacher education programs for discussion and dissemination of these new guidelines.

Benevento also mentioned the SLOM project, in which committee members evaluated various kinds of materials, including textbooks and computer software, in thirteen languages. In combination with Middlebury College, ACTFL was continuing its project to develop proficiency-based activities in Chinese, Japanese, and Russian. In fact, the *ACTFL Chinese Proficiency Guidelines* were first published in the October 1987 issue of *FLA*, and the *ACTFL Japanese Proficiency Guidelines* appeared in the December 1987 issue. She also mentioned ACTFL's development of a computer-adaptive test in reading proficiency, begun in 1985.

In the summary of the Executive Council May 7-9, 1987, minutes published in the October 1987 issue of *FLA*, Executive Director Scebold reported on the very positive trends that had developed since the President's Commission in 1979, which marked the beginning of the revival of foreign languages in the U.S. He pointed out that the JNCL office, which had opened on a relatively small budget in 1980, was operating on a budget of $125,000 in 1987. Scebold said both ACTFL's situation and the foreign language instruction profession in general were continuing to improve.

ACTFL's financial statement (*FLA*, Vol. 20, No. 5 (October 1987), pp. 494-501) showed a marked rise in assets from 1985 to 1986. The Fund for the Future was also growing: February 1987 saw 184 individual contributions and 22 contributions from associations and corporations. Through October 1987, these numbers had risen to 197 individual contributions and 28 from associations and corporations. Executive Director Scebold announced at the November 18-19, 1987, Executive Council meeting that the Fund for the Future had yielded an income of $26,670 to date. That certainly was a far cry from the $100,000 goal that had been set two years earlier!

According to ACTFL's accountants in their 1987 Financial Statement (*FLA*, Vol. 21, No. 4 (September 1988), pp. 376-383), while 1987 assets increased significantly from 1986 due to more grants and contracts, the organization had lost money regarding the general association, even though ACTFL had 14 projects for 1987-1988 already under way, 7 proposals pending, and 55 separate activities of the ACTFL staff for the year 1987. ACTFL's projects and activities were growing in number and in the breadth of areas: testing workshops, refresher workshops, advisory/consulting work, conference speeches and presentations, and curriculum/instruction workshops.

As President Tamarkin pointed out in her first "Message from the President," (*FLA*, Vol. 21, No. 1, p. 48a), ACTFL had been working to increase its services to the membership. It installed a membership hotline number; created a centerfold pullout section to provide news about ACTFL activities and services to be shared with colleagues; began an ACTFL column in regional newsletters through regional representatives to the Executive Council; drafted a resolution regarding ACTFL's

Toby Tamarkin
ACTFL President 1988

position on an English-only issue that had arisen. The SLOM project was to culminate in the publication of an annotated bibliography for materials in 12 languages. Furthermore, the Executive Council voted to offer two new awards: the Edwin Cudecki International Business Award for a person other than a foreign language educator who had helped promote a closer relationship between international business and language or international studies; and the Anthony Papalia Award for a foreign language educator who had demonstrated excellence in teacher training.

The year of 1988 saw the beginning of ACTFL's sponsorship of regional conferences on teacher education. These included three two-day workshops on the theme "Issues in Teacher Education" as part of a three-year grant from the U.S. Department of Education. Workshops were planned for Nashville, TN; Glastonbury, CT; and Greeley, CO. The *ACTFL Provisional Program Guidelines for Foreign Language Teacher Education* were published in the February 1988 issue of *FLA* (Vol. 21, No. 1, pp. 71-82). In the introduction to these guidelines, we find the following words of caution:

These guidelines should be used with caution. They do not represent a statement of minimum thresholds and therefor neither supplant nor correspond in purpose to current accreditation and monitoring instruments. Though professional consensus on minimal indicators may ultimately be gleaned from the statements in this document, these guidelines are intended to serve a program development function; that is to represent a forward-looking view as to what knowledge, skills and experiences are deemed by the profession as holding the most promise for the preparedness of foreign language teacher candidates.

These guidelines focused on three areas in the pre-service preparation of foreign language teachers:

1. *Personal Development:* the knowledge and skills derived from a strong liberal arts education;
2. *Professional Development:* the knowledge and skills derived from education and experience in the art and science of pedagogy;
3. *Specialist Development:* the knowledge and skills associated with being a specialist in the language and culture to be taught in the classroom.

Another set of guidelines appeared in 1988: the *ACTFL Russian Proficiency Guidelines*, which were published in the April 1988 issue of *FLA* (pp. 177-197). This set now brought to three proficiency guidelines for less-commonly taught languages: Chinese, Japanese, and Russian. The *ACTFL Arabic Proficiency Guidelines* appeared in the September 1989 issue of *FLA* (Vol. 22, No. 4), pp. 373-392. Truly proficiency had made incredible inroads into foreign language education. More and more people were being trained in the Oral Proficiency Interview (OPI) familiarization and refresher workshops.

ACTFL OPI Tester Certification was made available, and the new *Oral Proficiency Interview Tester Training Manual* became available for

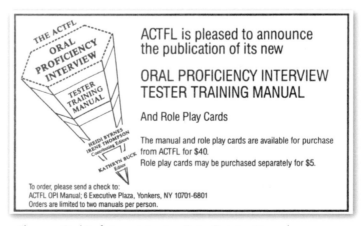

The new *Oral Proficiency Interview Tester Training Manual* became available for purchase in September 1989.

purchase in September 1989. The following Teaching for Proficiency workshops were offered:

- Textbook Adaptation and Instruction
- Teaching Reading and Writing: From Literacy to Literature
- Learning Strategies
- Learner-centered Instruction: Teaching Grammar and Vocabulary
- Curriculum Development.

More and more articles on proficiency were appearing in professional journals. For 1989, ACTFL announced two new workshops: (1) *Textual Levels and the Foreign Language Classroom: Overcoming the Authentic Text Barrier,* and (2) *Faculty Workshops on the Use of the Authentic Texts to Develop Cultural Understanding in Foreign Language Programs.* Many of these workshops were included in ACTFL's Professional Development Program for 1988-1989. Additional programs included: (a) instruction and textbook adaptation; (b) elements of successful grant writing; (c) fostering effective learning strategies; and (d) curriculum development. ACTFL was truly in the forefront as the proponent of proficiency in foreign language teaching and learning.

In April 1988, the Executive Council unanimously passed a motion to increase annual dues in order to provide and maintain a balanced budget. Domestic membership rose to $45/year, Student membership became $25/year, Retiree membership was $25/year, and International membership was $55/year. This change went into effect with the August billing for the 1989 academic year.

ACTFL staff member Patricia Dandonoli reported on the organization's financial history, pointing out that the OPI had begun initially in 1982 from money received from grant support. From 1980 to 1987, the total amount of income derived from this source increased significantly, from 15% in 1980 to 55% in 1987. A 1980-1988 summary of all funded projects ACTFL had obtained showed a $2.5 million over the 12 years. The number of workshop attendees since 1982 yielded a geometric increase in the numbers of trained testers and processed official ACTFL interviews. Dandonoli said the preceding seven years had seen a 74% increase in individual memberships, but membership income had risen by only 20%. Dues had last been raised in 1982. Finally, she pointed out that ACTFL had experienced tremendous growth in the preceding five years but it could not be sustained on a long-term basis. Though income had increased by 285% from 1982-1987, new ways to stabilize and maintain those gains had to be found.

The 1988 Annual Meeting in Monterey, CA, offered new exhibitions and events to attendees to refresh their spirit so their school could be effective in the 1990s. These included:

- a "Learning Technology Fair," in which teachers from all levels who were actively using computers, interactive video, audio, and satellite TV demonstrated their techniques and equipment;
- an "Exhibitor Forum" in which more than 100 exhibitors told attendees about upcoming changes in materials;
- "Networking Roundtables," in which attendees could meet with colleagues, share their concerns, and suggest solutions;
- post-conference workshops to be held in Honolulu, Hawaii, which were tax-deductible with discounted airfares and car rentals!

At the end of 1988, the Fund for the Future then had contributions from 210 individuals and from 29 associations and corporations. The elusive goal of $100,000 was still not within reach. Earlier in April 1988, Scebold had reviewed the years since 1980, recalling the ceasing of operations at Two Park Avenue, the move to

Hastings-on-Hudson, NY, the reduction of employees from 10 to 2, and the initiation of the rebuilding process. Scebold reported that 1988 operations resulted in a loss, largely because subcontract work brought returns under the budgeted income, and expenses were higher than expected. Then, in the December 1988 issue of *FLA,* ACTFL announced it had again moved—to 6 Executive Boulevard, Yonkers, NY.

The Yonkers Years

In early 1989, President Robert J. Ludwig (Mount Pleasant High School, Schenectady, NY) announced the invitational National Priorities Conference that would take place in Boston, preceding the 1989 Annual Meeting. This conference would be devoted to the planning of several Networking Roundtable Exchange Sessions on professional issues scheduled throughout the three days of the Annual Meeting. The discussions and recommendations would help the profession set its sights for the coming decade as we moved forward into the 21st century.

Robert J. Ludwig
ACTFL President 1989

This Annual Meeting would be a joint conference of ACTFL, AATG, AATI, the Chinese Language Teachers Association (CLTA), and the Massachusetts Foreign Language Association (MaFLA). Concurrently, the 4th International Conference on Second/Foreign Language Acquisition by Children would take place.

The April 1989 issue of *FLA* (Vol. 22, No. 2), was thematic, based on the three regional conferences on Issues in Teacher Education, which stemmed from the grant ACTFL had received in September 1985 to develop and disseminate guidelines for preservice foreign language teacher education programs. Based on a sampling of the papers delivered at these three conferences, this volume included such issues as:

- Reform, restructuring, change, and the examination of belief systems
- Credentialing
- Pre- and post-assessment of teacher candidates
- Model or innovative preservice programs
- Career ladders
- In-service models
- Development of teacher educators
- The preparation of FLES teachers
- Self-assessment
- Field experience and supervision
- TA development and supervision
- Undergraduate language programs
- Fostering cultural awareness
- Learner individuality
- Building management, decision-making and leadership skills
- Articulation
- Teachers and technology
- Consortia, collaboratives, networking

ACTFL announced in the February 1989 issue of *FLA* the publication of its Selected Listings of Instructional Materials for Elementary and Secondary School Programs (SLOM). This bibliography included Arabic, Chinese, French, German, Classical Greek, Modern Hebrew, Italian, Japanese, Latin, Portuguese, Russian, and Spanish, as well as a chapter detailing generic, non language-specific materials for the teaching of foreign languages.

The year 1989 saw a modest growth in ACTFL membership, yet the 1989 financial statement still showed a deficiency of income over expenses… albeit less than the very large deficiency of 1988. Due to ACTFL's financial situation, the Executive Council passed a motion that the Executive Director secure a new auditing firm for the organization, effective immediately after the final close-out of the 1988 financial statement.

In the second ACTFL Priorities Conference (the first had been held in Boston in 1980), invitees received a notebook that contained the working documents, followed by reaction documents, for that conference:

- "Addressing Curriculum Articulation in the Nineties: A Proposal" (Heidi Byrnes)
- "Integrating the Arts in the Second Language Curriculum: Fusing the Affective and the Cognitive" (Janet Hegman Shier)
- "The Global Imperative and Meta-language" (Donald Bragaw)
- "Literature and Communicative Competence: A Springboard for the Development of Critical Thinking and Aesthetic Appreciation" (Peter Schofer)
- "Applying Instructional Technologies" (James P. Pusack & Sue K. Otto)

- "Teaching All Students: Reaching and Teaching Students of Varying Abilities" (Jermaine D. Arendt & Helen P. Warriner-Burke)
- "Elementary School Foreign Language Instruction: Priorities for the 1990's" (Myriam Met & Nancy Rhodes)
- "Re-emerging Critical Instructional Issues: The Classics" (Martha Abbott)
- "Gaining Place: The Less Commonly Taught Languages in American Schools" (Galal Walker)
- "A Decade of Change to a Decade of Challenge" (Sen. Paul Simon)
- "Preservice and Inservice Teacher Education in the Nineties: The Issue is Instructional Validity" (Lorraine A. Strasheim)
- "Priority Issues in the Assessment of Communicative Language Abilities" (Grant Henning)

As can be readily seen, these topics and issues prove the adage that history repeats itself. These are not new topics at all, but new perspectives on issues we have continued to struggle to understand and make relevant to our situations at any given time. As we move into ACTFL's third decade, the 1990s, we will continue to revisit these issues and come to grips with new ones.

Appendix A

RECOMMENDATIONS TO THE PRESIDENT'S COMMISSION ON FOREIGN LANGUAGE AND INTERNATIONAL STUDIES

*AATF	American Association of Teachers of French
AATG	American Association of Teachers of German
AATI	American Association of Teachers of Italian
ADFL	Association of Departments of Foreign Languages
AATSEEL	American Association of Teachers of Slavic and East European Languages
AATSP	American Association of Teachers of Spanish and Portuguese
ACTFL	American Council on the Teaching of Foreign Languages
NABE	National Association for Bilingual Education
NFMLTA	National Federation of Modern Language Teachers Associations
TESOL	Teachers of English to Speakers of Other Languages

A Basic Premise

Many perceive that foreign language and international studies are separate and distinct, and that international education per se need not include foreign language instruction. In fact, foreign language and culture study is embodied in the concept of international education as a primary content source.

Understanding requires two interacting elements: knowledge about and experience of the phenomenon one seeks to grasp. One can only fully understand a second culture through experiencing the language of that culture, since the two are inseparable. The key concepts of a second language, which are embodied in its structure, its expression of feelings and attitudes, and its con notations are basic to creating a cross- cultural dimension in American education.

Priorities for New Legislation

RECOMMENDATION 1: Provision for Incentive Funding to Encourage and Improve the Study of Languages and Cultures

Legislation should be enacted by Congress to define a capitation formula that would provide funds for educational institutions at all levels, to support and encourage existing programs, and to foster the creation of new programs for the study of foreign languages and cultures. This legislation should encourage longer sequences of study through the provision of increasing levels of funding as students progress through the various foreign language and culture courses. Such funding would be allocated for teacher inservice programs, curriculum development, and the purchase of materials and media. A maximum of twenty-five percent of these funds may be allocated for the purchase of materials and media by each funded agency; no funding would be available for teacher salaries.

The formula might provide twenty dollars ($20) per student per year at the elementary or middle school levels. Similarly, students beginning foreign language and culture study at the secondary level, grades 7-12, would be subsidized at twenty dollars ($20) per student. During the second year of study, the funding level should be increased to thirty dollars ($30) per student per year; during the third year, the funding level should be thirty- five dollars ($35). The capitation formula should not provide support for the beginning levels of foreign language and culture study in higher education in order to encourage such study in the schools. The subsidy of students in higher education should begin at the level at which students would enter higher education after three years of high school. The suggested amount of support of students enrolled in the fourth year of the study of foreign languages and cultures, whether in schools or in higher education, should be forty dollars ($40) per student per year or per enrollment period (e. g., per semester in higher education). In order to encourage the creation of new programs such as African languages, Arabic, Chinese, Japanese, Portuguese, and Russian, a special category of incentive funding should be provided. Pro grams in any of these languages should be based on a capitation formula which provides an additional five dollars ($5) per student.

Incentive funding should be provided for an initial period of no less than ten years. As this program is implemented, steps should be taken to establish ongoing evaluation and assessment to carefully monitor its out comes. Periodic reports should be presented to Congress assessing the impact of incentive funding. Careful consideration should be given to the need for the continuation of incentive funding beyond the ten-year period or to the design of other incentive programs which will build upon the outcomes of the initial legislation and related professional efforts.

RECOMMENDATION 2: Creation of Model Programs

A minimum of thirty model programs should be created to study the effectiveness of alternative curriculum models, instructional strategies, and modes of inter disciplinary cooperation. In conjunction with the creation of such programs, funding should also be provided for the development of materials and teaching aids.

A special category of funding should be established in an existing Federal authority to support the creation of international high schools in ten major population centers in the country. Among the requirements for the designation as an international high school should be the provision for a minimum of three years of language study in any of ten languages, five of which should be wide-use languages not traditionally taught in American high schools (African languages, Arabic, Chinese, Japanese, Portuguese, and Russian), and for the interdisciplinary study of foreign languages and social studies content, along the lines suggested in the Recommendations to the President's Commission on Foreign Language and International Studies which were prepared by the National Council for the Social Studies (NCSS) and the American Council on the Teaching of Foreign Languages (ACTFL).

A special category of funding should be established in an existing Federal authority to support the creation of ten model programs providing a total school program of global education and foreign language study, elementary through twelfth grade. Each program should include global education curricula for the total school population at the elementary level, interdisciplinary curricula in the study of foreign languages and cultures at the middle or junior high school level, and various alternatives for studying foreign languages and social studies at the high school level.

A third special category of funding should be established in an existing Federal authority to support the creation of ten model programs which provide integration of the study of foreign languages, cultures, and global education in elementary grades through high school. These models could be based upon the combination of numerous components: early language training, such as was provided through foreign language in the elementary school programs of the 1960s; immersion programs, which employ the foreign language as the medium of instruction in other academic subjects, as well as in foreign language study; exploratory language and culture courses, which introduce the study of foreign languages and cultures, including the classical languages, to prepare and motivate students for future language study, to teach students techniques for learning other languages, to develop a basic understanding of the similarities and differences of cultures, to prepare for study abroad, and to aid in student placement in subsequent years of language and culture study; and the establishment or continuation of study abroad pro grams, including the possible creation of alternative intensive experiences in the United States which are designed to accomplish many of the same objectives as study abroad experiences.

Each category of model programs must provide careful articulation from the grade level of implementation through twelfth grade. Evaluation and assessment of each program must be conducted on a yearly basis. The provision for inservice training of teaching staff, development of curricula, and all other components of the program must be addressed in the design of such program models.

RECOMMENDATION 3: Creation of a National Assessment Program for Foreign Language and Culture Study

Funds should be provided through the National Institute of Education (NIE) for the creation of a national assessment program for the study of foreign languages and cultures.

Funding should be designated to support the needed research, test development, and coordination of this ongoing assessment effort. Categories of funding should be designated in the following areas:

1. The continual monitoring of enrollments in foreign language and culture study;
2. The assessment of foreign language skill learning and foreign language proficiency in existing programs both for students and teachers;
3. The assessment of foreign language skill and proficiency development in new or model programs of the study of foreign languages and cultures;
4. The assessment of cultural awareness, knowledge, and attitudes toward the target culture(s);
5. Evaluation of the quality and comparative effectiveness of existing and new learning models in foreign language and culture study.

Initially, extensive effort must be directed toward designing new instruments or modifying existing ones to evaluate foreign language skill and proficiency, as well as cultural awareness, knowledge, and attitudes toward the target culture. Once the instruments have been developed, funds should be made available to assess language skills, language proficiency, cultural awareness, knowledge, and attitudes in existing, new, and model programs. The Federal monitoring agency should assume responsibility for this effort.

Priorities for Existing Legislation

RECOMMENDATION 4: Creation of a Monitoring Agency at the Federal Level

Funding should be provided through an appropriate Federal authority to the creation of a monitoring agency to oversee all programs within the Federal government which provide funding for the study of foreign languages and cultures. This agency should be managed by a person at the Assistant Secretary level within the appropriate Federal agency and should maintain close contact with and access to the academic community through an advisory committee made up of no fewer than twelve persons working at all levels of education in the teaching and supervision of the study of foreign languages and cultures.

RECOMMENDATION 5: Funding of Language and Area Studies Centers, Support of Curriculum Development, and Establishment of a Teacher Inservice Program

Federal support of language and area studies centers and related programs designed to support research, international exchange, and teacher training should be in creased. The availability of specialists in languages and cultures of major importance to the U. S. national interest must be guaranteed. In establishing criteria for funding future programs of this type, careful attention should be given to outlining the types of outreach activities which should be conducted, to specifying the cultural component of such programs, and to assessing the outcomes of such programs in terms of language proficiency attainment, cultural awareness, cultural knowledge, and attitudes toward the target culture. Specific provision should be made for fostering the expansion of programs in wide-use languages such as African languages, Arabic, Chinese, Japanese, Portuguese, and Russian. Special emphasis should be given to providing support for the development of curriculum and teaching materials.

A national program of teacher inservice training should be established, similar in scope and purpose to the Institute Program funded in the past through NDEA, Title VI. The focus of this inservice program should be to improve the quality of foreign language and culture instruction, and to retrain current foreign language and social studies teachers for the task of teaching global education at all levels, as outlined in the second section of this report, Professional Priorities.

RECOMMENDATION 6: Establishment of a High Level of Priority for Foreign Language and Culture Projects Funded by Other Existing Federal Authorities

The Congress, working with and through the Federal monitoring agency, should establish a high level of priority for projects funded by other Federal agencies which support the study of foreign languages and cultures. As a first step, the Congress should formulate a clearly stated national policy in support of this need based upon our national priorities: (1) the growing dependence of the U.S. on foreign energy sources has resulted in an increasing trade deficit which must be reduced by increasing U.S. exports; and (2) the increasing interdependence of all nations demands increasing competence and understanding in dealing both individually and collectively with other peoples. Projects funded by the National Institute of Education, National Endowment for the Humanities, Fund for the Improvement of Post Secondary Education, Teacher Centers Program, Office of Bilingual Education, and other agencies concerned either directly or indirectly with education, should be linked to the recommendations outlined in the Professional Priorities section of this report.

Professional Priorities

RECOMMENDATION 7: Implementation of a National Public Awareness Program

The major, national professional organizations which represent those engaged in teaching foreign languages and cultures, in cooperation with the National Council for the Social Studies and the National Association for Bilingual Education, should undertake a national media campaign to inform the American public of the need for knowledge of other languages and cultures. Initial funding should be sought from the members of the Joint National Committee for Languages. Matching funds should be sought from private foundations and organizations concerned with ethnic and international studies. This campaign should be conducted with the sponsorship of the National Advertising Council, under its program of public service advertising.

As the national campaign is implemented, a simultaneous effort must be organized to assist local educators in conducting activities which will bring to the attention of the general public the values of foreign language and culture education. The sponsorship of town meetings, festivals, international fairs, and other activities which have traditionally been conducted in conjunction with National Foreign Language Week and other locally sponsored public awareness programs must be encouraged and expanded.

RECOMMENDATION 8: Establishment of a Congressional Liaison Office in Washington, D.C.

Funding should be provided by the major, national language- and culture-related organizations to establish a Washington liaison office during the fall of 1979. Those persons employed for this purpose would have as their major responsibility the establishment and maintenance of close cooperation with members of Congress, the staff of the U.S. Office of Education, and those in other agencies directly concerned with the implementation of the recommendations of the President's Commission on Foreign Language and International Studies.

In conjunction with this effort, a national communications network must be established to provide immediate access to key members of the education community, as well as a mechanism for alerting the profession to changes in policies and programs affecting language study, both nationally and locally.

RECOMMENDATION 9: Funding of an Interdisciplinary Effort for the Development of Global Education Curricula

Global education is a concept which could help U.S. citizens attain global literacy: an awareness of global conditions and problems; an understanding of the planet and the interconnectedness of the world social order; a respect for the concepts of multi-ethnic, polycultural, and multilingual education in pluralistic societies at home and abroad; communication and career competencies. It is a concept which must be implemented in curricula at all levels. The needs of American society and the major international issues which face our nation argue for introducing students to foreign language and culture study at an early age. It may motivate them to pursue the study of foreign languages and cultures as they progress through the secondary schools. The desired result of such programs is a population aware of the whole world context in which they live and able to communicate in languages other than English.

Incentive funds for the development of global education curricula could come from existing agencies such as the National Institute of Education and the National Endowment for the Humanities. In order to provide for the coordination and dissemination of the work under taken by the various agencies and institutions, a consortium of associations concerned with the teaching of foreign languages and cultures should be created and should work closely with the Federal monitoring agency. Support for the maintenance of the consortium would be provided through various sources, including the following: money allocated to the support of the consortium by each association member; projects conducted by the consortium or individual members of the consortium with grant support; fees paid to the consortium by other institutions or agencies which have received global education grants in payment for specific services, e.g., evaluation.

RECOMMENDATION 10: Continuation of Inservice Teacher Preparation in Foreign Language and International Studies

Funds should be appropriated through existing legislation to launch a major inservice program for current teachers. Statistics indicate that the majority of current teachers are "tenured in," therefore, few new teachers will enter the profession during the next decade. Initially, the inservice program should focus on the retraining of current foreign language and social studies teachers to teach global education in the elementary grades. The second phase of the program should focus on the retraining of foreign language and social studies teachers to teach courses of an interdisciplinary nature at the secondary level, based upon the concepts and purposes of global education.

Within the context of creating an interdisciplinary foreign language and global education curriculum, foreign language teachers have particular needs: maintaining and increasing proficiency in the foreign language; maintaining and increasing cultural knowledge about and sensitivity to the people(s) whose language they are teaching; improving teaching through increased awareness of and experience with strategies for teaching a foreign language; developing knowledge of the purposes and concepts of global education, as well as experience with relevant global education teaching strategies. Within this same context, social studies teachers also have particular needs: developing greater awareness and knowledge of the relationship between language and culture; experiencing another culture; learning another language; and improving teaching through increased awareness of and experience with strategies for teaching global education. The needs of foreign language and social studies teachers can be met in joint programs where both groups interact. The vehicles for such interaction are several, such as intensive summer workshops, intensive weekends, and academic year programs, held under the auspices of teacher centers or local education agencies. Foreign programs sponsored by consortia of local education agencies should also be considered.

Funds for such efforts should be granted only through consortia of associations or local education agencies which show specific needs and exhibit a plan, including evaluation, for inservice programs. Such consortia would work closely with the Federal monitoring agency. Although funds for inservice programs could be granted directly to institutions of higher education, only those institutions which demonstrate follow-up to the inservice activities by implementing these changes in their ongoing curricula will be eligible for future grants.

RECOMMENDATION 11: Availability of Training in Foreign Languages and Cultures in Non-Academic Settings

At present, private agencies are often called upon to provide training in foreign languages and cultures, due to the absence of such offerings at all levels of education. Therefore, funds should be made available through the National Institute of Education and the National Endowment for the Humanities for the design of curricula and the implementation of programs which address two significant segments of the adult audience: (1) Persons in business, industry, trade, and government who require skills in foreign languages and cultures in order to conduct their business; and (2) persons who wish to pursue the study of foreign languages and cultures as a leisure-time activity.

Any attempt to implement a program of global awareness at all levels of education must take into account the growing adult population of the U. S., because it is responsible for the conducting of business, industry, trade, and government affairs. In addition, as this segment of the population reaches retirement age, it has the opportunity to pursue study and travel and other leisure activities. Within this group, many have the need for or interest in the study of foreign languages and cultures.

RECOMMENDATION 12: Development of a Ten-Year Plan to Implement Curricula for Global Education, Teacher Inservice Continuing Preparation, and Language Learning in Non-Academic Settings

A ten-year plan for the implementation of the recommendations contained in this document is a necessity if the profession, through its own efforts and with the help of Federal funding, is to demonstrate the ability to respond to a renewed interest in the study of foreign languages and cultures.

A process which implements and accounts for change in the study of foreign languages and cultures must be composed of the following elements:

1. Assessment of the current state of the profession in preparation for the development of a renewed effort in foreign language and culture study;

2. Setting of goals for foreign language and global education in different education environments: elementary and secondary schools, colleges, and adult education;

3. Development of curricula for foreign language and global education in varied educational environments;

4. Preparation of current teachers to teach the new curriculum;

5. Development of instrumentation for the assessment of learning and programs;

6. Program implementation;

7. Evaluation and assessment of foreign language and culture learning and program evaluation.

All of the proposed projects in this document fall within the process outlined. This process would help insure orderly progress toward the use of time, would require accountability to the profession for its effort, would create a mechanism for reports to the Federal government for the expenditure of money, and would provide information which might help the profession in the continued development of optimal learning conditions in different learning environments.

Foreign Language Annals, Vol. 12, No. 5 (October 1979), pp. 387-391.

Appendix B

ACTFL IN RETROSPECT: A COMMENT ON TWO CULTURES*
BY FRANK M. GRITTNER,
WISCONSIN DEPARTMENT OF PUBLIC INSTRUCTION

My task is to give a brief, historical overview of ACTFL. In order to be brief, I have focused my remarks on two concepts: One is a hypothesis, the other a contrary-to-fact, conditional proposition. The contrary-to-fact part comes from the James Stewart film classic, *It's A Wonderful Life*, in which a guardian angel gives the hero an opportunity to see what the world would have been like if he had never existed. Similarly, I want to look at a "what if" clause relating to ACTFL. That is, "What would the profession be like today if ACTFL had never been created?"

The hypothesis part is simply this: I maintain that there are two distinct and separate cultures that operate within the foreign language field: One culture is devoted to literary and linguistic scholarship; the other is involved in the art of teaching people to communicate in a foreign language. I am using the word "culture" here in the sense that C. P. Snow used it in his book *The Two Cultures* in which he differentiated between the culture of literary intellectuals and that of scientists. And he said, "Without thinking about it...(people in

each culture) respond alike. That is what culture means...the members of each culture have...common attitudes, common standards and patterns of behavior, (and) common approaches and assumptions!" And each culture is distinctly different in these respects.

Now, I submit that significant differences also exist between the scholars of literature and the practitioners of teaching in the foreign language profession. It is true that, on occasion, a renowned scholar is also sufficiently bicultural to be a good teacher. But this skill tends to be regarded as little more than an interesting if not dysfunctional idiosyncrasy. It is seldom a major factor for getting promoted in a literature department. The key words here are "scholar" and "teacher." Or, to rephrase C. P. Snow, "We are not dealing here with common patterns of behavior, common attitudes or common approaches and assumptions!" Let me clarify this with a few examples: In the literary culture one goes to a conference to read a paper on a topic like "Proto Indo-European Nasals in Old Church Gothic?" or on "Franz Kafka's Prose Riddles: Oedipal Structures?" The pattern of behavior is clear. In this culture one reads a paper on a topic in one's area of specialization.

By contrast, in the pedagogical culture one gives a presentation, ideally supported by slides (or at least by a pile of transparencies). And the topics sound like this: "Supplementing the Foreign Language Curriculum with Available High Interest Materials," or "Using Pair Work to Maximize Communicative Interactions in the Classroom."

In the culture of the literati, success depends on one's individual performance: the scholar must be cautious, careful and slow to generalize. Research must be meticulously documented to protect one's reputation. In the culture of the language teacher success depends on getting others to perform. This means promoting risk taking, inferencing, quick application of generalizations and tolerance for error in communicative interchanges. The point here is that the status markers, performance standards and professional behaviors are totally different between cultures. Hence the complete futility of trying to establish continuity between them. In fact, trying to articulate the language teaching profession with the literary scholarship profession is like trying to articulate a dock worker's union with the local yacht club on the grounds that they both use the same waterfront. It really cannot be done. Cross cultural understanding is the best we can hope for.

To relate this to the topic at hand let me point out that 20 years ago, some very perceptive people in the Modem Language Association saw a need to provide funds to start a national association that would serve those who were dedicated to the teaching of foreign languages. This was formally announced in *Foreign Language Annals* in April 1967, with the statement that, "The MLA secretariat is authorized to initiate immediately necessary steps to organize a new association with individual membership open to persons engaged in the teaching or supervision of any foreign language at any level of education…." And it further stated that: "The new organization shall be called the American Council on the Teaching of Foreign Languages (ACTFL). ACTFL will seek to become a unifying focus for efforts to advance pedagogical and professional aspects of the teaching of all foreign languages at all levels."

The key phrases here are "unifying force" and "foreign languages at all levels." I am emphasizing this because another new pedagogical organization had been started in the mid 1960s. It was called The Department Of Foreign Languages Of The National Education Association. Let me list the names of some of the people who started this organization: Lester McKim, Nelson Brooks, Jerry Arendt, Emma Birkmaier and Frank Grittner. Within a few years all of the people listed above had opted for ACTFL and, in fact, several eventually served as presidents of ACTFL. And the reason why they changed allegiances was quite simple; going the Department of Foreign Language route with NEA would have tended to split the high school and university methods people into two non-communicating groups. So, back to the question: What if there had been no ACTFL? One answer is that we might now be split into two divisive segments according to instructional level.

However, ACTFL did become the organization chosen by those from the pedagogical culture. A former high school French teacher and State Foreign Language Supervisor, F. Andre Paquette, became the first Executive Director. And, under his editorship, *Foreign Language Annals* went from a newsletter to a professional pedagogical journal in just one year. Vol. Two of Annals in 1968 contained an article by John Carroll on "Proficiency Attained by Foreign Language Majors in Higher Education." It was a report on his extensive study involving the commonly taught languages. This was the first major use of the FSI proficiency tests for non-governmental research. Also, it was the forerunner of the present ACTFL Proficiency Guidelines. So, the seeds for this present-day development were already planted in ACTFL's second year of existence. Incidentally, in his report, Carroll deplored the fact that most college majors scored only at level 2 on the proficiency scale. This fact would surprise no one today, but it typified the over expectation of the times. We tended to expect miracles to happen as a result of new methods, FLES programs, language laboratories, programmed instruction, and other innovations.

However, there was a positive side to our naiveté. The professional atmosphere in which ACTFL was born was full of challenge and excitement. There were tens of millions of federal dollars for equipment, materials, pedagogical research and teacher summer institutes. And the choices were simple: there were only two main methodological bandwagons, and you could stay with one or jump on the other. The issues were clear-cut: You knew precisely whom to admire and whom to despise at the drop of a phrase. You were either "New Key" or "Old Hat;" audio-lingual or traditional; a Skinnerian structuralist or a Latinizing grammarian.

In fact, those who opted for the new movement rapidly became proficient in "audio-lingualeze". And there were certain buzz-words that instantly projected a person into the vanguard. For example, you could casually work the term, "Minimal phonemic pair" into a conversation, and eyes would widen. Follow that with the term "operant conditioning" and heads would nod knowingly. But then, just slip in the words "SUPRASEGMENTAL PHONEME" and people would swoon! Those were the days.

Today, bandwagon-jumping has become downright hazardous. There are so many of them going simultaneously in all directions. For example, in one foolproof modern method the teacher shuts up, and the students do all the talking. (It's called the "Silent Way.") But in another, equally foolproof method the teacher talks and the students shut up. (Now, for some reason, this is not called the "noisy way"—It's known as the "natural method.") However, in contrast to the 19th-century natural method, the new one has modernized its rhetoric. So, we now have COMPREHENSIBLE INPUT. This term is based on the impeccably reasonable belief that students should be able to derive meaning from the material they are learning. However, overemphasizing the use of the term conveys the unflattering implication that all previous practitioners have been ardent advocates of gibberish. Another item in the new version of the old natural approach is the possession of an AFFECTIVE FILTER that can be cranked up and down. (It's supposed to be down.) In fact, your filter can get so far down, that you can even lapse into "SUGGESIOPEDIA" where language is absorbed subconsciously to the rhythms of baroque music. Also, you can be counseled into learning, and even find old François Gouin updated into TOTAL PHYSICAL RESPONSE. And, of course, you can also get yourself notionally functioned, communicatively competented and even proficiently oriented.

Now, I'm not trying to offend everyone in the profession. (I'll settle for 80 percent.) Actually, I think this kind of methodological ferment is good. I believe in eclecticism, simply because there is no solid research base to prove the efficacy of any one method. And, when you consider that following World War I as the profession stagnated for over 40 years on the grammar-reading method, this diversity can only be regarded as healthy. Would all of this have happened without the national pedagogical forum that ACTFL has provided? Would it have happened without the right leadership? I don't think so.

What would be missing without ACTFL? Let me cite just a few examples:

- First, we would not have the Foreign Language Education Series reporting annually on new developments in the field and providing an historical record of pedagogical trends;

- Second, a major pedagogical journal, *Foreign Language Annals,* would be unavailable;
- Third, there would be no Annual Meeting to discuss pedagogical concerns with colleagues from across the nation;
- Fourth, there would be no vehicle for nationwide coordination of foreign language teaching efforts;
- And fifth, an information center across language lines would be missing. For example, who would collect and record enrollment information to let us know the status of the profession?

In short, what would our pedagogical culture be like today without ACTFL? The answer, I think, is clear. We would be what we were in the 1950's: a balkanized, decentralized, scarcely visible scattering of professionals in search of an organization. We now have that organization, and we need to find ways to better support it with money and members. ACTFL was important 20 years ago; it is essential today; it will be indispensible for tomorrow. We can be proud to have been part of it.

*From a speech delivered November 12, 1986 at ACTFL's Twentieth Anniversary Meeting held in Dallas, Texas.

Appendix C

MANHATTAN COLLEGE/ACTFL STUDY OF THE FOREIGN LANGUAGE TEACHING PROFESSION

1. Which one of the following best describes your work?: (circle one)
   a) teaching foreign language(s);
   b) management/administration;
   c) management/administration with foreign language teaching responsibilities;
   d) retired from foreign language teaching;
   e) other (please indicate) _____
2. Where do you do (or have you done) most of your teaching? (circle one)
   a) secondary school (high school);
   b) undergraduate (two or four year college);
   c) graduate or professional school;
   d) adult training;
   e) other (please indicate) _____
3. Are you a member of the American Council on the Teaching of Foreign Languages (ACTFL)?
   Yes _____ No _____

4. If you are a member of ACTFL, please indicate how many years you have belonged to the organization.
   _____ Years
5. Are you tenured (or the equivalent) at the institution where you currently work?
   Yes _____ No _____ Does not apply _____
6. Approximately how many jobs have you had as a teacher of foreign languages in your career? _____
7. For approximately how many years have you worked as a teacher of foreign languages? _____ Years
8. At the institution where you do most of your teaching, approximately how many students are enrolled? (circle one) a) fewer than 500; b) 500 to 2000; c) 2001 to 5000; d) 5001 to 10,000; e) more than 10,000.
9. Is the area where your school is located considered: (circle one) a) inner city?; b) urban?; c) suburban?; d) small town?; e) rural?; f) not sure.
10. Please indicate the five-digit postal zip code for the institution where you do most of your teaching:
    _____

Questions 11 through 17 are about you, your experience and your background.

11. What was the last level of school you completed? (circle one) a) four-year college graduate; b) some graduate credits; c) masters completed; d) credits beyond masters; e) doctorate completed; f) other (please indicate) _____
12. Was your undergraduate degree in foreign language(s)?
    Yes _____ No _____
13. Was your graduate work mainly in foreign language(s)?
    Yes _____ No _____
14. Please list below the languages you teach in the order you teach them, with the most frequently taught language first and so on.
    1. _____ 2. _____
    3. _____ 4. _____
15. Please let us know how you acquired your own proficiency in the language you most often teach by circling one or more of the following responses:
    a) formal education; b) travel and / or school abroad ; c) spoken at home in the U.S.; d) raised in a country where it is a first language.
16. Please indicate your gender: _____ Male _____ Female
17. Which of the following categories best describes your 1986 income derived from teaching, before taxes? (circle one) a) $15,000 or less; b) $15,001 to $20,000; c) $20,001 to $25,000; d) $25,001 to $30,000; e) $30,001 to $35,000; f) $35,0001 to $40,000; g) over $40,000.
18. Have you ever seriously considered leaving teaching to go into some other occupation? _____ Yes _____ No

19. Within the next five years how likely is it that you will leave the teaching profession to go into some different occupation? (circle one) a) very likely ; b) fairly likely ; c) not too likely; d) very unlikely.

20. All in all, how satisfied would you say you are with your job? a) very satisfied; b) somewhat satisfied; c) somewhat dissatisfied; d) very dissatisfied; e) not sure.

In the remainder of this questionnaire, we present a number of statements about your profession and where you work. Please let us know your opinion by indicating how much you agree or disagree with each statement. In doing so, select the appropriate number from the following scale and write it on the line before the statement you are considering. For example, if you "strongly agree," you would write a "5" on the line before the statement. If you "strongly disagree" with the statement, you would write a "1."

5	4	3	2	1
Strongly Agree	Agree	Neither Agree nor Disagree	Disagree	Strongly Disagree

_____ 21. Young people should be encouraged to have a career in foreign language teaching.
_____ 22. By and large, the demand for foreign language teaching is increasing.
_____ 23. One has reasons to be optimistic about the future of foreign language teaching as a career.
_____ 24. Compensation for foreign language teaching is adequate.

The following statements pertain to the organization where you work. Please use the same scale as above to respond to each statement which is prefaced with "Where I work."

WHERE I WORK:
_____ 25. The teaching of foreign languages is highly regarded as a profession by co-workers and others.
_____ 26. Foreign language instruction is a high priority.
_____ 27. Generally I am satisfied that enough emphasis is placed on the teaching of foreign languages.
_____ 28. The size of the work force is steadily increasing.
_____ 29. Faculty and staff generally respect and help one another.
_____ 30. Chaotic conditions prevail.
_____ 31. Objectives are well-defined.
_____ 32. Faculty members perform their assignments competently.
_____ 33. Administrators perform their assignments competently.
_____ 34. The quality of work done is of high caliber.

_____ 35. People are generally well-qualified for their responsibilities.
_____ 36. People trust each other.
_____ 37. There are enough qualified teachers of foreign languages to meet the demand for foreign language instruction.
_____ 38. The encouragement of foreign language instruction is a clear objective of the organization.
_____ 39. The channels of communication are poor.
_____ 40. It is hard to understand the direction or purpose of the organization.
_____ 41. People are often frustrated because of communication problems.
_____ 42. The organization is flexible enough to take on new missions and tasks.
_____ 43. Employees seem to get along well with each other.
_____ 44. We deserve a solid reputation for doing our jobs well.
_____ 45. When a change is required, people adjust.
_____ 46. The volume of work accomplished is quite large.
_____ 47. People are kept informed about things that affect their work.
_____ 48. People welcome change.
_____ 49. I anticipate an increase in the number of people hired.
_____ 50. Can be characterized as stable and smoothly functioning.
_____ 51. There are too many poorly qualified people with important assignments.
_____ 52. Those in positions of authority listen to those who work with them.
_____ 53. I look forward to going to work each day.
_____ 54. There is an overall emphasis on increased productivity.
_____ 55. People have a clear understanding of what the organization expects from them.
_____ 56. Those in charge generally plan their work in advance and are well organized.
_____ 57. Most people are personally motivated to perform well.
_____ 58. The organization provides positive incentives for exceptional performance.
_____ 59. Up-to-date technology is available to aid the teaching of foreign languages.
_____ 60. Professional development activities (conferences and the like) are actively supported by the organization.
_____ 61. Foreign language instruction receives its fair share of resources from the organization.

Foreign Language Annals (Vol. 20, No. 6) (December 1987)), pp. 576-577.

Maya Angelou was the keynote speaker at the 1990 ACTFL Annual Meeting in Nashville, TN. ACTFL's annual convention experienced rapid, dramatic growth in the 90s, reflecting its growth in membership. At the conventions, the expo area was also flourishing, with exhibitors showcasing the latest technology.

CHAPTER 4

THE 1990s

The Decade of Professional Priorities

Diane W. Birckbichler of The Ohio State University took the helm of ACTFL as the 1990 President. In her first "Message from the President" in *FLA*, Vol. 23, No. 1 (February 1989), p. 49, she follows the custom of beginning a decade with reflections on the past 10 years and with a plan of action for the next decade. She said, "For many, the 80s represent the 'proficiency' generation, a decade in which ACTFL and its Proficiency Guidelines have set the tone for the profession. However controversial the Guidelines may have become, they have clarified for the first time in many years a common goal for language learning at all levels: the development of the linguistic and cultural proficiency of our students." She went on to say that the 80s had also been marked by a series of dichotomies that had separated the profession needlessly on important issues. She said that "If we are to succeed in the 90s, we can no longer afford, for example, to separate theory from practice, to distinguish between teacher and researcher, to oppose learning to acquisition. Furthermore, we know far too little about second language learning to allow methodological preferences, bandwagons, and guruism to guide our thinking and prevent us from investigating all aspects of the teaching/learning process" (p. 49). Shades of Frank Grittner's retrospective speech in the middle of the 1980s! As the French saying goes...*Plus* ça *change, plus c'est la même chose* [The more things change, the more they stay the same].

The Fund for the Future was struggling along. Through the end of January 1990, 231 individuals and 32 associations and corporations had contributed to ACTFL—still a far cry from the anticipated 1,000 contributors.

President Birckbichler envisioned the 1990s as a decade for establishing professional priorities, a process that had begun with the 1989 Priorities Conference in Boston. Discussions of these important concerns continued throughout the year and especially at the 1990 Annual Meeting where a group of priorities became the sub-themes:

Diane W. Birckbichler
ACTFL President 1990

curriculum/articulation; culture/literature; advanced levels; technology; early language learning; political/professional research; teacher education; evaluation/measurement; less commonly taught languages. Some of these issues were familiar because they were ongoing concerns. Other issues represented new or renewed emphases for the profession.

The next phase of the process took place at the 1990 Annual Meeting, at which special focus sessions had been scheduled for culture, less commonly taught languages, assessment, teacher education, and research. As President Birckbichler pointed out: ACTFL is not a single issue organization; nor was it an organization that could focus its attention and limited resources equally on the many issues that surfaced at the 1989 Priorities Conference. It would be through discussion, future meetings, and through reactions, ideas, and comments sent to ACTFL by its members that the organization could begin to address those concerns that were indeed our priorities.

It was announced that the 1990 Annual Meeting, which had originally scheduled for New Orleans, LA, but was changed—both the location and the dates—to accommodate the wishes of attendees and the requirements of a convention that was experiencing rapid, dramatic growth (ACTFL '89 had 3,666 attendees!). The 1990 meeting, "Acting on Priorities: A Commitment to Excellence," was held at the Opryland Hotel, Nashville, TN, November 17-19, in conjunction with SCOLT, AATG, AATI, CLTA, and the Tennessee Foreign Language Teachers Association (TFLTA). Maya Angelou was the keynote speaker.

As can be seen from the theme of the Annual Meeting, "Acting on Priorities: A Commitment to Excellence," the focus on priorities was to move from discussion to action. President Birckbichler wrote that the first phrase in the clarification and establishment of our professional priorities was the 1989 Boston Priorities Conference, which

was not designed to find "quick fixes" for difficult problems or easy solutions to complex issues. Instead, the conference, the papers, and the recommendations that came from them should be viewed as points of departure for continued discussion, reflection, and refinement. The next phase would be the publication and dissemination of the recommendations of the different strands. The commissioned priorities papers and selected written reactions to them would appear in special issues of *FLA*.

At the Annual Meeting, there were Focus Sessions designed to build on discussions begun in 1989: Teacher Education, Research, Assessment, Culture/Authentic Texts, Less Commonly Taught Languages. Interestingly, the Research focus group would see the creation of a special-interest group (SIG) for ACTFL members interested in conducting research and in developing a research agenda for the profession. The establishment of this SIG represented an important direction for ACTFL—an enhancement of the organizational structure to accommodate both the general interests of its members as well as groups with special interests and areas of expertise.

The 1990 Annual Meeting was a success:

- Final attendance figures reached 3,200.
- Participation in pre- and post-conference workshops was the largest ever.
- Maya Angelou's audience numbered over 2,500 conference attendees, the largest ever at an opening session.
- The Opryland Hotel and surrounding hotels saw more than 1700 rooms booked.

It was also announced at that meeting that Gerard L. Ervin of The Ohio State University had been elected President of ACTFL for 1992.

ACTFL planned numerous workshops throughout 1990-1991, including oral proficiency interviewing and rating in Hawaii, Minnesota,

British Columbia, Kansas, Tennessee, and Colorado. An Oral Proficiency Interviewing Refresher workshop took place in Aptos, CA. There were also two post-conference workshops: Instructional Video Modules in Foreign Language Teacher Education, and Taming Technology: The Practical Use of Video in Foreign Language Instruction. 1990 also saw the appearance of the *ACTFL Hindi Proficiency Guidelines* (*FLA*, Vol. 23, No. 3 (May 1990), pp. 235- 252).

In her third message to the membership, President Birckbichler wrote about the work of JNCL-NCLIS. She talked about the outstanding leadership of Director J. David Edwards and Assistant Director Jamie Draper, and how JNCL-NCLIS was monitoring budget and legislation at the national level, translating professional priorities into legislative terms, providing professional updates and alerts, conducting political action workshops, and generally keeping the membership aware of the political and legislative contexts in which we were working (*FLA*, Vol. 23, No. 3 (May 1990), p. 223).

The September 1990 issue of *FLA* (Vol. 23, No. 4), was the first in a series of special issues in which selected topical papers and representative reactions were published throughout the 1990-1991 academic year in an effort to effect more wide-scale sharing of the positions and deliberations put forth at the 1989 National Conference on Professional Priorities. The September issue focused on three areas identified as priorities for the decade of the 1990s: Articulation, Integrating the Arts in the Second Language Curriculum, and Literature and Communicative Competence.

The October 1990 issue of *FLA* (Vol. 23, No. 5) was the second special issue focusing on papers about three additional priorities: instruction; teaching all students: reaching and teaching students of varying abilities; and foreign languages in the elementary school, and selected reaction papers.

ACTFL was experiencing growth along with its successes. The office staff at headquarters in Yonkers now had 10 full-time employees, four part-time employees/ consultants, and two students. Robert Katz of Combined Business Services was retained as a financial consultant in order to secure ACTFL's financial status. The position of Editor of *FLA* came available since the term of the current editor ended with the December 1991 issue.

1991: ACTFL's Silver Anniversary

In 1991, ACTFL celebrated its silver anniversary—25 years of growing leadership in the field of foreign languages. Two unsigned documents on retrospect and prospect were written, one in early 1991, the other in early December of 1991 (See Appendices A & B). Leading the organization during 1991 was President, Lynn Sandstedt, from the University of Northern Colorado, Greeley, CO. In his first Message from the President in *FLA* (Vol. 24, No. 1 (February 1991), 39), Sandstedt reflected on the accomplishments of not only ACTFL but also the profession in the past two and a half decades. He said that ACTFL had adhered to its mission through an ever-expanding range of projects and services that included:

Lynn Sandstedt
ACTFL President 1991

MEMBERSHIP SURVEY

ACTFL, as part of its 25th Anniversary Celebration, is conducting the following membership survey in order to give each of you the opportunity to evaluate the quality and effectiveness of the numerous services and activities of the Association. Suggestions for other services and projects that ACTFL might pursue in the future are also being requested.

PLEASE TAKE TIME TO COMPLETE THE SURVEY. YOUR RESPONSE WILL HELP ACTFL TO MEET YOUR PROFESSIONAL NEEDS.

I. For each of the following items, circle one of the numbers, 5 high to 1 low. 0 = NA. (Written comments are strongly encouraged.)

1. 5 4 3 2 1 0   ACTFL Annual Meeting
Comments: _____

2. 5 4 3 2 1 0   The ACTFL journal, *Foreign Language Annals*
Comments: _____

3. 5 4 3 2 1 0   The *ACTFL Newsletter*
Comments: _____

4. 5 4 3 2 1 0   The ACTFL Foreign Language Education Series
Comments: _____

5. 5 4 3 2 1 0   ACTFL Professional Development Program
Comments: _____

6. 5 4 3 2 1 0   ACTFL Professional Testing Certification and Recertification Process
Comments: _____

7. 5 4 3 2 1 0   The responsiveness of ACTFL Headquarters to individual member needs and requests
Comments: _____

8. 5 4 3 2 1 0   ACTFL dues structure
Comments: _____

9. 5 4 3 2 1 0   ACTFL's cooperation with other language associations
Comments: _____

10. 5 4 3 2 1 0   ACTFL as an effective voice for the profession
Comments: _____

(Cont...)

11. 5 4 3 2 1 0   ACTFL Awards Program
Comments: _____

12. 5 4 3 2 1 0   The Special Interest Group (SIGS) concept for addressing special concerns of the profession
Comments: _____

13. 5 4 3 2 1 0   The "Priorities Process" conducted every ten years to define the primary issues confronting the profession
Comments: _____

14. 5 4 3 2 1 0   Relationship of ACTFL with regional and state organizations
Comments: _____

15. 5 4 3 2 1 0   The Summer Seminar Program designed to find solutions for some of the problems of the profession
Comments: _____

16. 5 4 3 2 1 0   The overall effectiveness of ACTFL as a professional organization
Comments: _____

II. Suggestions for future projects and activities for ACTFL that you feel would benefit and strengthen the profession.

_____
_____
_____
_____

PLEASE SEND THE COMPLETED SURVEY FORM TO:

**ACTFL
6 Executive Plaza
Yonkers, New York 10701-6801**

THANK YOU.

Number of years member of ACTFL _____

Languages _____

Levels _____

Number of years teaching_____

Membership Survey from 1991, when ACTFL celebrated 25 years.

- an annual national convention and workshop program
- a journal, *Foreign Language Annals*
- a newsletter, the *ACTFL Newsletter* (first begun as *Accent on ACTFL*)
- the ACTFL Foreign Language Education Series
- the ACTFL Materials Center
- the ACTFL Professional Development Program
- ACTFL Special Interest Groups (SIGs)
- the ACTFL Summer Series, focusing on issues in second language education.

He also cautioned that we had no room for complacency. The 1989 Priorities Conference in Boston had indicated that there was much work yet to be done. Papers from this conference had appeared in *FLA*—September 1990, October 1990, February 1991, and April 1991. The February 1991 issue of *FLA* included papers and reactions on two more priorities: Public Relations and the Classics. The April 1991 issue contained the final papers based on the priorities Research, Teacher Education, Instruction, and Curriculum.

Now, as ACTFL was about to enter a new quarter century of leadership, the organization's leaders wanted to know what the members would suggest regarding the role that ACTFL should play in the coming years to help maintain the health of the profession.

Along with OPI workshops for 1991 given all over the U.S. as well as in Quebec City, Canada, ACTFL was also initiating a series of summer seminars, the first of which was held in Denver, CO, on July 29-30, 1991, addressing the area of Foreign Language Teacher Education. This seminar looked at the development of strategies to solve problems related to the effective education and training of competent foreign language teachers for our nation's schools.

In 1991, a new membership campaign saw an increase of over 700 new members in ACTFL, but also a loss of members due to an increase in membership dues:

- Regular:
  - 1 year $65
  - 2 years $120
  - 3 years $170
- International $75
- Joint $85
- New Teachers $45
- Student $25
- Retired $25

Financial consultant Robert Katz pointed out that membership dues actually amounted to 16% of ACTFL's annual budget, while the annual meeting and workshops each provided 30% of annual funds. As of the end of February 1991, the Fund for the Future included 241 individual and 33 association and corporation contributors. After much discussion by the Executive Council, Katz's recommendation to move income from Fund for the Future to the general operating fund passed unanimously.

Executive Director Scebold reported on a recent initiative at the May 1991 Executive Council meeting: an update on the National Education Goals Panel Hearings, at which people presented oral testimony on the six goals the nation's governors and the Bush administration had established for American education. While frustrating, the nationwide hearings had also been successful: language educators had represented the concerns of the profession well, and the testimonies they had presented were apparently being heard, would positively affect the final statements of the goals and objectives, and would influence future steps taken at the federal and state levels (*FLA*, Vol. 25, No. 1 (February 1992), pp. 74-75). Thus the groundwork was being laid for foreign languages to become part of core curricula and for development of national standards for foreign languages.

The Message from the President (*FLA,* Vol. 24, No. 4 (October 1991), p. 415) summarized the first ACTFL summer seminar. Seminar participants outlined and discussed major concerns the profession had to address to influence reform efforts:

- Recruiting and retraining new teachers;
- Developing a common set of teacher education program guidelines endorsed by all foreign language organizations;
- Providing relevant instruction, information, and experience for all in the three areas of Personal, Professional, and Specialist development at the preservice level;
- Providing useful, relevant inservice education: what should be offered, and who should offer it;
- Upgrading methods courses to reflect today's classroom realities: who should teach them, and what should be taught;
- Making the clinical and student teaching experience more meaningful and valuable;

- Establishing better liaisons and communication between the university and public schools, including formation of collaboratives and partnerships;
- Defining more effective procedures for supervision of student teachers by encouraging greater cooperation between the college supervisor and the cooperating classroom teachers;
- Studying the effects of both state and national external certification requirements on foreign language teacher education programs;
- Developing a plan for affecting the accreditation and certification of teachers;
- Assessing teacher competence, including language proficiency;
- Training foreign language teachers for the elementary schools;
- Encouraging more research related to second language teaching, learning and acquisition.

The dialogue that began at this summer seminar would continue at ACTFL '91 in Washington, DC. The 1991 annual meeting, now called ACTFL '91 Annual Meeting and Exposition, included a new Learning Technologies Fair, an informative program of the best technology-based second language instruction available. More than 3,500 had preregistered for this meeting—a new attendance record. Representation at this fair included major hardware manufacturers and distributors. Apple Computers and IBM provided workstations to enable participants to experiment with software of specific interest and application to their language instruction programs. Six ACTFL Corporate Sponsors provided private demonstrations and discussions of their newest and best software.

Honorees at the meeting included the ACTFL charter members—those who had joined it in 1967 and were still members in 1991 (see Appendix B). It was announced in the December issue of *FLA* for 1991 (Vol. 24, No. 6) that Ray T. Clifford, Provost of the DLI, had been elected President of ACTFL for 1993. The 1992 OPI testing and refresher workshops were announced, again ranging all over the US as well as in Toronto and Quebec. Several new SIGs were organized under the ACTFL umbrella: Teacher Development, Research, and Elementary School Language Issues. Finally, Frank Grittner was named editor of *FLA* in 1992, replacing Vicki Galloway.

The Next 25 Years

ACTFL 1992 President Gerard L. Ervin of The Ohio State University set membership as his term's priority, indicating that membership in ACTFL was surprisingly low throughout the US. He called for a grassroots, bottom-up movement for current members to work with him in reaching and recruiting non-members.

Ervin was presented with a challenge as a new president: how could he make the year following ACTFL's twenty-fifth anniversary a significant one for the organization? He offered three possibilities. Members could (1) share their enthusiasm for foreign language teaching and learning; (2) seek opportunities for growth as a teacher; and (3) support their local, regional, and national foreign language associations and urge their colleagues to do likewise.

Gerard L. Ervin
ACTFL President 1992

In the February issue of *FLA* for 1992 (Vol. 25, No. 1), Frank Grittner summarized the history of the journal:

[...] As a charter member of ACTFL, I clearly remember its inception. In fact, FLA pre-dates the existence of ACTFL itself. It was published in great quantity by the Modern Language Association in two issues in 1967 and sent gratis to foreign language teachers all over the nation. The first issue of FLA went to more that 60,000 teachers, the second to more than 85,000. Its initial purpose was to generate interest in the newly-formed American Council on the Teaching of Foreign Languages and to solicit members. Subsequently it was intended to be "an occasional newsletter of significant current events." That statement was made in the 1967 April issue of FLA. However, by December 1968 it had become a quarterly journal, the stated purpose of which was to "serve as a chronicle of information of current significance to the teacher, administrator, or researcher, whatever the education level or the language with which he is concerned." In 1971 the number of issues increased to six per year, but its function as ACTFL's refereed journal remained. (p. 9)

Grittner pointed out that some ACTFL members had objected to the use of the journal for the inclusion of practical teaching tips, directories, calendars, news items, and conference schedules that displaced space for theoretical and research-oriented articles. So an effort was under way to deal with such questions and problems with a survey sent to the general membership and to 75 article reviewers. Changes were to be made based on feedback.

The second ACTFL Summer Seminar, on the theme of "research in second language acquisition," took place in Monterey, CA, in early August. *FLA*'s May 1992 issue announced the ACTFL '93 program theme: "Enhancing Our Professional Status."

THE ACTFL '93 PROGRAM THEME:
Enhancing Our Professional Status

International economics and recent political events have increased public awareness of the importance of foreign languages. Standing in the spotlight has been flattering to our egos, but the harsh lights of center stage have also exposed some of our blemishes. Professionally, we are doing more than ever before, but more is also being demanded of us. Not only education, but business, trade, local service agencies, international commerce, and the Congress are asking for someone to step forward and assume the mantle of leadership for the foreign language teaching profession. These national leaders have many questions. The profession has the answers, but these answers are not being consistently, clearly, and succinctly communicated at the national level. It behooves ACTFL to respond and fill this information gap. No one is better prepared or better situated. The time is right; the direction we must go is clear.

If we want increased recognition as a profession, then we must have credibility. If we want credibility, we must have publicly announced professional policies and standards. The current furor over teacher certification will touch all disciplines. The call for revision of our schools' curricula, the push for national goals to implement *America 2000,* the publications of the Council on Basic Education, and the possibility of including foreign languages in the National Assessment Educational Progress will affect every foreign language teacher in America. We must actively participate in these forums, discussions, and decision processes. If we don't, we will have to live with what others from outside the profession decide is best for us.

Join with us as we work with state and regional delegates to define issues and respond to policy questions. Make ACTFL your national representative on professional issues.

Here we clearly see the impact of the National Education Goals Panel Hearings and testimonies Scebold had reported on in mid-1991. ACTFL was now the national representative on professional issues. Momentum was gathering, which would move foreign language education to a new level.

This same May issue of *FLA* included a job announcement for a Director of Professional Development at ACTFL headquarters. The new director would:

- manage the organization's professional development program, including the Oral Proficiency Workshops Program and instructional workshops;
- manage the OPI Interview Certification Program;

- explore new topics for funded projects and design new workshop formats, including training consultants; and
- coordinate Oral Proficiency Workshops.

Clearly the impact and importance of proficiency on the profession were becoming too great for headquarters staff to handle as "just another project."

The year 1992 was a year of great foreshadowing. The public's eye seemed to be on international events more broadly, directly, and consistently than at any time in recent memory, which implicitly underscored the importance of foreign language and international studies. Business and industry demands for ACTFL's language testing service increased. A new era of communication and cooperation among many foreign language organizations was dawning. At the national level, ACTFL and several language-specific organizations had begun discussions to put forth minimum standards for foreign language teacher education. State and regional multi-language associations and ACTFL had begun to develop a model in which issues of importance to all could be discussed, prioritized, and passed on for further consideration, leading to a proactive professional policy. Finally, task forces were being formed to work directly with ACTFL Executive Council to undertake the discussion and study needed for ACTFL to deal with the issues before it: articulation, elementary school foreign language study, inter-organizational communication, membership, public awareness and the media, proficiency guideline revision, student achievement goals, teacher education standards, and a written proficiency test (*FLA*, Vol. 25, No. 4 (September 1992), p. 335).

The great interest in the Oral Proficiency Interview (OPI) that was increasing in business and industry was causing ACTFL to investigate a separate entity that would deal with this interest: a for-profit venture. President-elect Clifford highlighted the OPI's development to show just why the organization was the logical originating and controlling source for this new business:

- Professional standards (level definitions) were first established in 1956 by FSI (initial step: one sentence statements);
- By 1960, Civil Service Requirements provided a paragraph on each level, which were used by various government agencies;
- In 1980, an effort was launched to create a Common Yardstick (later called the Common Metric) by Educational Testing Service. The project was funded by the U.S. Department of Education, and the project directors were Protase Woodford and John L. D. Clark; the Common Metric Conference was held later that year in Boston, MA, in conjunction with the ACTFL convention;
- In 1981, the Interagency Language Roundtable brought together representatives of all government agencies; they collectively identified fifteen proficiency-related issues which needed to be addressed;
- In 1982, ACTFL published the *Provisional Oral Proficiency Guidelines* (the academic version of work earlier completed by government agencies), which provided significant improvements and enhancements of the original work;
- Ten years later, we are beginning to see the benefits:
  a. The immediate credibility now established by statements of outcomes of instruction was not present before;
  b. People are aware of the existence of standards for performance in foreign language education; The guidelines and the OPI give the profession visibility and credibility;

c. We have a metric which can be used to quantify standards (expected outcomes) of instruction at the various levels of education in the U.S.;

• In 1992, legislation has been introduced recognizing ACTFL as the national voice on issues related to foreign language testing.

ACTFL financial consultant Robert Katz reported to the Executive Council at its May meeting in Colorado Springs that ACTFL had changed audit firms and the new firm had deemed ACTFL's accounting procedures to be sound. Katz added that ACTFL's financial situation was under control despite its negative fund balance.

At the November 1992 meeting of the Executive Council in Rosemont, IL, Katz announced the launching of Language Testing International (LTI). On the LTI website, we find this information:

Language Testing International is the exclusive licensee of the American Council on the Teaching of Foreign languages (ACTFL). ACTFL is a leader in the development of proficiency testing instruments and the training of language professionals in proficiency-based teaching and testing. ACTFL licensed LTI to act as the official ACTFL Testing Office in 1992. Since then, LTI has organized and administered proficiency assessments for hundreds of companies, universities, State Boards of Education and other state and federal government agencies. Clients have included the DLI and the Department of Homeland Security. LTI conducts hundreds of thousands of language proficiency assessments every year and delivers testing in over 40 countries. (Retrieved from http://www.languagetesting.com/ about-lti)

At this point in ACTFL history, it was no longer possible to ignore the elephant in the room—technology. In prior years, a sprinkling of articles in *FLA* had discussed the use of technology in foreign language education. President Ervin, in his fifth Message from the President, addressed technology as follows:

[...] the advance of technology in our field continues unabated. Coupled with good courseware, computers and interactive videodiscs, for example, can provide far more sensory input (both in terms of quantity and variety) for our students than we teachers can. Moreover, hardware enhancements and new developments are taking place all the time. Still, while technology can present material vividly and coherently and can tirelessly offer students in groups or as individuals practice in various skills and modes (grammar, vocabulary, and listening comprehension just for starters), the role of the human teacher in providing students with communicative development in the productive skills remains secure. But the handwriting is on the wall: Our responsibility is to understand the processes of foreign language teaching and learning, master and implement the aspects of technology that can aid in those processes, and use the element of teacher-student contact for the things that technology cannot do (FLA, 25, No. 5 (October 1992), p. 433).

Under 1993 ACTFL President Ray T. Clifford (Defense Language Institute, Monterey, CA), changes continued in the organization. For example, *FLA* changed its design, format, and publication frequency. It now appeared four times a year rather than six. A new special section was added to each issue, focusing on instructional application in the classroom and innovative approaches to curricular content. A "Point/Counterpoint" section also appeared periodically.

Sadly, it was announced that Lorraine Strasheim, Executive Council member (1974-1976) and ACTFL President in 1978, died in early 1993. In an obituary submitted to the *Modern Language Journal*, Martha Nyikos wrote:

Ray T. Clifford
ACTFL President 1993

In 1993, *FLA* changed its design,
format, and publication frequency

Many of Lorraine's innovative ideas have become part of the accepted professional body of knowledge which will continue to guide classroom teachers and foreign language educators. [...] she never forgot the classroom teacher. She will always be respected for her honesty and deep concern for the practitioners whose job it is to implement ideas emerging from theory. Her input was always valuable, her sense of humor keen, and her warm-hearted helpfulness appreciated by those who worked with her. (Retrieved from http://www.iflta.org/grants/strasheimhistory.pdf)

The ripples that began with the National Education Goals Panel Hearings had been transformed into a major effort: the development of foreign language standards. The first announcement of this initiative appeared in *FLA*, Vol. 26, No. 1 (Spring 1993), p. 9:

The U.S. Department of Education (ED) and the National Endowment for the Humanities (NEH) announced on January 8 that the American Council on the Teaching of Foreign Languages (ACTFL) is the recipient of a $211,494 grant to 'develop and disseminate voluntary national standards for foreign language education, kindergarten through 12th grade.' ACTFL will be joined by the American Association of Teachers of French (AATF), the American Association of Teachers of German (AATG) and the American Association of Teachers of Spanish and Portuguese (AATSP) to form a consortium that will guide the project.

The final standards were to be funded as part of the Bush administration's America 2000 strategy to achieve the six National Education Goals. "Foreign language standards are crucial if our children are going to live, work, and compete in the entire world," said Secretary of Education Lamar Alexander. June K. Phillips directed the standards initiative. Christine Brown headed the task force charged with developing the standards, whose members were announced in the Summer 1993 issue of *FLA* (Vol. 26, No. 2), p. 365:

June K. Phillips, Project Director
USAF Academy, CO

Christine Brown, Chair
Glastonbury Public Schools (CT)

Martha Abbott
Fairfax County Public Schools (VA)

Keith Cothrun
Las Cruces Public Schools (NM)

Beverly Harris-Schenz
University of Pittsburgh (PA)

Denise Mesa
Dade County Public Schools (FL)

Genelle Morain
University of Georgia (Athens)

Marjorie Tussing
University of California (Berkeley)

Ronald Watson
National Foreign Language Center,
Washington, DC

John Webb
Hunter High School, New York, NY

Thomas Welch
Kentucky Department of Education,
Frankfort

President Clifford, along with John L.D. Clark and Pardee Lowe, were developing a writing test for proficiency ratings in that skill. The original test was developed for Spanish and English as a Second Language and focused on the Superior and near-Superior levels due to the needs of the business community. The test became available in the fall of 1993.

Language Testing International was growing gradually at its headquarters in Rye, NY. Members of the ACTFL Steering Committee, Robert Terry and Gerard Ervin, along with Robert Katz, visited LTI headquarters and discussed a variety of issues facing LTI in terms of OPI testing, including the need for additional products—a written test, a marketing test (knowledge of cultural issues), and a translation test—and the need to provide more than test results, e.g., a means for improving competence after a person is tested. At the end of 1993, financial consultant Katz discussed the revenues generated for ACTFL through royalties from the OPIs administered: the amount generated was less than anticipated.

John E. Miles
Director of Professional
Development

At the Executive Council meeting at the November 1993 Annual Meeting in San Antonio, Executive Director Scebold reported that ACTFL had changed from a structure of Executive Director and Assistant Director to a department-oriented structure that decentralized authority to department heads who reported directly to the Executive Director (*FLA,* Vol. 27, No. 2 (Summer 1994), p. 129). The departments were Accounting, Professional Development, Conventions and Meetings, Production, and Membership and Special Projects. The position of Director of Professional Development Programs, one of the departments, had been recently given to John E. Miles.

ACTFL had recently begun a membership rebate campaign in which $25 was paid to each participating organization for each new regular ACTFL membership, with smaller rebates for other categories of membership. At the end of 1993, new memberships totaled more than 300 as a result of this campaign. Jamie Draper, Special Projects Manager and Membership Liaison, reported that the biggest challenge facing the organization was retaining members.

In the ongoing effort to boost membership, President Clifford's Message from the President in the summer 1993 issue of *FLA* included this piece of news:

Because of ACTFL's central role in much of what is happening nationally in support of second language education, there is a great potential for organizational growth. Therefore, a new membership committee was created to find ways of increasing teachers' awareness of ACTFL's services to the profession. The committee will include volunteers from the Executive Council and other ACTFL members from around the nation. (p. 265)

In late 1993, Clifford announced, "Our efforts to gain recognition for foreign languages as critical to our nation's future has paid off. Foreign languages have been formally included as a core subject in the version of the administration's reform bill, *Goals 2000*" (*FLA*, Vol. 26, No. 4 (Winter 1993), p. 399). The exact wording that passed in that act read:

3. American students will leave grades 4, 8, and 12 having demonstrated proficiency in challenging subject matter including English, mathematics, science, foreign languages, arts, history, and geography…

This was indeed a major accomplishment. Goal 3 provided the preparation that would allow accomplishment of Goal 5: "Every adult American will be literate and will possess the knowledge and skills necessary to compete in a global economy and exercise the rights and responsibilities of citizenship."

However, Clifford warned that this formal recognition was still more symbol than substance:

If this rewording survived the House-Senate conference committee, the greatest advantage of this formal recognition of foreign languages at the national policy level was not what it would do for foreign languages, but what it would allow us to do—we would have a strong foundation from which we could more effectively continue our efforts to expand our nation's linguistic awareness and second language skills…. We are still living in a nation where the value of foreign language competency is more underrated than understood (p. 399).

Year I of the foreign language standards project was proceeding well, but it had been under-budgeted, so the U.S. Department of Education supplemented the grant. Year II was then budgeted with this in mind—with money allocated to underwrite presentations at local conferences to enhance public awareness and encourage public input.

Project Director June K. Phillips reported that ACTFL had been invited to submit a proposal to the Fund for the Improvement of Postsecondary Education (FIPSE) for the preparation of entry-level teacher standards and accomplished teacher standards.

In 1994, work on the national standards was fully under way. In his first Message from the President, 1994 ACTFL President Robert M. Terry (University of Richmond), reported that in early February ACTFL had been formally notified that Year II of the National Standards in Foreign Language Education, K-12 Project, had received full funding for the amount requested. Several representatives of ACTFL participated in an invitational Forum on Standards and Learning, held in New York and sponsored by the College Board. The field of foreign languages was "the new kid on the block" regarding the then-current stage of development of our national standards, yet there was a remarkable degree of mutual support, common interests, and concerns among the six national organizations invited to participate in this forum: ACTFL, the Music Educators National Conference, the National Council for the Social Studies, the National Council of Teachers of English, the National Council of Teachers of Mathematics, and the National Science Teachers Association. All were collaborating by agreeing to play a key role with the federal government in assuring the validity and quality of our standards in the nation's education system.

Robert M. Terry
ACTFL President 1994

Strategic planning became a primary focus in 1994. ACTFL's mission, its current status, its needs, and its future direction were discussed. At the May 21-23, 1994, Executive Council meeting in New York City, five issues that were (and still are) central to any ACTFL strategic planning were raised:

- achieving financial stability and building a reserve for the future;
- increasing membership;
- planning and pursuing growth and development within the various departments at ACTFL headquarters;
- continuing to improve relationships with ACTFL's organizational members;
- enhancing ACTFL's role as the national professional policy organization.

Despite the recent success of ACTFL and foreign language study, Terry cautioned that, lest we be complacent, we had to recognize significant impediments to institutionalizing our new-found status: (1) limited human resources, (2) apparent lack of professional unity and commitment, (3) underutilization of resources available, (4) the profession's aging leadership, (5) lack of integration of less commonly taught languages into the mainstream of foreign language education, and, perhaps most important of all, (6) lack of a clear vision for the future of our profession.

These impediments must be confronted and addressed with professional unity before foreign language education can truly assume its place of national acceptance and importance. ACTFL has been and continues to be a major, although often unacknowledged, aggressive player in this climb to the current level of national recognition and acceptance. (FLA, Vol. 27, No. 2 (Summer 1994), p. 265)

In late July 1994, an invitational Standards and Articulation Conference took place in Baltimore. National Standards Task Force members presented the draft copy of those standards to about 50 attendees, who, along with members of the Standards Advisory Board, reacted to them very positively. Changes and amplifications were made in the draft document, which was then sent to Standards Board of Reviewers members and others for reactions and comments.

LTI's business was expanding. The number of academic OPIs had increased, and a contract had been signed with the NYNEX Corporation. ACTFL and LTI were developing Spanish and Chinese writing tests.

In late summer 1994, President Terry worked at ACTFL headquarters for several weeks and gained great insight to both the daily workings at headquarters and new projects the organization was engaged in:

1. ACTFL was ready to seek funding for year III of the joint National Standards project, a year that would see field testing and validating the standards; making recommendations on appropriate strategies and assessment instruments to assess the standards; designing a professional development program to provide assistance on teaching and assessment strategies; and publishing the standards and teaching strategies.
2. ACTFL was preparing a proposal to "revisit" the 1986 Proficiency Guidelines, to make necessary changes in them that reflected the results of current research in second language acquisition and to address the possible need for a parallel set of standards for young learners and a new professional development program for training OPI testers and trainers.
3. A Mexican company had expressed interest in working closely with ACTFL to disseminate OPI materials and training.

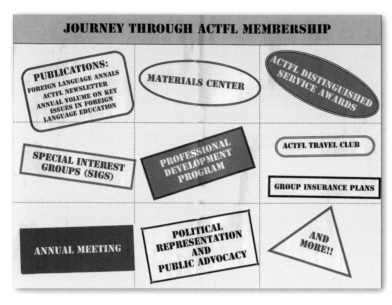

JOURNEY THROUGH ACTFL MEMBERSHIP

PUBLICATIONS: FOREIGN LANGUAGE ANNALS ACTFL NEWSLETTER ANNUAL VOLUME ON KEY ISSUES IN FOREIGN LANGUAGE EDUCATION

MATERIALS CENTER

ACTFL DISTINGUISHED SERVICE AWARDS

SPECIAL INTEREST GROUPS (SIGS)

PROFESSIONAL DEVELOPMENT PROGRAM

ACTFL TRAVEL CLUB

GROUP INSURANCE PLANS

ANNUAL MEETING

POLITICAL REPRESENTATION AND PUBLIC ADVOCACY

AND MORE!!

A new Member-Get-a-Member Campaign, the Passport to Your Professional Future, ran from 1994–1995.

4. A draft copy of the Proficiency Guidelines in French had been prepared at McGill University, Montreal.
5. A new *Handbook on Nominating Procedures— Officers and Awards* was prepared.
6. A draft copy of an *ACTFL Oral Proficiency Interview Familiarization Workshop Manual* was written.
7. A grant proposal for a new survey of foreign language enrollments in public secondary schools was in progress.
8. The ACTFL constitution and by-laws were updated.
9. An *Executive Council Handbook* was written.

By the end of 1994, ACTFL membership had reached over 6,000, which had not been seen in over 10 years. A new Member-Get-a-Member campaign had begun: the Passport to Your Professional Future was to last through May 1, 1995. Individuals who recruited more than one member would have their names placed in a series of raffles for prizes ranging from a year's free membership in ACTFL to discounts on the 1995 annual meeting in Anaheim to two airline tickets to anywhere in the continental United States.

In the summer, Terry had challenged the Executive Council to address head-on the five professional issues ACTFL faced, and the Executive Council aggressively took up the challenge. Executive Council members wanted the organization, for example, to reexamine its current committee structure, to consider making changes, and to assume a strong, proactive stance on concerns of teachers in the field: languages across the curriculum, alternative scheduling, school-to-work, block scheduling, site-based management.

The 1995 ACTFL President, Kathleen M. Riordan (Springfield (MA) Public Schools) shepherded the organization through the release of the *Standards for Foreign Language Learning: Preparing for the 21st Century*. She talked about "our" foreign language education reform, but cautioned that we must work within the context of "the" broader education reform effort now under way, especially with President Bush's Goals 2000. She said "our" reform could not succeed if we were not part of "the" reform. As we moved to bring foreign languages to all children and into the mainstream of American education, we had to work toward shared decision-making, community involvement, and inclusive educational environments. We, the foreign language profession, had to join locally, at the state level, regionally, and most importantly at the national level to meet the new opportunities before us (*FLA*, Vol. 28, No. 1 (Spring 1995), pp. 11-12).

The national standards were being field-tested in six pilot sites around the US: Edmonds School District, Lynwood, WA; Gwinnett County, Lawrenceville, GA; Houston, TX Public Schools; Springfield, MA Public Schools; Clovis Unified School District, Fresno, CA; and Williamston, MI Community Schools. Riordan announced that a new draft of the standards had been released in April 1995 and that their final version would be presented officially to the U.S. Department of Education at the 1995 annual meeting in Anaheim, CA, in November. The theme of the ACTFL '95 Annual Meeting was "Standards and Assessment: Implementing the Vision."

The success of proficiency and the appearance of national standards for foreign languages were the source of much activity. Refresher workshops for certified OPI testers were offered through the regional conferences. ACTFL and LTI had jointly created a writing proficiency test for commercial settings. At that time, the test was available in Spanish and Chinese (Cantonese and Mandarin). ACTFL had been working with the Texas Education Agency in creating tape-mediated tests of speaking and listening comprehension to be administered to all graduating seniors in Texas. State foreign language frameworks were under development throughout the U.S., most based on national standards.

The National Standards Task Force met in June 1995 in Salt Lake City with representatives from the six pilot sites, state departments of education, state associations, and national language-specific associations to: (1) share the work to date, (2) plan the dissemination and implementation of the standards, and (3) devise short- and long-term strategies to capture the power and expertise within the foreign language profession. This dissemination plan had a broad scope: within our profession, within the broader education field, and in the general public.

Riordan mentioned the growth of language enrollments at all levels, some increasing markedly. Yet, with this growing need for more knowledge of languages and cultures came drastic reductions in funding for education in general and for second language education in particular. As she exclaimed, "Such a lack of logic!" (*FLA,* Vol. 28, No. 3 (Fall 1985), p. 307). Reminiscing on her year as President of ACTFL, Riordan called it a "wonderful year for professional collaborations and coalitions" (*FLA,* Vol. 28, No. 4 (Winter 1995), p. 475).

ACTFL had collaborated—often as a leader—with various educational, language-specific and regional associations, which was reflected in the National Standards Project's success. In addition to the original coalition members, many language-specific organizations had provided input and feedback in the creation of this achievement. Another sign of professional unity and cooperation was the meeting of the joint Central States, Southwest, and Pacific Northwest regional organizations in Denver on March 30–April 1, 1995.

At the May 20-21, 1995, Executive Council meeting in New York City, it was recommended that "ACTFL create a Home Page in the World Wide Web (WWW) to provide information" (*FLA,* Vol. 29, No. 1 (Spring 1996), p. 15). Past President Terry created the original home page for ACTFL and presented it at the November 16, 1995, Executive Council meeting in Anaheim, CA. Past President Ervin's comments about the role of technology in foreign language instruction were proving accurate: not only were the number of articles on this subject increasing in professional journals, but also the general use of technology in general was expanding, and the Internet was becoming more and more pervasive. Looking forward, she pointed out that the professional unity

Kathleen M. Riordan
ACTFL President 1995

In 1995, ACTFL worked on the *Standards for Foreign Language Learning: Preparing for the 21st Century.*

June C. Hicks, Member Liaison (L) and Jamie Draper, Special Projects Manager & Member Liaison (R)

New ACTFL membership cards in 1996

of the Standards project would bear fruit at the 1997 ACTFL annual meeting in Nashville.

The ACTFL Accounting Manager announced that the negative fund balance from the 1994 audit had been eliminated in 1995. This was very good news for ACTFL, which had been suffering for so long with negative balances at the end of each year. While the rebate membership program was working very well, the new Member-Get-a-Member campaign had proved rather unsuccessful: only 35 new members had joined.

The 1995 annual meeting in Anaheim, however, had been very successful, with more than 3,800 attendees. The new national standards were formally introduced and an Executive Summary was available there. The complete standards document was available to the public in mid-January 1996 for $20. It was announced at ACTFL '95 that Ann Tollefson, Natrona County School District #1, Casper, WY, had been elected ACTFL President for 1997.

As promised, the national standards became available for purchase in early 1996. The Standards Project's Board of Directors created an independent fund to provide money to support future work on the standards. Approximately $10 from the sale of each document was deposited in this special fund for initiatives that aimed at continuing their work: (1) for developing language-specific standards documents, (2) for professional development and dissemination activities, and (3) for informing those outside the foreign language education profession about this work. Some of the funds were also used for creating entry-level teacher standards and for writing a new draft of the 1987 Teacher Education Standards, which were available on the ACTFL web page.

ACTFL's membership was at its highest point in nearly 10 years, with 6,600 individual members and an additional 100 subscribers to *FLA*. The Executive Director told the Executive Council that ACTFL needed additional office space that would allow it to save money on meeting expenses by eliminating meeting space charges, reducing food and beverage costs, and reducing other meeting-related expenses. This space would also accommodate an expanding staff and new office equipment associated with expansion, and would also allow the option of moving LTI to Yonkers to facilitate a closer working relationship. The space at ACTFL headquarters in Yonkers was doubled by the end of 1996. LTI itself had a stable business, with about 3,000 OPIs administered per year, and it remained apart from headquarters.

The new membership cards were of benefit to both ACTFL members and staff—a cost-effective way to improve staff productivity and enhance service to members. The cards had information on both sides: membership information on the front, including a member number; the reverse contained the information necessary to contact ACTFL. The organization had recently begun holding ACTFL regional membership meetings that had proved to be very helpful. Similar meetings were planned to continue in 1997 and hopefully in the future.

Work continued toward the addition of foreign languages to the subject matter areas that were regularly tested through the National Assessment of Educational Progress (NAEP), a step that would greatly enhance the status of foreign languages as a core subject. In addition, ACTFL, AATF, AATG, and AATSP had planned follow-up activities to the work on the standards and had launched a series of workshops to provide assistance and support to those seeking to implement the standards. A special team met at ACTFL headquarters in the summer of 1996 to begin developing a series of new workshops on implementing the standards. The first was "Breaking New Ground, Exploring the Potential of Standards."

Since the 1996 Annual Meeting in Philadelphia would be the 30th anniversary meeting, ACTFL's 151 original charter members were recognized in the Fall 1996 *FLA* (p. 302). At the top of the list of those members was the statement:

Elvira Swender
Professional Programs Director

Over the past three decades, the following men and women have maintained their ACTFL membership year by year, without any lapses. On the occasion of ACTFL's 30th anniversary, we mark this occasion with a salute to these 151 charter members. Not only did they found this organization, but they have also continued to guide and support it. On behalf of all our members, we extend to each of you our deep appreciation for your leadership and your commitment and dedication to our profession. Your contribution has had a profound impact on a generation of teachers and students. [See Appendix C]

The Professional Development Department of ACTFL began a "limited" OPI project that would provide workshops and "limited" certification for those who had not previously sought OPI certification because of time and/or money constraints. Headquarters had also received a grant to revisit the 1986 ACTFL Proficiency Guidelines and to create guidelines for younger learners. In the summer of 1996, Elvira Swender became the ACTFL's Director of Assessment Initiatives, and in 1997 she assumed the position of Director of Professional Development that John Miles had held. The ACTFL Professional Development Workshop offerings and brochure were redesigned to include workshops on new topics such as block scheduling, alternative assessment, and teaching *all* students.

At its May 1996 meeting, the Executive Council accepted the Professional Issues Committee's recommendation to change the organization's name to the American Council on the Teaching of Languages, though the acronym ACTFL would stand. This proposed name change would take place over the next three to five years in the interest of economy. (This was not the first or last time such a discussion has taken place.)

However, the name change was defeated in an ACTFL membership vote during the 1996 elections.

Valorie S. Babb
ACTFL President 1996

Ann Tollefson
ACTFL President 1997

President Valorie S. Babb (Minot [ND] Public Schools) announced in her Message from the President in the Fall 1996 issue of *FLA* (Vol. 29, No. 3) that the 1997 Annual Meeting would take place at the Opryland Hotel in Nashville. ACTFL would be joined by AATF, AATG, AATI, CLTA, NCSTJ, and the Tennessee Foreign Language Teachers Association (TFLTA), making it the largest annual meeting to date (p. 301). This issue of *FLA*, devoted to "Strategies and Techniques in Foreign Language Teaching," was a special expanded issue encompassing a large backlog of articles that had been accepted for publication.

In her final Message from the President, Babb wrote about being an "occasional member" who joined ACTFL when she planned to attend the Annual Meeting but then let her membership lapse or did not remember to send in her last membership renewal. She also said that, as a foreign language teaching professional, she could not afford *not* to be a member of the member of the organization that represented her at the national level. Referring to the ACTFL membership brochure, she said membership means access to the latest developments in foreign language methodology and pedagogical research, to nationally recognized leaders in the field, to colleagues across the nation and around the world, to the professional development opportunities needed to enhance one's career; and to a competent, professional staff who always have our needs in mind (*FLA*, Vol. 29, No. 4 [Winter 1996], p. 537).

In 1997, ACTFL's 31st year, President Ann Tollefson of Wyoming was at the helm. After a major anniversary, it was time to reexamine the vision for the foreign language teaching professional's future and to revisit the organization's mission and priorities, in order to determine the framework for the intelligent, proactive planning necessary to maintain strong, well-directed leadership in the profession. Based on membership input, a new draft of ACTFL's strategic plan was issued.

In her first Message from the President (*FLA*, Vol. 30, No. 1 [Spring 1997], p. 13), Tollefson asked members to consider two extracts from that draft: a Vision statement and a Mission statement. From this context would come the strategic plan that would guide ACTFL in the coming years. Members were urged to remember that such planning was a process, not a final product, and were encouraged to participate in developing the strategic plan. (See the ACTFL Membership Survey, Appendix D.) The final document was presented to the Executive Council in New York in May 1997.

The National Teacher Professional Standards Board (NTPSB) had asked ACTFL to nominate foreign language educators to develop teacher standards for them. ACTFL and other language-specific organizations submitted approximately 50 nominations, all on the National Standards Collaborative Project letterhead—yet another sign of increasing professional unity.

ACTFL's infrastructure was reorganized to strengthen the organization's effectiveness for the future, and to serve its members better. For example,

- The Delegate Assembly was reorganized and given much more responsibility and power within ACTFL.
- The Professional Development Program was totally revamped to provide what was needed at greater convenience and reduced cost.

- The Executive Council's Publications Committee was renamed the Membership Services Committee, and its duties were expanded to determine what services were needed and wanted and to develop and provide them. (*FLA*, Vol. 37, No. 2 [Summer 1997], p. 171)

At its May meeting, the Executive Council again addressed increasing its funding to JNCL-NCLIS after that organization had presented draft copies of its new strategic plan. Also, Scebold said that significant progress made by the foreign language profession in the U.S. Foreign languages had been reported in the National Assessment of Educational Progress (NAEP): the federal government was now willing to include traditionally marginalized foreign languages, civics, the arts, and other disciplines in the core curriculum. Congressional recognition of foreign languages was positively affecting national assessment. Finally, foreign languages had been added to the list of disciplines that would soon receive a national credential for recognizing excellence in teaching. Scebold also reported that the national standards for foreign languages were

flourishing—more than $200,000 in sales had been received since they were first released—and language-specific standards were being developed in Chinese, French, German, Italian, Japanese, Latin, Russian, and Spanish.

LTI was doing extremely well ever since it had been spun off from ACTFL into a private corporation: it had been conducting many OPIs for both commercial and academic clients, and this market was growing consistently. LTI's testing office was now in White Plains, NY, with Robert Katz, President, and Helen Hamlyn, Vice-President.

Professional Programs Office Head Elvira Swender reported that the Professional Development Program of the 21st century would be entirely standards-based and assessment-driven, which would guide instruction to assure that teachers were teaching what students needed to know to function in the real world. The program was fully accredited, offering graduate and CEU credit to all of its teacher trainees. In 1997, such credits were offered through Manhattanville College in Purchase, NY.

The announcement for the 1998 ACTFL Programs for Language Professionals (*FLA*, Vol. 30, No. 3 (Fall 1997), p. 445) included:

Elizabeth Hoffman
ACTFL President 1998

The ACTFL *Performance Guidelines for K-12 Learners* was published in the fall of 1998, along with the new, multi-language *Standards for Foreign Language Learning in the 21st Century.*

We now understand foreign language learning to be a process whereby linguistic and cross-cultural competence are best developed over time, through critical reflection, and with optimum linkage to appropriate subject matter knowledge as this relates to the total curriculum. Implicit in our understanding is an expanded and multidimensional definition of the role of the teaching professional.

The ACTFL '97 Annual Meeting in Nashville, themed on "National Challenges—Professional Priorities," had 295 exhibit booths, 642 sessions, 28 workshops, 70 booths at the Technology Fair, and more than 5,500 attendees, many of whom spent "An Hour with Maya Angelou," the keynote speaker. The theme of the year for Elizabeth Hoffman, 1998 ACTFL President from the Nebraska Department of Education, was "Winds of Change," reflecting not only the 1998 annual meeting's Chicago location, but also new initiatives of ACTFL and other foreign language professional organizations from the national level to individual classrooms across the country.

Hoffman announced that ACTFL membership was steadily increasing and at its highest level since the mid-1980s, having grown by more than 1,000 in 1998. She attributed this to advocacy, professional development initiatives, and the new ACTFL website—a growing number of international inquiries, the first online registrations for ACTFL '98, and the convention program, which would be made available later in 1998 (*FLA,* Vol. 31, No. 2, 1998, p. 155).

Hoffman also announced that on May 14, 1998, ACTFL and TESOL had been notified that both organizations had been ratified as constituent members of the National Council for Accreditation of Teacher Education (NCATE), a partnership of national organizations that sets professional standards for teacher-preparing colleges and universities. ACTFL's membership was supported by collaboration with 10 language-specific associations, including AATF, AATG, AATSP, AATI, ACTR, ATJ/NCSTJ, and CLASS/CLTA. ACTFL joined 30 other national organizations that represent teachers, teacher educators, state and local policy makers, and school specialists. In addition, the Foreign Language Committee of the National Board for Professional Teaching Stand (NBPTS) had met and begun work on its goal of creating the foreign language credential.

The new language-specific standards, created by the 10 language-specific associations, were to be released in Chicago at ACTFL '98. Also the ACTFL *Performance Guidelines for K-12 Learners* were published in the fall of 1998. These *Performance Guidelines,* which described "how well" language learners were expected to do the "what" from the standards—the *Standards for Foreign Language Learning* that were first released in 1996. In late spring of 1998, the new, multi-language *Standards for Foreign Language Learning in the 21st Century* was released.

A new campaign for ACTFL's endowment fund was designed: 2000 x 2000, in which pledges would be obtained from individuals and foundations. Money from the current endowment fund was to be put aside so that those who contributed to the Fund for the Future would understand that ACTFL was serious about building its reserve.

The 1997 joint Annual Meeting in Nashville was a success, but Executive Director Scebold stated that there was little chance that ACTFL would be joined by AATF or AATSP again anytime in the near future, because the joint convention was too large and they were lost in the process of meeting with other organizations.

ACTFL had indeed made progress as a presence in the larger professional arena—membership in NCATE, along with the ACTFL Professional Development initiatives. But the organization had to continue its efforts to seek broader collaboration and to find new funding sources to reach its full potential in this larger arena. Technology had to be embraced as a tool to support language programs, professional development, teachers and students if P-16 standards were to be implemented nationwide.

In her first Message from the President in 1999, Emily Spinelli (University of Michigan-Dearborn) focused on teacher preparation, a matter that was becoming increasingly important as a national issue. The voice of foreign language professionals had to be among those heard by the policy- and decision-makers. According to Spinelli, ACTFL's most important role over the next few years was in pre-service and inservice foreign language teacher development, and the discussion focus was on not only teacher-training programs, but all areas of foreign language education from pre-K through Ph.D. One area of concern included recruitment to address the teacher shortage, including foreign language teachers. ACTFL was exploring alternative certification and the retraining of existing language teachers.

Another area of concern was teacher development, in which ACTFL had already become involved by becoming a constituent member of NCATE, thereby helping to establish foreign language and culture standards as well as methodology standards for college and university programs that prepare foreign language teachers. ACTFL was also represented on the Foreign Language Committee of the NBPTS, whose goals are to recognize accomplished foreign language teachers and to work toward creation of a foreign language credential.

Spinelli's final concern was inservice and pre-service teacher preparation, particularly initiating change within the college and university undergraduate language and teacher education programs for better pre-service teacher preparation (*FLA*, Vol. 32, No. 1 (Spring 1999), pp. 9-10). This concern, at the close of the 1990s, echoes President Birckbichler's similar statement that opened the decade and Grittner's comments from the mid-1980s.

To fully capitalize on the potential of the general public's recognition of the value of proficiency in a second language and culture, as well as school boards and government agencies, ACTFL entered into an important initiative, "New Visions for Foreign Language Education" (later New Visions in Action) in June 1999, in conjunction with the National K-12 Foreign Language Resource Center at Iowa State University, under the leadership of Marcia Rosenbusch. New Visions was funded by five grants from the U.S. Department of Education and two from the National Network for Early Language Learning (NNELL). In a brochure prepared for this new initiative, we find the following statement:

Emily Spinelli
ACTFL President 1999

The goal of New Visions in Action is to study and redirect where necessary the actions of the profession so that we can more effectively realize our goal of foreign language proficiency for every American…. New Visions in Action is a project involving PreK-16+ foreign language educators from every state in a collaborative effort to improve the profession. Open to all, New Visions in Action is identifying and implementing the actions necessary to improve foreign language programs throughout the United States.

At New Visions' initial meeting, approximately 40 participants representing a broad range of foreign language associations explored the organizing question, "What could we do?" They discussed such critical issues as: (1) professional development; (2) research; (3) curriculum, instruction, assessment and articulation; (4) teacher recruitment and retention. These four items became the work of four task forces, who sent draft issue papers on them to a Board of Reviewers for discussion at the 1999 ACTFL conference in Dallas. A June 2000 priorities conference focused on these same topics. In November 2000 at the ACTFL conference, these issues were further discussed and refined. At that time, the profession would decide "What will we do, and who will do it?" When the New Visions initiative concluded, the profession would have a well-defined action plan for the future.. Key characteristics of this New Visions initiative included:

- New Visions was participatory. Many language organizations were represented and actively involved in every step of the process.
- The New Visions process was forward-looking. Participants were asked to think "outside the box" and seek new solutions.
- New Visions was action-oriented. Its aim was to go beyond yet another description of the status

quo or a new list of priorities. New Visions would actually establish a how-to plan for implementing our professional agenda. (*FLA*, Vol. 32, No. 2 [Summer 1999], p. 157)

In her Fall 1999 Message from the President, Spinelli announced that ACTFL had received funding for three major new programs. Since the new projects all involved the use of new technologies, her announcement appropriately appeared in the special Fall issue of *FLA* devoted to the use of technology to support foreign language education.

1. ACTFL received three-year funding (1999-2002) to develop, in collaboration with Weber State University (Ogden, UT), an on-line methods course that would reflect state-of-the-art research and practice in foreign language education. The course would be made available to post-secondary institutions that wished to offer the entire course on their own campuses, ,or to supplement their existing methods course by taking advantage of professional expertise on certain topics.
2. ACTFL received a subcontract grant with the National Foreign Language Center (NFLC) to assist in the continued development of the LANGNet system. LANGNet was funded by the Fund for the Improvement of Post-Secondary Education (FIPSE) for the creation of a website pertaining to the less commonly taught languages. This site listed and described peer-reviewed materials, as an important resource for LCT teaching and learning. The new FIPSE funding would enable NFLC to expand the project, including materials for German, Japanese, Spanish, and general pedagogical resources.
3. The National Assessment Governing Board (NAGB) awarded a 14-month contract to the Center for Applied Linguistics (CAL)

to prepare for 2003 a framework and specifications for the National Assessment of Educational Progress (NAEP) of America's foreign language ability. The American Institutes of Research (AIR) and ACTFL were subcontracted to CAL. The project, beginning with Spanish, was designed to seek national consensus on various issues that would lead to the development of the framework of goals, objectives, and content for the secondary school level NAEP, as well as the task and item specifications.

In her third Message from the President (*FLA*, Vol. 32, No. 3 (Fall 1999), pp. 277-278), Spinelli said that, despite ACTFL's success in receiving grants and implementing many worthwhile projects, funding would stop when a granting-period was completed, forcing many projects to curtail activities or shut down completely. ACTFL simply could not rely solely on grant funding or other soft monies. She announced ACTFL's capital campaign to create an endowment that would fund many projects into the future.

Another important initiative in 1999 concerned *FLA* and its role in the year 2000 and beyond. This journal was undergoing an expansion in size and scope. Volume 32, No. 4 (Winter 1999) was the final issue of *FLA* in its current format. Beginning in 2000, *FLA* was to be published six times per year in a larger size and in four-color design, but would continue to run high-quality, refereed articles on current research in second-language acquisition and foreign-language education.

A most fitting end to this decade can be found in *An ACTFL Retrospective*: comments made at the ACTFL '99 Annual Meeting in Dallas by André Paquette, an ACTFL founder in 1967 and its first Executive Secretary (Director):

An ACTFL Retrospective
By F. André Paquette

I would like to sketch for you briefly the highlights of the socio-political and professional contexts within which ACTFL was created in the 1960s.

"It was the best of times, it was the worst of times"
This phrase, written by Charles Dickens in 1859 about conditions in two cities in Europe, could just as appropriately have been written more than one hundred years later about conditions in many cities in the United States of America. In the U.S. :

It was a time when we were frightened by the space race, by Sputnik.

It was a time when we were challenged by the space race, to put a man on the moon.

There was a Cold War—with the Soviet Union and its satellites.

There was a Hot War—in Vietnam and Cambodia.

There were antiwar demonstrations from East to West and North to South.

There were civil rights demonstrations from Birmingham to Berkeley to Washington, D.C.

Campuses were surrounded, and in some cases occupied, by troops and tanks.

Students in higher education were shot and killed by National Guardsmen.

Political leaders were assassinated in Texas and California.

Political activists were murdered in Mississippi and Tennessee.

"Radicals" were building bombs and blowing up others and themselves.

They were kidnapping and shooting individuals with impunity.

The Beatles invaded the Colonies, and Bob Dylan epitomized the protest musicians.

The "baby boomers" were also listening to Leary and wending their way to Woodstock.

Feminists were bashing *Playboy*, while others published *Playgirl*.

Man of La Mancha, Funny Girl, Fiddler on the Roof, and *Hello Dolly* reflected the vibrancy of Broadway.

It was, in short, a period that took us from Camelot to Cam Ranh Bay.

Many of us still cherished the promises and hopes of Camelot, but our socio-political leaders could barely "keep hope alive."

Eventually, we would walk from Woodstock to Watergate.

In the profession…

McLuhan was the messenger

McLuhan was the messenger, and he told us that the medium was the message.

A debate raged in higher education between schools of education and liberal arts institutions, about the quality of teacher preparation—including foreign language teachers—and who was better equipped to provide it.

In the mid-1950s, the Ford Foundation began to show interest in supporting efforts in the foreign language field. In addition to supporting the Foreign Language Program of the Modern Language Association (MLA), one of its other early projects was the founding of the Center for Applied Linguistics. This reflected the growing belief that structural and contrastive linguistics could play a significant role in foreign language education. Among other charges, the Center was asked to take a leadership role in the teaching of English as a Second Language; this reflected social and educational concerns for non-English-speaking Americans and immigrants.

The leaders of the Foreign Language Program of the MLA had lobbied to include foreign language study along with the study of mathematics and science in The National Defense Act of 1958. They persuaded Congress that the development of foreign language competence

in the population was "in the National interest." The impact of that legislation affected all levels of foreign language education in every section of the country, through, for example, FL institutes, state FL coordinators, and proficiency tests for teachers and advanced students.

With respect to the last of these activities, it must be noted that beginning in the late 1950s, the FL teaching profession was the first subject matter group to promote the importance of competency testing and of "recognizing competency, however acquired." These two principles would have significant impact on the entire teaching profession in the decades to come.

Whether in response or not to the publication, in 1958, of *The Ugly American*, the U.S. Departments of State and Defense were expending enormous resources on teaching their personnel foreign languages…. In the 1960s, regional foreign language conferences were becoming key annual leadership events…. Language-specific and multi-language associations at the state level increased in numbers and in strength of membership and programs…. FL programs reached into elementary, middle, junior high, and high schools. In 1966, the National Federation of Modern Language Teachers Associations celebrated its "Golden Anniversary)" of publishing *The Modern Language Journal* (Vol. L, No. 6, October 1966).

The Federation had constituents that included five language-specific associations, three regional language groups, and one (NY) state federation of language associations.

That same year—1966—was marked by numerous, repeated, and sometimes acrimonious discussions among any leaders in the profession about the need for a national organization that would bring together teachers of all foreign and second languages at all levels of American education. It would achieve this by providing linkage for all the national, regional, and state foreign language groups to a national organization, which would in turn provide leadership for its members and its constituted organizations through research, publications, meetings, and other means. It would provide a "national voice" for the profession.

At that moment in the history of the profession, it proved impossible to restructure any existing entity into the one envisioned. Thus, under the auspices of the MLA, and with the encouragement and support of key leaders from throughout the country, ACTFL was created.

ACTFL was born of necessity, guided by key leaders

Who were some of the key leaders?...William Riley Parker, Indiana University and Executive Secretary, MLA, MLA FL Program, "Foreign Languages and the National Interest," "The Case for Latin"... George Winchester "Win" Stone, New York University and Executive Secretary, MLA, Executive Director, MLA, seminal essay, "Central Educational Purposes," *MLJ*, Golden Anniversary issue...Theodore "Tug" Anderson, University of Texas, FLES, Research in FL teaching... Emma Birkmaier, University of Minnesota, Graduate FL Program, Research in FL teaching...Donald D. Walsh, The Choate School, noted Hispanist and Neruda translator, Director, MLA FL Program...Mel Fox, Program Officer of the Ford Foundation...Kenneth H. Mildenberger, English Scholar, U.S. Office of Education, MLA...Robert F. Roeming, University of Wisconsin, Editor, *MLJ*... Stephen Freeman, Director, Language Schools, Middlebury College, Vermont, France, Germany, Italy, Spain, and Soviet Union...Howard L. Nostrand, University of Washington, Research in FL Teaching... And so many more, such as Elton Hocking, William Edgerton, William Moulton, Austin Fife, Norman Sacks, Nelson Brooks, William Locke, Gordon Silber, and Kai-yu Hsu.

Then and now: *"Lever les yeux"*

In the 1960s, the Internet did not exist, except for a handful of people; today, the opposite is true.

Yet in the U.S. the debate over internationalism versus isolationism continues.

In the "new world order," many national identities are giving way to ethnic identities—with the attendant issues of language and culture. Ironically, at the same time, English is becoming more universal as a second language. In the "new world order," the leadership role of the U.S. (including its armed forces) has been redefined, not reduced or eliminated. The violence that marked the 1960s has become the terrorism—domestic and international— that marks the beginning of the new millennium.

In our country, family has been redefined at the same time that the role of schools acting *in loco parentis* is virtually passé.

And schools are no longer just schools, they are total social institutions.

As the same time, we are facing educator shortages that will make all previous ones pale in comparison.

The birth of the global village makes competence in more than one language more compelling than ever.

Finally, the need for vision and leadership in the language-teaching field is as great as it was thirty years ago.

These and other factors in today's world make ACTFL more necessary than it was three decades ago.

But we must remember to lift our vision. I am reminded of an incident that occurred just a few months ago: I had visited the church of St. Martin, in St. Remy, France. A little while later, I inquired about an organ I had seen pictured on a postcard. I told the tourist bureau agent that I hadn't seen it when I had visited St. Martin's. She responded, "*Eh bien, Monsieur, il faut lever les yeux!*" "Well, sir, you have to raise your eyes!"

I am in awe of what ACTFL has become and has achieved in thirty years. Now, "*Il faut lever les yeux.*" We must lift our eyes and create a new vision for the future.

Foreign Language Annals, Vol. 33, No. 1 (pp. 133-134)

RETROSPECT AND PROSPECT

December 8, 1991

In the late 1950s, William Riley Parker, Executive Secretary of the Modern Language Association, saw his long-term interest in improving foreign language education in the United States begin to bear fruit. With its inclusion in the National Defense Education Act of 1968, foreign language teaching was changed in significant ways, Millions of dollars flowed into NDEA programs and out to the field, supporting the purchase of language laboratories, textbooks and materials. An extensive program of institutes and other programs trained a generation of teachers in new methodologies.

Reacting to this new-found national interest in second language matters—and burgeoning enrollments— the MLA power structure decided that a new professional entity was needed to deal specifically w1th these issues. And so, in 1966, a project was undertaken to create and launch what we today know as ACTFL—the American Council on the Teaching of Foreign Languages.

The mission of the American Council on the Teaching of Foreign Languages is to promote and foster the study of languages and cultures as an integral component of American education and society and to provide effective leadership for the improvement of teaching and learning at all levels of instruction in all languages.

As ACTFL enters its 25th year of service to the profession, it is important to review our accomplishments, look at where we are now and consider new initiatives that will lead us into the next 25 years and beyond.

LEADERSHIP ON PROFESSIONAL ISSUES
Past Accomplishments:
- Proficiency Projects
- Professional Development Program

Current Projects:
- The New England collaborative, College Board and ACTFL are seeking funding for a project to build a process for articulating foreign language programs around the ACTFL Proficiency Guidelines.
- AT&T Language Line has contracted with ACTFL to use the OPI for screening potential employees.

- The ACTFL OPI is being studied by the Immigration & Naturalization Service for possible use in screening current and future employees, as well as determining advancement and salary increments based on language competence.

Future Directions:
- The ACTFL Proficiency Guidelines must be updated and reworked in the commonly taught languages if they are to serve projects such as the College Board initiative.
- ACTFL must seek consensus among language association on a coherent set of guidelines for teacher education programs and recruitment of new teachers.
- Promotion of the OPI should be undertaken to expose other corporations to the potential of this instrument for purposes of screening prospective and current employees. In anticipation of this:
  a. Current certified tester rosters must be reviewed to measure the amount of future work which can be accommodated.
  b. Recruitment of trainees must be undertaken in 1anguages where the number of certified testers is below the minimum needs projected,
- We must add components to the Professional Development program which will provide training and expertise in association management and discussions of professional issues to provide focus to ACTFL's efforts at the national level.
- ACTFL must find ways to refocus its programs to deal aggressively with professional issues such as:
  a. promoting second languages and cultures study to the general public;
  b. guidelines for teachers education programs;
  c. teacher recruitment.

BUILDING AN ORGANIZATIONAL STRUCTURE FOR ALL LANGUAGE EDUCATORS MEMBERSHIP
Past Accomplishments:
Current Projects:
- The establishment of the ACTFL Special Interest Groups (SIGs) has been met with

great enthusiasm by many who felt their special needs were not being adequately addressed through current programs.
- A membership campaign is being developed.

Future Directions:
- The message and the image of ACTFL as "Your Professional Voice" (vs. the "Your Voice in Washington" image of JNCL-NCLIS) must be sharpened.
- We must monitor and guide the development of SIGs to ensure they integrate and focus our efforts, rather than diffuse them.
- We must focus membership promotion efforts on those language groups with whom we have the greatest rapport (AATI, CLTA) and the greatest potential for rapport (ATJ).
- Member services should be expanded to include such things as a job service to aid in the placement of existing teaching personnel.

Publications
Past Accomplishments:
Current Projects:
- ACTFL publications are doing an adequate (but not outstanding) job of informing professionals of our work.

Future Directions:
- We must update, refocus and redesign ACTFL's publications to improve interest and readability.

Annual Meeting
Past Accomplishments:
- The ACTFL Annual Meetings have become "the event of the year" for many foreign language teachers.
- The support of AATI and CLTA are stronger than ever in terms of joint convention sponsorship.

Current Projects:
Future Directions:
- We must broaden the constituency of the Annual Meeting by offering more of interest to more language groups, while focusing on commonalities and bringing the profession together.

Ties to Other Professional Organizations
Past Accomplishments:
Current Projects:

Future Directions:
- We must greatly enhance the relationship between ACTFL and the state and regional organizational members, including:
  a. arranging regular exhibits at these meetings which focus on the (organization)-ACTFL connection, with appropriate brochures and other materials;
  b. urging greater involvement of board members and ACTFL consultants in the programs of the various meetings.

Promoting the Study of Foreign Languages and Cultures

Past Accomplishments:
- Involvement in the President's Commission on Foreign Language and International Studies
- Establishment of JNCL-NCLIS

Current Projects:
- The National Education Goals and America 2000 initiatives provided incentive for us to strongly focus on the issue of foreign languages as part of a "core" curriculum.

a. We reactivated our networks and ensured foreign language representation at the various hearings of the National Education Goals Panel.

b. We wrote and talked to those issues in many forums, including the preparation of an overview paper on foreign languages for the U. S. Department of Education.

Future Directions:
- ACTFL should use JNCL-NCLIS as a forum and a sounding board for establishing our legislative agenda, focusing more on building consensus on key issues. Legislation should grow directly out of professional concern rather than address peripheral issues or issues that our Hill colleagues feel will be "good for us." Immediate topics for consideration include:
  a. links between second language education and vocational/technical/professional education; and
  b. incentives for students to continue second language study for extended sequences.

- ACTFL must take steps to demystify the political process for its members in order to attract more people to work on pubic policy. We must continue to educate our constituency on issues of "how" and "why" this focus is crucial to our efforts.
- A series of projects must be undertaken to provide "ammunition" for our efforts at expanding public awareness, including:
  a. an annual survey of foreign language enrollments to better track trends in foreign language education; and
  b. a survey of high-school seniors to obtain a clearer picture of precisely who studies foreign languages, and for how long.
- We must establish a program to reach into other constituencies, including presenting at the conventions of associations such as ASCD, School Boards, AASA and NASSP.
- We must remain vigilant, aggressively seeking inclusion in all initiatives such as America 2000, and jumping at every opportunity for input.

Appendix B

ACTFL CHARTER MEMBERS [ORIGINAL LIST]

James E. Alatis†	Mildred V. Boyer†	Joseph T. Connell	Roland E. Durette	Eva M. Fuld
Edward Allen†	Laurel A. Briscoe	Marilyn J. Conwell	F. Alan Duval	Philip A. Fulvi
Howard B. Altman†	John H. Brown	Margaret M. Corgan	Esther M. Eaton	Estella M. Gahala
Donald H. Anderson	Frederick R. Burkhardt	Jacqueline S. Cork	Walter G. Eggmann	Alan B. Galt
Keith O. Anderson	E. H. Butkus	Norman R. Cote	Marilyn C. Eisenhardt	Paul A. Garcia
Jermaine D. Arendt†	Anita L. Byler	Joanna B. Crane†	Jacqueline C. Elliott	Alan Garfinkel
Edwin P. Arnold	Frederic J. Cadora	Leonard R. Criminale	Maurice G.A. Elton	Francoise P. Gebhart
Sheila S. Ashley	June A. Calen	William C. Crossgrove	Margritt A. Engel	Hanna Geldrich-Leffman
Robert P. Austin	Benita B. Campbell	David Crowner	Edward T. Erazmus	William Gemmer
Herbert L. Baird	Juanita Carfora	Norman G. Damerau	Thomas H. Falk	Robert A. Gilman
Reid E. Baker†	Lolita Carfora	Bruna B. Danese	Victor Maurice Faubert	Anthony Gradisnik†
Robert L. Baker	Louise A. Carlson	Francis J. Dannerbeck	Eveline Felsten	Virginia L. Gramer
Alice R. Balk	Mary M. Carr	John M. Darcey	Edward G. Fichtner	Carolyn M. Gray
Marilyn J. Barrueta†	Jane J. Chamberlain	John Defrancis	Mario Fierros	Frank M. Grittner†
John W Barthel	Barbara M. Chandler	Carl Dellaccio†	Mary L. Finocchiaro†	Ida Grober
Irving H. Becker	Walter L. Chatfield	William E. Delorenzo	Ellouise M. Ford	Michio P. Hagiwara
Jacqueline D. Benevento	Marianne C. Ciotti	Gerard A. Desjardins	James F. Ford	Milton R. Hahn†
John P. Berwald	Joan E. Ciruti	Georges R. Desrosiers	Joanne Foster	Pollyanna P. Hale
Ann A. Beusch†	John L. D. Clark	Antonio Diaz	Robert R. Fournier	Clemens L. Hallman
Amalia Biester	Margaret B. Clark	Robert J. Di Pietro†	Nancy Frankfort	Bernard P. Hardy
Dorothy E. Bishop	Elizabeth W. Cloud	Guy G. Di Stefano	Ernest A. Frechette†	William N. Hatfield
George R. Bishop	Pedro I. Cohen	Mildred R. Donoghue	Herschel J. Frey	Maurice M. Heidinger
Herman F. Bostick	Mary C. Colin	R. Thomas Douglass	Bruce Fryer	Mary L. Hellen
Richard E. Boswell	Pensacola Christian College	Phyllis J. Dragonas	Joe K. Fugate	Margarete L. Hilts

Robert L. Hinshalwood
Wilma Hoffmann
Frederick W. Holda†
Dorothy B. Holland-Kaupp
Dolores R. Hudson
Geraldine M. Huhnke
George M. Hyland
Don R. Iodice
James L. Jacobs
Gilbert A. Jarvis
William N. Jeeves
Ruth L. Jeismann
Albert Wjekenta
Valentin Kamenew
Mary Helen Kashuba
Patricia Keenan
Leo L. Kelly
Thomas W. Kelly
Dora F. Kennedy†
Joseph R. Kennedy
Elizabeth A. Kiefer
Terence C. Kiernan
Sumako Kimizuka
Arthur S. Kimmel
Yvonne J. King
Max S. Kirch
Max Klamm
Wallace G. Klein
Constance K. Knop
Betty J. Koenig
Marlise C. Konort
Christopher Koy
Shirley F. Krogmeier
Astrid B. Kromayer
Edward L. Kruse Jr.
Robert LaBouve
Robert C. Lafayette
Wallace P. Lagerwey
Dale L. Lange
Edgar L. Langevin

Judith A. Laurie
George J. Lauscher
Bernard P. Lebeau
Victor F. Leeber
Ellen L. Leeder
Kenneth A. Lester†
Kurt L. Levy
Stephen L. Levy
Lavinia L. Lile
Gladys C. Lipton
Rebecca M. Liskey
Helene Zimmer-Loew
Gerald E. Logan
Paul F. Luckau
Robert A. MacDonald†
Bruce H. Mainous
Barbara A. Maitland
Sara E. Malueg
Andre Maman
E. Jules Mandel
Patricia Manfredi
Edward Marxheimer
Robert J. Mautner
J. Oscar Maynes Jr.
Richard J. Mcardle
Robert H. McGlynn
Lester W. McKim†
Robert G. Mead Jr.†
David T. Mensing
Helmut Meyerbach
Donald J. Meyers
Judith M. Michaels
Joseph Michel
Arthur L. Micozzi
Marcia S. Miller
Jane T. Mitchell
Marlin M. Mittag
Jack R. Moeller
Hans-J G. Mollenhauer
Karen S. Montgomery

Raymond A. Moody
J. Michael Moore
Merriam M. Moore
Genelle G. Morain
Robert R. Morrison
Klaus A. Mueller
Maria Olivia Munoz
Oliver T. Myers
Donald S. Nash
Richard W. Newman
Samuel Nodarse
Frances B. Nostrand†
Howard L. Nostrand†
Leroy A. Oberlander
Chester W. Obuchowski
Jude T. O'Donnell
Josefina V. O'Keefe
Argentina Palacios
G. Cherie B. Palmer
Anthony Papalia†
Mary Anne Brown Parenty
Charles A. Partin
Arsilia L. Pellegrino
Paul W. Peterson
Erwin A. Petri
Edward S. Phinney†
Geoffrey Pill
Travis B. Poole
Elaine S. Potoker
John M. Purcell
Dorothea R. Rahn
Raji M. Rammuny
Gerhard Rauscher
DonaB.Reeves-Marquardt
Margaret C. Rehring
Constance L. Reid
Andrew I. Rematore
William R. Rice
Albert I. Richards
Charles P. Richardson

Leo N. Rinaldi
Wilga M. Rivers†
Rose A. Rose
Celesta Rudolph
Ferdinand A. Ruplin†
Norma D. Rusch
Norman P. Sacks
Victor Sampon
Lynn A. Sandstedt†
Richard T. Scanlan
C. Edward Scebold†
Frances Schering
Gerd K. Schneider
Shirley J. Schreiweis
Maryalice D. Seagrave
H. Ned Seelye†
Mary E. Sexton
Richard K. Seymour
Mary C. Shapiro
David C. Siebenhar
Cyril Siegel
Juliana Sienko
Robert E. Simmons
Pierre B. Simonian
Grace C. Skelley
Anne Slack
Russell J. Sloun
Alfred N. Smith Jr.
Philip D. Smith
Philip E. Smith
Ronald E. Smith
Sara K. Smith
Flint Smith
Luis Soto-Ruiz
Edra P. Staffieri†
James R. Stebbins
Gabriele R. Stiven
Rebecca J. Stracener
Lorraine A. Strasheim†
Rosalie Streng

Helena Stuart
Janet Susi
Rodney N. Swenson
Alex L. Szaszy
Mahmood Taba Tabai
Pearl G. Tarnor
Anna Taussig
Jean H. Teel
Esther S. Tillman
Paul E. Tully
Albert Turner
Patricia V. Egan Turner
Joseph A. Tursi†
Albert Valdman†
Rebecca M. Valette
Eduardo E. Vargas
Morris-Vos
Louis A. Wagner
Helen P. Warriner-Burke
Ellen F. Williams
Kathe P. Wilson†
Harold B. Wingard†
Joseph A. Wipf
David Wolfe
Mary Lou M. Wolsey
James J. Wrenn
Winfred O. Wright
Bernice B. Yarbro
John D. Yarbro
Charles H. Yeager
Valois A. Zarr
Dorothy M. Zimmerman
Carrie May K. Zintl

† –deceased

ACTFL CHARTER MEMBERS, THIRTIETH ANNIVERSARY— 1996

Over the past three decades, the following men and women have maintained their ACTFL membership year-by-year, without any lapses. On the occasion of ACTFL's 30th anniversary, we mark this occasion with a salute to these 151 charter members. Not only did they found this organization, but they have also continued to guide and support it. On behalf of all our members, we extend to each of you our deep appreciation for your leadership and your commitment and dedication to our profession. Your contribution has had a profound impact on a generation of teachers and students.

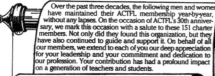

ACTFL Charter Members

Charles H. Ahnert
James E. Alatis
Howard B. Altman
Keith O. Anderson
Jermaine D. Arendt
Edwin P. Arnold
Sheila S. Ashley
Reid E. Baker
Marilyn J. Barrueta
Jacqueline D. Benevento
Jean P. Berwald
Herbert H. Boswau
June A. Calen
Benita B. Campbell
Juanita Carfora
Lolita Carfora
Mary M. Carr
Jane J. Chamberlain
Barbara M. Chandler
Walter L. Chatfield
John L. D. Clark
Elizabeth W. Cloud
Pedro I. Cohen
Rose A. Collins
Marilyn J. Conwell
Jacqueline S. Cork
Joanna B. Crane
William C. Crossgrove
David Crowner
Norman G. Damerau
Francis J. Dannerbeck
John M. Darcey
John DeFrancis
Carl Dellaccio
William E. DeLorenzo
Gerard A. Desjardins
Phyllis J. Dragonas
F. Alan Duval
Walter G. Eggmann
Jacqueline C. Elliott
Maurice G. Elton
Margritt A. Engel
Victor Maurice Faubert
Eveline Felsten
Mario Fierros
Joanne Foster
Robert R. Fournier
Herschel J. Frey

T. Bruce Fryer
Joe K. Fugate
Estella M. Gahala
Paul A. García
Alan Garfinkel
Hanna Geldrich-Leffman
William Gemmer
Anthony Gradisnik
Virginia L. Gramer
Carolyn M. Gray
Frank M. Grittner
Ida Grober
Michio P. Hagiwara
C. L. Hallman
Bernard P. Hardy
William N. Hatfield
Margarete L. Hilts
Robert L. Hinshalwood
Dorothy B. Holland
Don R. Iodice
Gilbert A. Jarvis
Albert W. Je Kenta
Sr. Mary Helen Kashuba
Dora F. Kennedy
Elizabeth A. Kiefer
Max Klamm
Constance K. Knop
Edward L. Kruse Jr.
Robert LaBouve
Robert C. Lafayette
Wallace P. Lagerwey
Dale L. Lange
Edgar L. Langevin
Judith A. Laurie
George J. Lauscher
Ellen L. Leeder
Kenneth A. Lester
Stephen L. Levy
Gladys C. Lipton
Rebecca M. Liskey
Walter F. Lohnes
Lena L. Lucietto
Paul F. Luckau
Dennis D. Magnuson
Bruce H. Mainous
Barbara A. Maitland
E. Jules Mandel
Patricia Manfredi

J. Oscar Maynes Jr.
Helmut Meyerbach
Judith M. Michaels
Joseph Michel
Arthur L. Micozzi
Jane T. Mitchell
Raymond A. Moody
Genelle G. Morain
Maria Olivia Muñoz
Donald S. Nash
Howard L. Nostrand
Erwin A. Petri
Travis B. Poole
John M. Purcell
Raji M. Rammuny
Dona B. Reeves-Marquardt
Constance L. Reid
Leo N. Rinaldi
Wilga M. Rivers
Ferdinand A. Ruplin
Norman P. Sacks
Lynn A. Sandstedt
C. Edward Scebold
Gerd K. Schneider
Shirley J. Schreiweis
Mary C. Shapiro
David C. Siebenhar
Pierre B. Simonian
Russell J. Sloun
Alfred N. Smith
Philip D. Smith
Luis Soto-Ruiz
Edra P. Staffieri
Charles W. Stansfield
James R. Stebbins
Rebecca J. Stracener
Rosalie Streng
Helena Stuart
Rodney N. Swenson
Alex L. Szaszy
Mahmood Taba-Tabai
Jean H. Teel
Paul E. Tully
Albert Turner
Patricia V. Egan Turner
Joseph A. Tursi
Rebecca M. Valette
Morris Vos
Louis A. Wagner
Helen P. Warriner-Burke
Harold B. Wingard
Joseph A. Wipf
David Wolfe
Mary Lou M. Wolsey
John D. Yarbro
Helene Zimmer-Loew

MEMBERSHIP SURVEY

ACTFL, as part of its 25th Anniversary Celebration, is conducting the following membership survey in order to give each of you the opportunity to evaluate the quality and effectiveness of the numerous services and activities of the Association. Suggestions for other services and projects that ACTFL might pursue in the future are also being requested.

PLEASE TAKE TIME TO COMPLETE THE SURVEY. YOUR RESPONSE WILL HELP ACTFL TO MEET YOUR PROFESSIONAL NEEDS.

I. For each of the following items, circle one of the numbers, 5 high to 1 low. 0 = NA. (Written comments are strongly encouraged.)

1. 5 4 3 2 1 0   ACTFL Annual Meeting
    Comments: _____

2. 5 4 3 2 1 0   The ACTFL journal, *Foreign Language Annals*
    Comments: _____

3. 5 4 3 2 1 0   The *ACTFL Newsletter*
    Comments: _____

4. 5 4 3 2 1 0   The ACTFL Foreign Language Education Series
    Comments: _____

5. 5 4 3 2 1 0   ACTFL Professional Development Program
    Comments: _____

6. 5 4 3 2 1 0   ACTFL Professional Testing Certification and Recertification Process
    Comments: _____

7. 5 4 3 2 1 0   The responsiveness of ACTFL Headquarters to individual member needs and requests
    Comments: _____

8. 5 4 3 2 1 0   ACTFL dues structure
    Comments: _____

9. 5 4 3 2 1 0   ACTFL's cooperation with other language associations
    Comments: _____

10. 5 4 3 2 1 0   ACTFL as an effective voice for the profession
    Comments: _____

(Cont...)

11. 5 4 3 2 1 0   ACTFL Awards Program
    Comments: _____

12. 5 4 3 2 1 0   The Special Interest Group (SIGS) concept for addressing special concerns of the profession
    Comments: _____

13. 5 4 3 2 1 0   The "Priorities Process" conducted every ten years to define the primary issues confronting the profession
    Comments: _____

14. 5 4 3 2 1 0   Relationship of ACTFL with regional and state organizations
    Comments: _____

15. 5 4 3 2 1 0   The Summer Seminar Program designed to find solutions for some of the problems of the profession
    Comments: _____

16. 5 4 3 2 1 0   The overall effectiveness of ACTFL as a professional organization
    Comments: _____

II. Suggestions for future projects and activities for ACTFL that you feel would benefit and strengthen the profession.

_____
_____
_____
_____

PLEASE SEND THE COMPLETED SURVEY FORM TO:

ACTFL
6 Executive Plaza
Yonkers, New York 10701-6801

THANK YOU.

Number of years member of ACTFL _____

Languages _____

Levels _____

Number of years teaching_____

ACTFL Newsletter, FLA, Vol. X, No. 1 (Fall 1997), pp. 15-16.

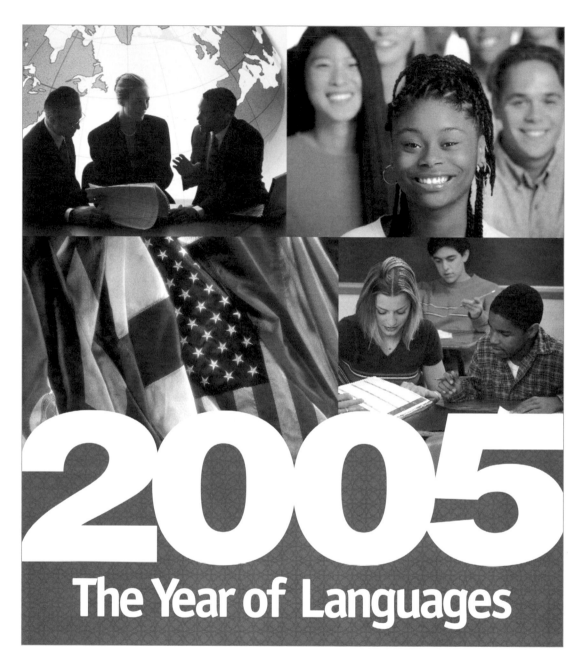

2005

The Year of Languages

The *2005: The Year of Languages* campaign solidified ACTFL as the leader of language education advocacy. The U.S. House of Representatives, U.S. Senate, governors, and other government officials passed resolutions and proclamations recognizing 2005 as the Year of Languages.

CHAPTER 5

THE 2000s

The Decade of Big Changes

We now arrive at the beginning of a new century. ACTFL was operating smoothly and moving into the 2000s, boosted by the widespread global acceptance of new proficiency guidelines. Also, new national standards for foreign languages were bringing about refreshing changes in language classrooms, accountability and responsibility for ACTFL's various departments was being restructured, and the ACTFL organizational budget and audits were more stable and positive.

Paul A. Garcia was the President who was to lead ACTFL forward. His theme for the year was *Language Learners in the 21st Century: Every One, Every Day, Every Where,* a theme that stressed both the unity and the diversity that "our profession must achieve and nourish as our world continues to change" (*FLA*, Vol. 33, No. 1, p. 135).

Emily Spinelli had assisted Frank Grittner, Editor of *FLA,* beginning in early 2000. When he officially retired from that position after eight years, Spinelli became Editor of *FLA* at the annual meeting held in Boston. There were several new initiatives under Spinelli and Grittner's editorships:
- an editorial board of 10 was established;
- forms were distributed to potential reviewers (Spinelli noted that each article had two reviewers);
- the journal was now appearing six times a year (once every two months);
- it had a new cover design;
- its size was larger;
- the *ACTFL Newsletter* was incorporated into a section entitled *Member News*;
- advertising revenue was increasing.

In the January/February 2000 issue of *FLA* (Vol. 33, No. 1, p. 13-18), the *ACTFL Proficiency Guidelines—Speaking (Revised 1999)* were published, 13 years after the

Paul A. García
ACTFL President 2000

FRANK GRITTNER AND FRIENDS — ACTFL 1999
A RECEPTION TO HONOR THE RETIRING EDITOR OF *FLA*

Left and bottom right:
Frank Grittner, Editor, *Foreign Language Annals*; Ed Scebold, Executive Director, ACTFL

Top right: Emily Spinelli, 1999 ACTFL President; Liz Hoffman, 1998 ACTFL President; Frank Grittner; Constance Knop, University of Wisconsin

original guidelines had appeared in 1986. Also in this issue (pp. 103-122) was *In a Class by Itself: Focus on Instruction,* concerning the use and implementation of the *Standards for Foreign Language Learning.*

The New Visions 2000 initiative was under way after a planning meeting in June 1999, at which the participants discussed what the profession might do to address five critical concerns in foreign language education: (1) the architecture of the profession; (2) curriculum, instruction, articulation and assessment; (3) research; (4) teacher development; and (5) teacher recruitment.

In June 2000, a retreat was held in Leesburg, VA, at which the registrants refined the work done to date and answered the following questions:

- What can the profession do?
- What are the priorities for these actions?
- Who will do the work—the individuals, organizations, associations, and related agencies that would collaborate to achieve the agreed-upon objectives in a non-duplicative manner?

In the "Member News" section of *FLA*, Paul Sandrock of the Wisconsin Department of Public Instruction, who was Task Force Coordinator of ACTFL's Standards Assessment Design Project, explained the PAU [Performance Assessment Unit] Project. The PAU was designed to forge the last link in the chain that began with the creation of the Standards for Foreign Language Learning in 1996, evolved through the *ACTFL*

Summary of ACE Credit Recommendations for Official ACTFL OPI Ratings

Official OPI Rating	Category I Dutch, English*, French, Haitian Creole, Italian, Norwegian, Portuguese, Spanish, Swahili and Swedish.	Category II German, Modern Greek, Hindi, Indonesian, Punjabi and Urdu.	Category III Cambodian, Czech, Hmong, Hebrew, Hungarian, Lao, Polish, Russian, Serbo-Croatian**, Slovak, Tagalog, Turkish, Thai, Ukrainian and Vietnamese.	Category IV Arabic, Cantonese, Japanese, Korean and Mandarin.
Novice High/ Intermediate Low	2 LD	2 LD	3 LD	3 LD
Intermediate Mid	4 LD	5 LD	6 LD	6 LD
Intermediate High/ Advanced Low	8 LD	8 LD + 2 UD	6 LD + 3 UD	6 LD + 3 UD
Advanced Mid	10 LD	8 LD + 4 UD	6 LD + 6 UD	6 LD + 6 UD
Advanced High/ Superior	10 LD + 2 UD	8 LD + 4 UD	6 LD + 6 UD	6 LD + 6 UD

Legend

*English is treated as a foreign language.
** Serbian and Croatian have been combined to Serbo-Croatian.
Credit recommendations are based on a semester hour.
LD = Lower division baccalaureate/associate degree category.
UD = Upper division baccalaureate degree category.

The 10 ACTFL OPI language proficiency ratings are: Superior, Advanced High, Advanced Mid, Advanced Low, Intermediate High, Intermediate Mid, Intermediate Low, Novice High, Novice Mid, Novice Low.

Figure 1. ACE Credit and the OPI. From *FLA*, March/April 2000, Vol. 33, No. 4, p. 457

Performance Guidelines for K–12 Learners in 1998, and culminated in the creation of an assessment mechanism to measure student performance in standards-based programs (*FLA,* Vol. 33, No. 2, p. 237).

In the spring of 1996, a major U.S. Department of Education grant for the development of model licensing standards for entry-level foreign language teachers K–12 was announced, virtually assuring a complete standards- and performance-based approach to foreign language education. The Council of Chief State School Officers (CCSSO) received a $330,000 award for over two years to establish model licensing standards for beginning teachers. This project was administered by the CCSSO's program arm, the Interstate New Teacher Assessment and Support Consortium

(INTASC). The standards developed by INTASC would become part of the dialogue about statewide criteria for education. ACTFL's voice in the process was strengthened by its collaboration with the National Board for Professional Teaching Standards (NBPTS), its work with the National Standards in Foreign Language Education Collaborative Project (NSFLECP) consortium, and its 1998 membership in NCATE.

Another positive development in 2000 was the American Council on Education (ACE) College Credit Recommendation Service's favorable review of the ACTFL Oral Proficiency Interview (OPI). This approval meant that demonstration of spoken language abilities, as evidenced by an Official ACTFL OPI rating, could be presented to individual colleges and universities for the

ACTFL HEADQUARTERS STAFF—2000

L to R: Norma Strauss, Exhibits and Meeting Manager; Cynthia Galik, Assistant to the Executive Director; Louise Patierno, Convention Services Director

June C. Hicks, Staff Writer; Adam Stryker, Professional Development Specialist

Elvira Swender
Professional Programs Director

Stephen L. Levy
Professional Programs Associate

Jamie B. Draper
ACTFL Consultant

awarding of undergraduate college credit upon recommendation by ACE (Fig. 1).

On April 19, 2000, President Clinton issued an Executive Memorandum to the Heads of Executive Departments and Agencies regarding the importance of international education: "To continue to compete successfully in the global economy and to maintain a role as a world leader, the United States needs to ensure that its citizens develop a broad understanding of the world, proficiency in other languages, and knowledge of other cultures…" (*FLA*, May/June 2001, Vol. 33, No. 3, pp. 364-366). ACTFL Executive Director Scebold was one of 30 invited attendees at a forum held at the French Embassy in Washington, D.C., that day to discuss postsecondary education in the U.S. and the U.S. Department of Education's role in it.

In early 2000, Lynne McClendon, Executive Director of the Southern Conference on Language Teaching (SCOLT), approached Steve Levy, Associate for ACTFL's Professional Development Programs, about the feasibility of incorporating ACTFL Professional Development

Workshops within a regional conference program. Such a collaboration would expand the availability of the existing training programs, bringing the possibility of attending such workshops to all attendees at a regional conference. The first of such regional workshops was in 2001: "Measuring Up to Standards: Practical Applications of the *ACTFL Performance Guidelines for K–12 Learners.*"

Late in the summer of 2000, President García wrote to some 200 ACTFL members selected randomly as part of a test launch for the organization's newly planned capital fundraising effort, "Campaign for the 21st Century: Better Beginnings." With this campaign, ACTFL was hoping to raise $2.1 million over the next four years to capitalize on the current unrivaled opportunities for the profession. In a parallel but separate mailing, Past Presidents Ann Tollefson and Kathy Riordan wrote similar letters and conducted personal follow-up with another segment of ACTFL colleagues. Initial response to this campaign saw more than $15,000 pledged during the first week. The fund was to be used for two purposes:

- direct funding in teacher development and recruitment, development of student assessment instruments, and promotion of language study for all learners, especially in the primary grades; and
- creation of an endowment fund that would generate interest income to give ACTFL more independence from limited avenues of revenue.

Amid these positive signs for foreign language education in general and for ACTFL in particular, Executive Director Scebold had become seriously ill and was forced to curtail much of his daily work. So he announced his retirement for Fall 2001, after 32 years at the helm of an organization in which he fervently believed. An announcement was published so that a search for his replacement could begin immediately, with the goal to announce an Executive Director-Designate in the summer of 2001.

At the November 2000 Executive Council meeting in Boston, it was announced that the two-year ACTFL-NFLRC collaborative "New Visions" would terminate at the end of that year.

A grant that Ann Tollefson and Myriam Met had submitted to continue the New Visions initiative enabled the New Visions Steering Committee to continue to consult and meet.

Scebold could not attend ACTFL 2000 in Boston because of his illness, but he remained in touch with the Executive Council's Steering Committee and the staff at headquarters. He learned that this annual meeting was a great success, with attendance at 6,535, exceeding all projections and expectations. The keynote speaker was a first: the famous Latina writer Esmeralda Santiago. ACTFL now had 7,800 members, with an 85% renewal rate. Adam Stryker had joined the Professional Development department. Department head Elvira Swender mentioned an increase in all aspects of OPI and MOPI (Modified Oral Proficiency Interview) testing.

June K. Phillips
ACTFL President 2001

Executive Director
American Council on the Teaching of
Foreign Languages

The American Council on the Teaching of Foreign Languages invites applications and nominations for its Executive Director. ACTFL is an 8,000-member organization located in Yonkers, north of New York City, dedicated to promoting and enhancing the study of languages and cultures in educational institutions at all levels.

Responsibilities of the Executive Director:
• Promote the interest of ACTFL at the national level, interpret the mission to the membership, public, and potential funders.
• Provide leadership in the development and implementation of ACTFL professional services.
• Have operational responsibility for the organization including management of its staff, finances, facilities, technological support and programs.
• Report to a Council elected by the membership.

Qualifications:
• Masters degree required/doctorate preferred in related field.
• Total of 8 years combined experience in foreign language teaching, research, or administration and association, non-profit, education, governmental, or business management.
• Demonstrated ability to work collaboratively with constituents, members, staff, professional organizations, and government entities.
• Success in grant and development activities.
• Ability to create and implement projects/initiatives/policies important to the foreign language profession.
• Demonstrated commitment to the role of languages and cultures in a diverse U.S. education system.

◆◆◆◆◆

Nominations and applications should be submitted in a confidential envelope to Search Committee, ACTFL Headquarters, 6 Executive Plaza, Yonkers, New York 10701-6801. Applicants should include a detailed letter describing their experience and qualifications as they relate to the position, a current Curriculum Vitae, and names and contact information for three professional references. All applications will be acknowledged and held in the strictest confidence. Review of applications will begin March 1, 2001, and continue until the position is filled. Starting date on or about August 15, 2001. ACTFL offers a competitive salary and benefits package. ACTFL is an equal opportunity employer. For further information consult www.actfl.org.

Figure 2. Advertisement for Executive Director of ACTFL. From *FLA*, January/February 2001, Vol. 34, No. 1, p. 1.

2001: The End of an Era (Annus horribilis)

June K. Phillips from Weber State University, Ogden, UT, was President of ACTFL in 2001—a year filled with tragedy on the national scene and surprise and grief for the organization. A search committee for the new Executive Director of ACTFL had been selected, a timetable was set, and nominations were being received (Fig. 2, p. 118). The year was beginning rather favorably. In her first Message from the President (*FLA*, Vol. 34, No. 1, p. 67), Phillips welcomed *FLA* readers to "the real millennium"—a time to reflect on the past and envision the future. Her theme for the 2001 annual meeting was "A Professional Odyssey: Exploring New Spaces," inviting ACTFL members to "disdain the comfort of the status quo so that as members of a dynamic profession, we dedicate this year to working together to improve the position of our discipline among students, parents, public, and other stakeholders" (*FLA*, Vol. 34, No. 1, p. 67).

Phillips also called 2001 a "momentous year in the life of our organization," referring to the current Executive Director's retirement, the search for a new leader to carry forward the mission of the organization, and the need to continue expanding its membership so its professional voice would be heard. She concluded with "Let the odyssey begin" (*FLA*, Vol. 34, No. 1, p. 67).

New Visions 2000, the initiative supported by funds from the U.S. Department of Education awarded to the National K–12 Foreign Language Resource Center (NFLRC) at Iowa State University and administered by ACTFL, had met in Leesburg in June 2000 and had established priorities for each of the five Action Groups (see Appendix A). New standards initiatives were under way: NCATE and the Interstate New Teacher Assessment and Support Consortium (INTASC)—the former for new foreign language teacher education program standards, the latter for model licensing standards for beginning teachers of foreign languages. A new set of standards was presented by the National Board for Professional Teaching Standards (NBPTS): *World Languages Other Than English Standards* (for teachers of students aged 3–18+).

A special message from the President of ACTFL appeared in *FLA*, Vol. 34, No. 2, p. 166: Executive Director Scebold could resume his work, and he agreed to continue his position through the summer of 2002. This issue also announced that Scebold had received the NECTFL Nelson Brooks Award for Outstanding Leadership in the profession (pp. 165–166). NECTFL Executive Director Rebecca Kline lauded him as follows:

Special Message from the President of ACTFL

During the course of the NECTFL Conference, the ACTFL Steering Committee discussed new developments in the search for a new Executive Director. Concurrently, we were deeply relieved and gladdened to learn that Ed Scebold's recuperation from illness has been so significant, his doctors have determined he is now able to continue to work if he wishes to do so. Accordingly, we have asked him to stay on as Executive Director at least through the summer of 2002. Ed has told us he is more than willing to do this. Therefore, the search for a new Executive Director, while not abandoned, will proceed more slowly than anticipated. Again, we are delighted with this state of affairs. I will discuss this at further length in my next President's Message in the May/June issue of *Foreign Language Annals*.

June K. Phillips
President, ACTFL

Figure 3. Winning artwork by Kit Rees. (*FLA*, May/June 2001, Vol. 34, No. 3, p. 273).

When we think of leadership in foreign language education, we think of ACTFL. And when we think of ACTFL, we think of Ed. Yet it is always ACTFL that receives the recognition. Where would we be without Ed?

Ed's leadership has served as a model to associations, their leaders, and their members. He has actively sought to collaborate with the myriad organizations that dot our professional landscape...

ACTFL has had only two people at its helm—as a longtime ACTFL and NECTFL leader observed: "Andy Paquette got it off the ground, and Ed has put it where it is today." It is extremely rare for any professional organization to enjoy the same leadership—and benefit from it—for this length of time.

*If you have not been asking yourself that question during the last 30 years [Where would we be without Ed?], you may now be wondering, with the news of his retirement, where **will** we be without Ed? But rest assured, he leaves us in the best of shape: thinking ahead but conscious always of the foundation that is our past. Not only has Ed himself been an outstanding leader, but he has helped to develop the leaders of our future.*

...enjoy coming back to be with us when the burdens are on someone else's shoulders!

More good news: the ACTFL fundraising campaign was continuing to gain momentum. Its initial test phase had raised more than $22,000 in contributions and pledges toward its $2 million goal over the next four years. One key element of the Phase I development strategy was the acquisition of a building for use as ACTFL's permanent headquarters. Phase II of the campaign would establish an ACTFL endowment fund of $500,000 that would provide for ACTFL's future security, as a source of special support as future needs presented themselves.

In Memoriam

C. Edward Scebold
November 21, 1939 – September 16, 2001

✦

We dedicate this issue of *Foreign Language Annals* to C. Edward Scebold
for his vision for the Foreign Language profession, his dedication to ACTFL,
and his ongoing support of the research that this journal embodies.

FLA (Vol. 34,
No. 5, p. 495)

name, address and institutional information. Participating exhibit booths would have machines to read the card, eliminating the need to fill out endless registration forms. A new electronic registration system to streamline the registration process was also planned.

In her "Message from the President" in the July/August 2001 issue of *FLA*, Phillips updated readers on the search for a new Executive Director. The position was to be re-advertised in Fall 2001, with screening to begin early in 2002.

Then...the *annus horribilis* began: first the tragedy of September 11, 2001, with the terrorist attacks in New York, Washington, and near Pittsburgh. Five days later, on Sunday, September 16, 2001, long-time Executive Director C. Edward Scebold died.

In her "Message from the President" in the September/October 2001 issue of *FLA* (Vol. 34, No. 5, p. 495), Phillips called Scebold's death a personal and professional loss for those who had worked with him on hundreds of projects over the years of his leadership:

What binds all these events together is the larger goals we hold dear and in which Ed so strongly believed: to build cultural understandings through common languages so that the us/them mentality that nurtures such events might someday be quashed.

Ed ably led us in the spectrum of standards-related efforts that comprise the Professional Odyssey we celebrate as the theme of the 2001 Annual Meeting in Washington, DC.

Also, the ACTFL Member-Get-a-Member Drive began May 1, 2001, and would end October 5. Incentives included a pair of round-trip airline tickets to any destination in the continental U.S., free convention registration, or free ACTFL membership renewal.

President Phillips presented a winning idea: having a student design the artwork for the ACTFL 2001 theme: "A Professional Odyssey: Exploring New Spaces." The winning design was by Kit Rees, a Visual Arts major at Weber State University, Ogden, UT (Fig. 3).

Preparations were afoot for the annual meeting in Washington, DC, in November. One innovation for the 2001 meeting would be the availability of a "swipe card" for all attendees. This plastic card felt just like a credit card, with a backside magnetic strip containing the attendee's

Ed Scebold's obituary was printed in the November/December 2001 issue of *FLA* (Vol. 34, No. 6, pp. 609–611) and included tributes from Leo Benardo, ACTFL President, 1969; Dale L. Lange, ACTFL President, 1980; Kathleen M. Riordan, ACTFL President, 1995; Lynn A. Sandstedt, ACTFL President, 1991; and Helene Zimmer-Loew, ACTFL President, 1984. (See Appendix B.)

Christine L. Brown
ACTFL President 2002

Left: Acting ACTFL Executive
Director Stephen L. Levy and 2001
ACTFL President June K. Phillips

Ever the leader, Scebold had the smooth functioning of ACTFL in mind when he met with President Phillips during an earlier hospitalization in April 2001. He had told her what he wanted her to do and what to discuss with the headquarters staff. He also told her to work closely with Stephen L. Levy, who was appointed acting Executive Director in August 2001.

The 2001 annual meeting was held as planned Washington, DC, on November 16–18, despite the traumatic events that had unraveled in September. At the meeting, many initiatives important to foreign language education were highlighted: NCATE standards for accreditation of teacher education programs, INTASC standards for initial licensure, and NBPTS teacher certification. The revision of the proficiency guidelines for writing were also presented and were published in the January/February issue of *FLA* (Vol. 35, No. 1, pp. 9-15). As President Phillips said in her final Message from the President, "... our professional odyssey did explore new spaces and will continue to navigate the waters when they are rough and when they are calm" (*FLA*, Vol. 34, No. 6, p. 615).

Christine L. Brown (Glastonbury, CT, public schools) was the 2002 President of ACTFL, and Martha G. Abbott was 2003 President-elect. The Executive Director Search Committee included the Steering Committee, a past president, an Executive Council member, a peer, and a staff member (see Appendix C for the job description that advertised this search).

ACTFL signed a contract with WGBH, Boston's PBS affiliate, to collaborate on a series of foreign language professional development videos focusing on the best use of foreign language teaching standards in the classroom. The project, which WBGH was producing for Annenberg/CPG, was the last major subject area of Annenberg/CPB's satellite teacher training programs. ACTFL Professional Development Specialist Adam Stryker, June K. Phillips, and Kathleen Riordan were ACTFL's three core advisors to the project.

Plans were in progress for the 2002 annual meeting in Salt Lake City, on the theme of *Beyond Our Customary Borders: Language and Culture in Context*. At the annual meeting, three plenary sessions were planned around this theme:

- the essential role culture plays in language education;
- the context of our discipline in the broad spectrum of education today; and
- the preservation and teaching of indigenous native languages in the US today.

Allied to the 2002 theme was a Language and National Security Briefing held in Washington, DC, in January 2002, at which discussants addressed the widespread, urgent need for more foreign language proficiency nationwide among US citizens, especially in the light of the events of September 11.

The NCATE foreign language teacher education standards were nearing their final form for submission to NCATE for acceptance, release to the profession at the ACTFL 2002 conference, and implementation. These new standards were expected to significantly affect teacher education programs in three key areas:

Institutions seeking NCATE accreditation will need to submit evidence that their foreign language teacher candidates have the necessary knowledge, skills, and dispositions to help their students in grades P–12 learn. Foreign language teacher preparation programs must submit evidence that their candidates have met standards in six areas:

- *Language, linguistics, comparisons*
- *Cultures, literatures, cross-disciplinary concepts*
- *Language acquisition theories and instructional practices*
- *Integration of standards into curriculum and instruction*
- *Assessment of languages and cultures*
- *Professionalism*

Programs will need to develop an ongoing assessment system through which they gather candidates' evidence such as portfolios, lesson plans, case study reports, presentations, papers, examinations, interviews, projects, and P- 12 student work samples.

Teacher candidates must demonstrate proficiency in speaking and writing at the "Advanced- Low" level as described in the ACTFL Proficiency Guidelines (the level is "Intermediate-High" for candidates teaching target languages that use non-alphabetic writing systems)

Colleges of Education and Departments of Foreign Languages will need to engage in dialogue and collaboration in order to help their teacher candidates achieve the knowledge, skills, and dispositions in pedagogy and language, culture, and literature. (FLA, *Vol. 35, No. 2, p. 253*)

In the May/June 2002 issue of *FLA* (Vol. 35, No. 3, pp. 275 & 282) appeared a call for papers for a special issue of the journal along the theme "Assessment of Oral Proficiency." Ray T. Clifford was guest editor of this special issue that was to be published in early 2004 but actually appeared in the Winter 2003 issue.

Also in this issue, the new ACTFL Executive Director was announced: Dr. Linda M. Wallinger, who was Director of the Office of Secondary Instructional Services at the Virginia Department of Education in Richmond, VA. Wallinger began her new position in Yonkers on July 8, 2002. In her Message from the President (*FLA*, Vol. 35, No. 3, p. 363), President Brown said the Executive

Director candidate pool contained 35 applicants, eight semi-finalists, and three finalists. The search committee was composed of Paul García, June Phillips, Helene Zimmer-Loew, Rita Oleksak, Stephen Levy, June Hicks, Marty Abbott, and Christine Brown.

For the first time, in 2002 the SIGs each had ListServ services that let them communicate messages to all fellow members through one general e-mail address to the list. At this time, there were nine SIGs:

- Foreign Language and the African-American Student
- Community College
- Cinema
- Teaching and Learning of Culture

- Distance Learning
- Small German Programs
- Research
- Spanish for Native Speakers
- Teacher Development

Linda M. Wallinger
ACTFL Executive Director
2002–2003

By October 16, 2002, there were 105 contributors to the ACTFL Campaign for the 21st Century, including donations received in the Memorial Fund that the Scebold family had established.

The year 2002 was the 20th anniversary of the proficiency movement in foreign languages. In her article "The ACTFL Proficiency Guidelines: A Historical Perspective," Judith Liskin-Gasparro, who co-authored the first oral proficiency manual used in some U.S. government agencies at the time, wrote:

*In an earlier, more innocent era, one could accept the illusion that language study was a classroom activity with little or no application in the outside world. One could create a closed system of curriculum, textbook, and tests. Success could be efficiency gauged in terms of how well the students learned the material they were taught, i.e., by their level of achievement. The question of probable success or failure with the language outside the classroom was seldom asked. The only accountability was internal: whether the student measured up to the expectations of the teacher. (*Teaching for Proficiency, the Organizing Principle, *Theodore V. Higgs, Ed. (1984), Lincolnwood, IL: National Textbook Company, p. 12)*

In "Member News" in the September/October issue of *FLA* (Vol. 35, No. 5, pp. 581, 589-593), we read: "While in many classrooms across the country that 'earlier, more innocent era' still exists, the fact is that the quiet revolution that stood language assessment on its head twenty years ago has now come into its own" (p. 589). On this same page, a chart illustrates the ACTFL OPI training and testing milestones (Fig. 4, p. 124).

New Visions in Action was still at work and conducted a national survey, beginning in November 2002 for completion in February 2003, to determine whether there was professional consensus on important criteria for defining well-articulated curricula, effective instructional strategies, valid and reliable assessment practices, and exemplary professional development, recruitment, and retention programs (*FLA*, Vol. 35, No. 6, p. 610).

1982: Publication of the *Preliminary ACTFL Guidelines* and first workshop to train OPI Trainers and Testers

1986: Publication of the *ACTFL Proficiency Guidelines*.

1988: First use of the ACTFL Oral Proficiency Interview (OPI) as an assessment tool in the workplace.

1992: A relationship with ALC Press, Japan is established in order to conduct OPI Tester Training in Japan annually.

1992: Language Testing International (LTI) the ACTFL Testing Office, is established.

1997: Introduction of the Modified Oral Proficiency Interview (MOPI) Tester Training Workshops; proficiency training for those who teach and test primarily at the Novice and Intermediate levels.

1999: Publication of the *ACTFL Proficiency Guidelines – Speaking* (Revised 1999) and the new OPI Tester Training materials.

2000: The American Council on Education (ACE) College Credit Recommendation Service publishes college credit recommendations for official ACTFL ratings received through an ACTFL OPI.

2002: To date more than 5,000 language professionals have participated in ACTFL OPI and MOPI Tester Training Workshops in 17 languages, and many thousands more in Proficiency Familiarization Workshops. This year alone, ACTFL Proficiency Workshops are held in the U.S. (Berkeley, CA; Provo, UT; Tallahassee, FL; Chattanooga, TN; Wilmington, DE; Atlanta, GA; Princeton, NJ; Wilmington, DE; Kyle, SD; University Center, MI; Chicago, IL; New York, NY) and abroad (Tokyo, Japan; Cape Coast, Ghana; Edinburgh, Scotland; Berlin, Germany; Madrid, Spain; Beijing, China; and Leuven, Belgium).

2022: ??

Figure 4

The November/December issue of *FLA* (Vol. 35, No. 6, p. 617; 621) announced that, beginning with Vol. 36 in 2003, the journal would be published quarterly rather than bimonthly, and issues would appear in March, June, September, and December.

This issue also announced that NCATE had approved the New Teacher Preparation Program Standards at its board meeting on October 19, 2002. These new standards were a joint two-year project of the National Foreign Language Standards Collaborative and ACTFL. Beginning in 2004, foreign language teacher preparation programs seeking NCATE review were to submit program reports that addressed the new ACTFL standards. Also a call was put out for ACTFL/NCATE Program Reviewers, who would be trained to examine the reports and data submitted by institutions seeking NCATE accreditation for their foreign language programs. Reviewers were assigned to a three-person program review team and were to participate in at least one review per semester.

2003—Ongoing Changes

"I can best characterize our organization as one that is in transition— literally and figuratively!" said ACTFL 2003 President Martha G. ("Marty") Abbott, of the Fairfax County, VA, public schools, in her first Message from the President in *FLA* (Vol. 36, No. 1, p. 139). Transition? Yes, new Executive Director Linda Wallinger, had decided to pursue other career interests and had stepped down from her position in December 2002, putting ACTFL back in the throes of a search for a new Executive Director. This was an opportune time to move the organization to a location that would provide more visibility for language educators in the language policy and advocacy arena, in or near Washington, DC. A new office had been found in Alexandria, VA, just outside Washington, in a suite adjacent to the Teachers of English to Speakers of Other Languages (TESOL) offices. ACTFL would now be in an environment that would easily allow it to be a major player in education decision-making at all levels.

In the interim before a new Executive Director was found, the ACTFL Executive Council hired a consulting firm, Helming & Co., to handle the organization's daily administration. Former Executive Director Wallinger worked with this firm as a consultant. Staff members were offered the opportunity to transfer to the Alexandria office, but none accepted, and most staff members were let go. Of the two remaining, June Hicks left ACTFL to work for MLA, while Elvira Swender remained at ACTFL.

On a more positive note, President Abbott announced a collaborative project between ACTFL and the U.S. Department of Education: *2005, the Year of Languages in the United States*. The idea of the Year of Languages had been resoundingly endorsed by the ACTFL delegates at the 2002 Convention's Delegate Assembly. These delegates represented more than 130 foreign language professional organizations and 50,000 language educators across the country. An invitation was sent to Secretary of Education Roderick Paige to join ACTFL for the historic announcement. The initiative began in 2002 under President Christy Brown, who was key in setting the plan into motion. This year of celebration was to be based on the successful European Union campaign as a model.

ACTFL had received a contract from the DLI Foreign Language Center (DLIFLC) in the fall of 2002 to help the government increase its testing capabilities and expand the number of languages that could be tested on demand. The project was named "100 Days—100 Languages," referring to the testing of 100 languages and the estimated number of days of training required to build capacity in any given area. ACTFL was a natural source of what the government needed because—in addition to its own test, the ACTFL OPI—the organization had a test administration capability in its testing partner, Language Testing International (LTI) (*FLA*, 2003, Vol. 36, No. 1, p. 147).

The Summer 2003 issue of *FLA* (Vol. 36, No. 2, pp. 289 & 292) announced Bret Lovejoy's appointment as ACTFL's new Executive Director after a five-month nationwide search. The search committee was composed of President Marty Abbott, Past President Christy Brown, 2004 President-elect Keith Cothrun; John Grandin, representing the ACTFL Council; Lynn Sandstedt, Past President of ACTFL and former Executive Director of the American Association of Teachers of Spanish and Portuguese (AATSP); and Pat Barr-Harrison, representing the ACTFL Delegate Assembly.

Lovejoy was already well-versed in NCATE and had managed educational nonprofit organizations. He saw much opportunity for growth in ACTFL in membership, conventions, member services, and other areas, as his prior experience was in fostering such growth.

Lovejoy began his position at ACTFL on May 12, 2003. One of his priorities was to shepherd the move of the organization's headquarters to Alexandria in the summer of 2003.

Martha G. Abbott
ACTFL President 2003

Bret Lovejoy
ACTFL Executive Director
2003–2011

Figure 5. New ACTFL Headquarters, Alexandria, VA

He also stressed that the organization's bylaws mandated a treasurer for the association. The treasurer would be a non-voting member of the Steering Committee and would be appointed annually by the Executive Council; the same person could be reappointed. Executive Council member John Lalande was named ACTFL's first treasurer.

Plans were afoot for the 2003 Annual Meeting on November 21-23 in Philadelphia, at which language professionals nationwide would celebrate the official announcement of *2005 The Year of Languages in the United States* by Secretary of Education Rod Paige. Keynote speaker Andrew Cuomo, son of former New York Governor Mario Cuomo, was to discuss the linguistic and cultural insights he gained by interviewing more than 20 world leaders on the qualities behind leadership. NCATE program reviewer training was also planned for the annual meeting and other locations in 2004.

In the Summer 2003 issue of *FLA* (Vol. 36, No. 2, p. 304) appeared an update to New Visions

in Action (NVIA). Four task forces had been organized to address the work of New Visions: (1) Curriculum, Instruction, Assessment, and Articulation; (2) Professional Development; (3) Teacher Recruitment and Retention; and (4) Research. The link of task forces, sub-task forces, and professional organizations provided a healthy blend of national, regional, and grassroots efforts toward a common cause. Thus NVIA was moving rapidly toward its original vision of bringing together diverse communities of educators serving particular focus areas of the foreign language field to work collaboratively toward shared goals.

Toward the end of 2003, ACTFL had settled into its new headquarters at 700 South Washington Avenue, Suite 210, Alexandria, VA. Professional Programs remained in the now-smaller offices at Executive Plaza in Yonkers, NY.

The Winter 2003 issue of *FLA* (Vol. 36, No. 4) was a special issue focusing on Oral Proficiency Testing. Ray T. Clifford was Guest Editor, and Elvira Swender was Assistant Guest Editor. Its articles treated the history of oral proficiency testing, research, language analysis, and curriculum and instruction. As Clifford said in his editorial:

Since their first publication 20 years ago, the ACTFL Oral Proficiency Guidelines have been the focus of much interest, discussion, and debate. Some of those discussions have been productive; other have generated more heat than light and have evidenced more emotion than understanding…. The Guidelines were intended to be used primarily for proficiency assessment and not for other purposes, such as performance, achievement, or diagnostic testing. Yet, some are searching for a single scale that can assess both current communicative ability and validate the acquisition sequence of enabling linguistic features" (p. 481).

This issue was a tribute to C. Edward Scebold and other leaders who, decades before, had begun to prepare the profession to move beyond focusing on teaching methods and balancing concern for learner outcomes. The issue aimed to provide a substantive reference for teachers, researchers, and administrators.

At the Annual Meeting in Philadelphia, U.S. Secretary of Education Roderick Paige told the attendees, "Because of my belief that language education is necessary for a quality education, I strongly support your efforts to declare 2005 as the Year of Languages" (*FLA*, Vol. 36, No. 4, p. 599).

Cuomo called ACTFL's Year of Languages "an important step in broadening the horizons of Americans in a post-9/11 world" (p. 599). The goal of the Year of Languages celebration was to advance the idea that every American should develop proficiency in both English and another language.

Many of ACTFL's recent accomplishments were highlighted during the annual meeting:

Roderick Paige
U.S. Secretary of Education
2001–2005

- The hiring of the new Executive Director, Bret Lovejoy.
- The development of NCATE/ACTFL Program Standards for the Preparation of Foreign Language Teachers.
- The Complete Curriculum study by NASBE (National Association of State Boards of Education) detailing the state of foreign languages and the arts in the schools. (See *FLA*, Vol. 36, No. 4, pp. 607-609, for a full report on this study, and Appendix D for the ten recommendations from the study).
- The attendance of Past President Christy Brown at the 21st World Congress in South Africa of the *Fédération des Professeurs de Langues Vivantes (FIPLV)*, as part of ACTFL's commitment to the international language learning community.
- The Teaching of Foreign Languages K-12 Multimedia Project, in collaboration with WBGH and Annenberg/CPB.
- The creation of two new SIGs: Foreign Language in Elementary Schools (FLES) and the Less Commonly Taught Languages (LCTL).
- National Board certification.
- A new video promoting global knowledge, in cooperation with the Asia Society.

Keith Cothrun
ACTFL President 2004

At the conclusion of the 2003 meeting, Thomas Keith Cothrun (Las Cruces High School, Las Cruces, NM) assumed the presidency of ACTFL for 2004. In his first Message from the President (*FLA*, Vol. 36, No. 4, p. 603), Cothrun, a full-time classroom teacher of German, indicated that plans for ACTFL's immediate future included developing a new strategic plan for the organization, working hard to see that quality language learning opportunities were available to students throughout the educational continuum, and gearing up for the "greatest celebration of language learning this country has ever seen as we celebrate The Year of Languages in the United States!" With that he announced the theme of the 2004 meeting to be held in Chicago: *The Year of Languages: Celebrating Our International Spirit.*

Sen. Paul Simon

In this same issue of *FLA,* Executive Director Lovejoy gave a report on how far ACTFL had come and where it was headed for the future. He came to the job with two major objectives established by the Executive Council: (1) to begin moving the association headquarters to Alexandria, VA, and (2) to ensure that the association had a successful convention in Philadelphia; both were accomplished. Lovejoy reported more than 5,200 attendees, 500 educational sessions, and 330 exhibitors at ACTFL 2003 (p. 605).

Sad news was shared with the ACTFL membership: on December 9, 2003, Senator Paul Simon (D-IL) died at 75 from complications from heart surgery. The notice of his death in *FLA,* Vol. 36, No. 4, p. 625, commented: "Known for his trademark bow tie and his straight talking ways, Senator Simon was a lifelong supporter of the need for Americans to achieve competence in foreign languages." His book, *The Tongue-Tied American*, highlighted America's deficiencies in foreign language and how that had hindered our economic and diplomatic work around the world...and that book had appeared in 1980!

By the time of the Annual Meeting in Philadelphia, ACTFL had established its headquarters in Alexandria, and new staff had been hired in its Alexandria and Yonkers offices (Fig. 6, p. 129).

In early 2004, plans were in the works for celebration of The Year of Languages (YOL) in 2005. ACTFL and its affiliate organizations—along with U.S. Department of Education officials, government leaders at the federal, state and local levels, school administrations, and classroom teachers—were helping build greater public awareness of other languages and cultures through the YOL campaign. Celebrations were planned for a variety of settings, including elementary and secondary schools and postsecondary institutions. Special community events and other programs would focus on the increasing importance of foreign language learning in American education and American life (*FLA*, Vol. 37, No. 1, p. 151).

The year 2004 was very busy for both President Cothrun and Executive Director Lovejoy. They attended all of the regional conferences and spoke at each about ACTFL and the Year of Languages plans, under the leadership of co-chairs Marty Abbott and Christy Brown. A list of the ACTFL events for the YOL 2005 was being disseminated widely (see Appendix E). ACTFL's presence at these meetings was most welcome and appreciated.

The new Alexandria offices were already too small, and Executive Director Lovejoy discussed moving to larger space. Renovations were being completed at the New York office, and LTI had agreed to move into the Yonkers office and share space as well as rent. The financial situation of the organization had turned around, coming from a deficit in 2002 to a significant positive cash position in 2003.

ACTFL was moving forward with the Teacher of the Year Award. Five regional finalists would be chosen, and then the National Teacher of the Year would be chosen from these winners. New Visions in Action (NVIA) had committed to providing $8,000-$10,000 to ACTFL to launch the effort. The award was announced officially in the winter issue of *FLA* (Vol. 37, No. 4, p. 646); the first award was made in 2005 to Ken Stewart, a Spanish teacher in Chapel Hill, NC.

Figure 6. LEFT — ACTFL Staff, Alexandria (L to R): Regina Farr, Juliet Mason, Steve Ackley, Bret Lovejoy, and Tamisa Pope.

RIGHT — ACTFL Staff, Yonkers (L to R): Stephen Levy, Rochelle Render, Harriet Barnett, Elvira Swender, Hollie West, and Linda Kaplan.

On June 22–24, 2004, a National Language Conference took place at the University of Maryland at College Park, hosted by the Office of the Undersecretary of Defense (Personnel and Readiness) and the Center for Advanced Study of Language (CASL). ACTFL Executive Director Lovejoy and past presidents Abbott and Brown participated in the conference, along with many other ACTFL members from various sectors of the foreign language profession. The conference hosted over 400 individuals representing federal agencies, academia, the nation's educational system, industry, language experts, and researchers (*FLA*, Vol. 37, No. 3, pp. 500-501), and it led to major recommendations regarding the U.S. and its relationship with language learning.

As a follow-up to this conference, a National Language Policy Summit, themed *An American Plan for Action*, was to be held at The University of North Carolina at Chapel Hill on January 10–11, 2005. Since focusing and expanding America's language education policy was a top priority of the YOL initiative, leaders in education, business, and government were to meet at this summit to share ideas and begin to identify steps that could be taken to shape policy that would guide language education in the U.S. for many years. This summit was an international video-conference that focused on the issues surrounding language policies in the U.S. and how to forge a plan of action to promote language learning for all Americans. This undertaking would be the first official activity for the 2005 ACTFL President, Audrey Heining-Boynton, of the University of North Carolina at Chapel Hill.

In the fall issue of *FLA* (Vol. 37, No. 3, p. 340), a full-page ad appeared for the Grand Opening of The Year of Languages Logo Products Store, which sold bags, T-shirts, hats,

Audrey Heining-Boynton
ACTFL President 2005

Figure 7. Public Service Announcements for YOL 2005

cups, and many other items to show support for YOL.

The 2004 Annual Meeting in Chicago on November 19-21, themed *Celebrating our International Spirit,* officially kicked off the YOL celebration. People were invited to "Celebrate, Educate, Communicate...the Power of Language Learning." No longer simply a conference, it was now officially called the Annual Meeting and Exposition. And no wonder: it was the largest professional meeting of second language educators in the U.S. and the largest exhibition of teaching materials and technology for the foreign language profession. More than 5,300 attendees—1 in 5 of whom were there for the first time—participated in more than 500 program sessions and workshops and heard such speakers as Ambassador Michael Lemmon, Dean of the School of Language Studies, Foreign Service Institute; Jean-David Levitte, French Ambassador to the United States; and Chief Red Hawk, co-founder of the United Indian Nation, Inc.

At the meeting it was announced that Paul Sandrock, state consultant for World Languages Education at the Wisconsin Department of Public Instruction, was President-elect for 2006. Attendees also learned that ACTFL had drafted a strategic plan, which, by the end of 2004, was still in its early stages. The organization now had an excellent framework for approaching its future. A draft of the ACTFL Strategic Plan, endorsed by the Executive Council, was presented to delegates during the annual meeting and received a very positive reaction regarding the direction ACTFL was taking. A new mission statement was supported strongly by the majority of delegates: *ACTFL: Providing vision, leadership, and support for quality teaching and learning of languages.* Strategic plan goals were presented; each was targeted with several specific action items that were concrete and measurable (*FLA*, Vol. 37, No. 4, p. 655).

In her "Message from the President-elect," Heining-Boynton laid out a plan for each month of

2005 on a designated monthly theme that would help highlight existing events in our schools and hometowns, as well as assist in initiating new ones:

January	Language Policy
February	International Engagement
March	Connecting Languages to Other Areas
April	Higher Education
May	Language Advocacy
June	Adult Learning and Language Usage
July	Languages and Communities
August	Parents
September	Heritage Languages
October	Early Language Learning
November	Celebrating Accomplishment and Looking Ahead
December	Culture

(*FLA*, Vol. 37, No. 4, p. 648)

The YOL would culminate at the 2005 annual meeting in Baltimore on November 18–20. The theme was *2005–2015: Realizing Our Vision of Languages for All*. To publicize the Year of Languages, a series of public service announcements for media were prepared (Fig. 7, p. 130).

It was announced that 2003 ACTFL President Marty Abbott had joined ACTFL's staff as Director of Education. In her new position she led the coordination of the *2005: The Year of Languages* initiative and handled various language education-related issues.

New Visions in Action called for nominations of programs of excellence for the NVIA project. The project task forces were gathering information about exemplary programs in curriculum and instruction, teacher recruitment and retention, teacher development, and research around the country. The information, when gathered, would be made accessible online to the profession and the public, with the goal to improve and strengthen language learning throughout the nation by making information about exemplary pre-K–16 programs easily available (*FLA*, Vol. 37, No. 4, p. 668).

At then end of 2004, Executive Director Lovejoy announced that ACTFL had over $1 million in the bank—a far cry from its past economic woes! The organization's auditing firm had praised Lovejoy's financial management and austerity in spending for its turnaround of the financial picture...what they called "truly amazing."

The year 2005 was truly the year of languages! ACTFL was moving forward with great energy. In his Executive Director's report at the May 2005 Executive Council meeting, Lovejoy reported on the organization's activities since November 2004, including:

- passage of House and Senate Resolutions on the Year of Languages;
- 55 proclamations passed by governors and other government officials to recognize 2005 as the Year of Languages;
- 9 ambassadors added to the Honorary Council;
- more than $140,000 raised to help defray the cost of the YOL activities;
- implementation of the Teacher of the Year process, with sponsorship by McDougal Littell;
- training of more than 100 OPI testers in the past year;
- expansion to 60 of the number of languages tested;
- receipt of a three-year $420,000 grant for assessment review and development;
- the new member recruitment campaign and a lapsed member recruitment campaign;
- development of a new flyer with ACTFL achievements to promote the organization to members and non- members;
- a member needs assessment survey;
- plans for a new magazine;

- more than 60 articles in various publications about the YOL;
- many interviews for radio and television coverage;
- creation of a new postcard marketing strategy for early notification of the convention, along with e-mail blasts
- opening of convention registration and hotel registrations four months earlier than ever before.

2005: The Year of Languages

The House of Representatives passed H. Res. 122 proclaiming 2005 as the Year of Languages throughout the U.S., a resolution sponsored by Rep. Rush Holt (D-NJ) and Rep. Patrick Tiberi (R-OH). The Senate version (S. Res. 28) was passed on February 17.

The momentum from the June 2004 National Language Conference came to fruition at the "National Language Policy Summit: An American Plan for Action" in January 2005, at which more than 35 leaders representing academic, business, government, and humanitarian organizations met to set priorities and establish a U.S. language policy plan of action for the upcoming decade. Also included in the summit were thousands of videoconference participants worldwide. This initiative continued with the "Blueprint for Action on Language Education," the next steps from the January summit, including:

- raising the American public's awareness of the need and value of learning languages and understanding cultures;
- establishing a National Language Advisor at the federal level;
- surveying businesses to identify their language and cultural needs;
- partnering with CEOs of corporations to advocate for the importance of language and culture;
- creating a fully articulated Chinese language

program for students from kindergarten through college and subsequently expanding this model to other languages;
- developing effective assessment strategies for measuring students' language learning;
- implementing a civilian language corps;
- advocating for expanded language legislation. (*FLA,* Vol. 38, No. 1, p. 142)

The "Member News" section of every 2005 issue of *FLA* was crammed with examples of YOL activities throughout the country, with photos of students, billboards, groups, and classrooms involved in celebrating. Also included were articles on meetings that involved stakeholders from all over the world. Negotiations were going on between ACTFL and the National Network for Early Language Learning (NNELL) for the inclusion of NNELL on the ACTFL Executive Council. A new NNELL award for outstanding support of early foreign language learning was created; the first award was granted at the November 2005 annual meeting in Baltimore.

The Executive Council was at work on the strategic plan. The Mission Statement had been approved in November 2004, the amended Vision Statement awaited approval, and then the Council would turn its attention to the action plans. It was also revising the organization's bylaws, with ACTFL Past President Ray T. Clifford serving as Bylaws Committee chair.

ACTFL's budget showed that the organization's financial condition was better than ever. Projections showed that the year would end with a larger budget surplus than expected, which would enable the association to take another step toward the Council-approved goal for an association reserve fund. In addition, there was a significant sum in the endowment fund that was designated for awards to assist new teachers and new members to attend the annual meeting.

President Heining-Boynton, in her "Message from the President" (*FLA*, Vol. 38, No. 2, p. 299), recognized the efforts of Executive Director Lovejoy and the ACTFL staff: "His energetic work and that of our headquarters staff still continue to make us a vibrant, fiscally sound, goal-oriented organization, providing vision, leadership, and support for quality teaching and learning of languages. ACTFL's goal is to serve you and the profession at large."

FLA was ranked the highest among language journals in a study that established a rank order of the most prestigious foreign language teaching journals, and was recognized as the most frequently cited journal (*FLA*, Vol. 38, No. 2, p. 301). Nevertheless, editor Emily Spinelli announced her resignation from her position to become Executive Director of the American Association of Teachers of Spanish and Portuguese (AATSP), so a search for a new editor was announced in *FLA* (Vol. 38, No. 3, p. 328). This issue also announced that ACTFL would launch *The Language Educator*, a new language professions journal, in January 2006.

In 2005, the Global Learning and Observations to Benefit the Environment (GLOBE) Program joined with ACTFL to promote content-based language study around the world. GLOBE is a cooperative effort of schools led by a Federal interagency program supported by NASA, NSF, and the U.S. State Department in partnership with colleges and universities, state and local school systems, and non-government organizations. Internationally, GLOBE is a partnership among the U.S. and more than 100 other nations (*FLA*, Vol. 38, No. 2, pp. 308-311).

The National Association of State Boards of Education (NASBE) directly addressed the issue of creating a framework to provide foreign language education to all students. The article, "Building an Infrastructure to Meet the Language Needs of All Children," was written by ACTFL President-elect Paul Sandrock and Shuhan Wang from the Delaware Department of Education and published in the March 2005 issue of NASBE's *State Education Standard*. The authors write:

Figure 8. Opening NASDAQ, including Audrey Heining-Boynton (center), 2005 ACTFL President, and Bret Lovejoy (right), ACTFL Executive Director.

As tools of communication and windows for intercultural understanding, languages should be a core component of the education of every child in the United States. Whether the argument is made on the basis of academic and cognitive benefits, economic value, national security or simply to understand neighbors, all students need to learn more than their native language. State boards of education (SBEs) and state education agencies (SEAs) can make this happen (FLA, Vol. 38, No. 3, p. 449).

Senators Christopher Dodd (D-CT) and Thad Cochran (R-MS), co-chairs of the 2005 Year of Languages Honorary Council, introduced the International and Foreign Studies Act of 2005, which called for changes in Title VI of the Higher Education Act, including significant increases in the bill's spending authorizations.

On August 29, as part of the YOL national celebration, ACTFL representatives opened the NASDAQ stock market and conducted a language "pop quiz" in Times Square, New York (Fig. 8).

Figure 9. ACTFL Teacher of the Year 2005, Ken Stewart (center), President Audrey Heining-Boynton (left) and Dave Pieklo, McDougal Littell Vice President for Marketing (right).

Finally, the Fall issue of *FLA* (Vol. 38, No. 3, p. 454) ran a policy statement from the National Council for Languages and International Studies (NCLIS) responding to and supporting the National Language Conference White Paper the federal government had officially issued a few months prior.

At the 2005 Baltimore Annual Meeting, ACTFL's sustained campaign, *Discover Languages,* was introduced. It would build on the momentum of *2005: The Year of Languages* to continue to heighten public awareness on the critical importance of language education and proficiency in the U.S. Ken Stewart from Chapel Hill High School, Chapel Hill, NC, was announced as the first ACTFL National Teacher of the Year (Fig. 9). Membership was now up to about 8,400.

At the final Executive Council meeting for 2005, the Council's name was changed to the Board of Directors, and the Steering Committee became the Executive Committee. At that meeting, Lovejoy said ACTFL had outgrown its office space, and new space would be sought over the next year.

As 2005 wound down, the Year of Languages had truly brought foreign language study to the forefront of education concerns. ACTFL had become a known entity and had certainly helped to spearhead numerous initiatives with its concern about and vested interest in the study of foreign languages.

The year 2006 would bring *The Language Educator*, which would serve educators of all languages at all levels as a single, comprehensive source of news and information. It would be published six times a year. *FLA*, under the editorship of its new editor, ACTFL Executive Council member Sheri Spaine Long, would undergo a redesign that would premiere with its Spring 2006 issue (Vol. 39, No. 1). The journal would also return to its former 6" x 9" size—more traditional for academic journals—and have a slightly different format for the articles. *Member News* would no longer appear in *FLA*, but would become a feature of the new color magazine, *The Language Educator*.

In the "President's Message" of Vol. 39, No. 1 of *FLA* for 2006, President Paul Sandrock (Wisconsin Department of Public Instruction, Madison) presented the newly formatted journal, which focused even more on the mission of presenting through scholarly articles the best current research on language teaching and learning. *The Language Educator,* however, emphasized applications in our classrooms and communities. It offered concise articles about teaching languages including lessons learned, news and events connected to our profession, conferences and workshops of interest, and advocacy and policy updates (p. 7).

In celebration of the 2005 YOL, ACTFL had designed materials for an ongoing sustained advocacy campaign under the theme *"Discover Languages! Discover the World!"* The profession had gained the expertise and courage to make the case for languages and was determined to keep the enthusiasm alive, because there was more to accomplish. February was designated *Discover Languages Month* annually.

The U.S. Senate had passed resolution S. 308 designating 2006 as the "Year of Study Abroad": "Study abroad programs not only open doors to foreign language learning, but empower students to better understand themselves and others through a comparison of cultural values and ways of life"(cited in *FLA,* Spring 2006, Vol. 39, No. 1, p. 7). The

Paul Sandrock
ACTFL President 2006

The Language Educator magazine began in 2006, serving educators of all languages at all levels as a single, comprehensive source of news and information. Also in 2006, *Foreign Language Annals'* redesign premiered in its Spring issue.

theme of the 40th Annual Meeting and Exposition, held in downtown Nashville on November 16-19, 2006, was *Discover the Future...Discover Languages*, a variation on the theme of the follow-up campaign to the 2005 YOL. Because of earlier promotion and sign-up dates for the meeting, as of May 17, 2006, registration had increased 192%, and registration revenue was up 53%. In mid-October, ACTFL membership was at 9,022.

Clearly 2006 was a busy, exciting time for languages, with much interest from the media, along with President George W. Bush's message of support for foreign language instruction on January 5, 2006. Bush launched the National Security Language Initiative (NSLI), a plan to bolster national security and prosperity in the 21st century through education, and through developing foreign language skills in particular. In February, he sent a message supporting ACTFL's

Discover Languages campaign and, in particular, the celebration of February as *Discover Languages* month.

ACTFL was internally busy. The organization's bylaws were studied very closely and revised, led by Ray T. Clifford, Past President of ACTFL, who brought a fresh perspective to the task. Furthermore, the organization was outgrowing its office and exploring the purchase of a building or office condo. The creation of the national Foreign Language Teacher of the Year Award was endorsed by several Senators and Congressmen through press releases.

FLA's new editor, Sheri Spaine Long, and staff were examining web-based manuscript systems to streamline the submission and review process. This was announced in *The Language Educator (TLE)* (Vol. 1, Issue 6, p. 6) and *FLA* (Vol. 39, No. 4, p. 544). *TLE* was launched in January 2006

(Vol. 1, No. 1) under Sandy Cutshall's editorship and was widely accepted and read. In his "President's Message," Sandrock said, "*The Language Educator* is building on the long tradition for which ACTFL has always been known, namely the high quality of its publications, while also breaking new ground" (p. 7).

TLE's inaugural issue included the "Member Needs Assessment Survey Results" (Vol. 1, Issue 1, January 2006, pp. 24–25), discussing the 2005 survey findings. Interestingly, the most frequently identified issue facing the foreign language teaching profession was "the lack of perceived value by the public in general, and the government in particular, of learning foreign languages" (p. 24). The *2005: The Year of Languages* initiative had been a good start, but more effort was needed, in part because the No Child Left Behind (NCLB) Act lacked a foreign language measurement component .

In response to these concerns, ACTFL introduced the ACTFL Career Center to provide an easy, convenient meeting place for language educators seeking to enhance their careers and employers wishing to connect with the best in the profession. It was free to ACTFL members.

Another new development was the Integrated Performance Assessment (IPA), a prototype for assessing the progress language students make in achieving the K–16 standards and developing their language proficiency. This cluster assessment featured three tasks, each reflecting one of the three modes of communication, as outlined in the ACTFL *Performance Guidelines for K–12 Learners* (1998) and the *Standards for Foreign Language Learning in the 21st Century* (National Standards for Foreign Language Education Project, 1999) (*TLE*, Vol. 1, Issue 4, p. 38). In addition, a third revised edition of the national standards appeared in 2006, now including Arabic standards to offer standards for ten languages.

The National Assessment Summit of April 2005 kicked off action on an assessment literacy initiative to understand the key markers for moving from one proficiency level to the next; effective ways to evaluate students' skills in interpreting, presenting and exchanging information, ideas, and opinions; and analyzing provided information about student progress through the numerous forms of assessment available. ACTFL had received a U.S. Department of Education grant to develop the ACTFL Assessment of Performance and Proficiency of Languages (AAPPL) (*FLA*, Vol. 39, No. 3, p. 357).

The year 2006 ended positively. Although conference attendance was slightly down for ACTFL's 40th anniversary celebration in Nashville, the organization was on solid financial footing, and membership was over 9,000. An office was being purchased in a different building in Alexandria, with funds coming from the Scebold Building Fund. Executive Director Lovejoy recommended a plaque honoring Ed Scebold for the new office. Ray T. Clifford, President of ACTFL in 1993, was elected President for 2008. The second Teacher of the Year was announced at the Nashville meeting: Christine Lanphere from Natomas High School, Sacramento.

ACTFL President for 2007 Rita Oleksak (Springfield, MA, public schools) invited everyone to join her "as we continue the journey of discovery and celebrate the power of language" (*TLE*, Vol. 2, Issue 1, January 2007, p. 7). On January 26, 2007, President Bush voiced his support for the *Discover Languages Month* initiative:

Rita Oleksak
ACTFL President 2007

Effective communication can help build a world that lives in liberty, trades in freedom, and grows in prosperity. By studying languages, Americans can demonstrate a compassionate interest in the lives of others, learn about different cultures, and gain a better understanding of the world. Learning other languages will also help our troops, intelligence personnel, and diplomats communicate as they work to make our nation more secure. Discover Languages Month is an opportunity to celebrate the benefits of learning other languages and to promote cultural awareness throughout our country.... I appreciate those observing Discover Languages Month, and I am grateful for the teachers, administrators, and other dedicated professionals who promote language learning. Your efforts help enhance the ties between nations and build a brighter future for people everywhere. (TLE, Vol. 2, Issue 2, February 2007, p. 10)

In late January, President Oleksak represented ACTFL on Capitol Hill to testify before the Senate Subcommittee on Oversight of Government Management, the Federal Workforce, and the District of Columbia. She testified that American national security and economic vitality were now closely tied to our foreign language capability. She stressed the need for a comprehensive, coordinated plan to expand and strengthen school-based foreign language education in the U.S. The message to the subcommittee was clear: The goals of achieving a language-trained military and language-qualified personnel in embassies around the world will fail unless strong support is provided to our nation's K–20 foreign language education infrastructure. In her testimony, President Oleksak, representing ACTFL, proposed:

We must work to ensure that all languages are supported in our educational system, not just the languages deemed critical for today. Since research *supports the notion that after learning a second language, the third and fourth languages come more easily, it is important to support any language that a school system considers important for its community and for which teachers are available. (FLA, Vol. 40, No. 1, p. 5)*

ACTFL offered ten recommendations:

1. Ensure that all languages are supported, not just those deemed critical to the government.
2. Support articulated sequences of languages beginning in the earliest grades and continuing through the postsecondary level.
3. Include funding for the development of a consistent program of assessments.
4. Make foreign language truly a part of a core curriculum in every school.
5. Provide assistance to community colleges and universities offering specialized foreign language instruction focused on combining language instruction with other majors.
6. Provide incentives to enhance teacher recruitment and retention and ensure teacher quality through the teacher education and certification process.
7. Require intensive training for teachers recruited from abroad to work in American schools and provide professional development for incorporating standards-based teaching into the curriculum.
8. Develop and encourage the skills of our heritage language speakers.
9. Fund research into a wide range of areas.
10. Provide funding for public education initiatives such as the *Discover Languages...Discover the World* campaign.
(*TLE*, Vol. 2, Issue 3, April 2007, p. 7)

FLA editor Sheri Spaine Long announced three forthcoming special topics focus issues for three years:

Figure 10. (left) ACTFL Headquarters since September 2007 (1001 North Fairfax Street, Suite 200, Alexandria, VA 22314). (center) ACTFL Headquarters in New York, from July 2007–2013 (3 Barker Avenue, Suite 300, White Plains, NY 10601); (right) ACTFL Headquarters in New York (445 Hamilton Avenue, Suite 1104, White Plains, NY 10601), from 2013 to the present.

- 2009: Language Learning and Disabilities, Anxiety, and Special Needs
- 2010: Language Learning and Study Abroad
- 2011: Language Learning and the Standards

Long also said *FLA*'s shift to web-based management was overwhelming: manuscripts were being received from around the world (*FLA*, Vol. 40, No. 1, p. 7).

At their May 2007 meeting, the Board of Directors began to discuss aligning Linguafolio (based on the European portfolio program) with ACTFL's own professional guidelines in a way that could relate to students at different levels and integrate into ACTFL's framework. The checklist evaluation was described as a classroom-based assessment to benchmark where students werew in their language study and where they wanted to go, thus enabling them to take charge of their own learning. This assessment was not intended as a proficiency evaluation, since proficiency must have three separate components: (1) a situation or context, (2) a task, and (3) an expectation for accuracy.

STARTALK, an undertaking of the National Foreign Language Center (NFLC), began at the University of Maryland in the summer of 2007. This first year saw the initial planning phase of a multi-year project of the National Security Language Initiative (NSLI), a multi-agency effort to expand foreign language education, particularly in undertaught critical languages. That project provided funding for programs to offer Arabic and Chinese language study for 400 high school students and professional development opportunities for 400 teachers of Arabic and Chinese (*TLE,* Vol. 2, Issue 1, January 2007, p. 24).

The push for foreign language study recognition in core curricula was reflected in two additional moves in 2007: Russian President Vladimir Putin declared 2007 the Year of the Russian Language in Russia and abroad, and the United Nations named 2008 the International Year of Languages. In fact, U.S. Secretary of Education Margaret Spellings released a statement on International Education Week 2007, a joint initiative of the U.S. Department of Education and the U.S. Department of State, on the theme of *International Education: Fostering Global Citizenship and Respect.*

In the October 2007 issue of *TLE* (Vol. 2, Issue 5, p. 7), President Oleksak announced that more than 50 new Foreign Language Assistance Program (FLAP) grants had been awarded and that many districts were implementing new programs and expanding existing programs to younger audiences, often in less commonly taught languages. The annual meeting took place November 16–18 in San Antonio and was one of the largest in ACTFL history. More than 6,700 attendees took part in over 600 sessions, special events and meetings. By the time of the November Annual Meeting, ACTFL membership had climbed above 10,400! Janet Glass of Dwight-Englewood School in Englewood, NJ, received the 2008 ACTFL National Language Teacher of the Year Award.

ACTFL was again on the move. The New York office moved from Yonkers to larger space with LTI in White Plains in July, and the organization's headquarters moved into new office space at 1001 North Fairfax Street, Suite 200, in Alexandria in September (Fig. 10, p. 138).

In her final "President's Message" (*TLE*, Vol. 2, Issue 6, November 2007, p. 7), Oleksak said the overarching theme that surfaced since her January testimony before the Senate Subcommittee was collaboration, citing several ACTFL initiatives in 2007:

- with CLASS to offer the STARTALK program in Chinese;
- with NCSSFL and NADSFL to jointly plan the Assembly of Delegates, at which more than 150 state and local leaders discussed issues relevant to the profession;
- with JNCL-NCLIS, regarding issues at the national level.

She also said the most significant discussion was on assessment literacy. Building on the New Visions in Action 2005 Assessment Summit and the 2006 assessment plenary, another summit took place in November 2007, at which "Building a Framework for National Assessment Literacy" was discussed.

At its 2007 Annual Meeting in San Antonio, the Board of Directors made a number of decisions that would impact ACTFL's programs and policies:

- The formal dedication of the new headquarters would take place May 2, 2008, in Alexandria.
- For the 2007–2008 academic year, ACTFL would pilot a Mentoring Program designed to help early career language educators succeed in their current assignments and gain the skills needed for long-term success in the profession.
- The audit firm reported that the association was in excellent financial health and was operated in a fiscally responsible, cost-efficient manner.

Ray Clifford, now from Brigham Young University in Provo, UT, sounded a positive note of encouragement when, in his first "President's Message" in *TLE* (Vol. 3, Issue 1, January 2008, p. 7), he said "This is clearly an auspicious time for second language learning! As evidence of globalization becomes increasingly visible in our daily lives, the historically isolationist attitudes of the U.S. public appear to be changing." He added that, whether the topic was national security or economic competitiveness, the world

Ray T. Clifford
ACTFL President 2008

Figure 11. Past Presidents at the May 2, 2008, dedication of ACTFL Headquarters: (front row, from L to R) Emily Spinelli, Helene Zimmer-Loew, Liz Hoffman, Ann Tollefson, Christy Brown, Marty Abbott, Rita Oleksak, Paul García, Dale Lange, Ray Clifford; (back row, from L to R) Kathy Riordan, Leo Benardo, Helen Warriner-Burke, Lynn Sandstedt, Keith Cothrun, Bob Terry, Paul Sandrock.

was clearly becoming smaller. He then cited results of several recent studies that indicated a lack of knowledge about foreign cultures and foreign languages that threatened the security of the U.S., as well as its ability to compete in the global marketplace and produce an informed citizenry.

Following up on the assessment plenary session and ensuing discussions of 2007, Clifford informed ACTFL membership that the results of ACTFL's Assessment for the Performance and Proficiency of Languages (AAPPL) survey would soon be published, describing a national PK–16 assessment model for language education (*TLE,* Vol. 3, Issue 2, February 2008, p. 7).

The May 2, 2008 dedication of ACTFL's new home was attended by 17 of the organization's past presidents (Fig. 11), 10 ACTFL charter members, and more than 120 visiting dignitaries. Clifford said in his "President's Message" (*TLE,* Vol. 3, Issue 4, August 2008, p. 7):

With the purchase of its own office, ACTFL has reached a significant milestone of organizational stability and professional maturity, and we are now even better positioned to accomplish our mission of 'Providing vision, leadership and support for quality teaching and learning of languages'…. Over the years, Ed [Scebold] often mentioned his dream, his goal, his aspiration of having a permanent home for ACTFL headquarters. After his death, two memorial funds were established: one for professional development and the other for a building fund. Both of these initiatives were at the heart of Ed's dreams for ACTFL...[and] the vision for a permanent ACTFL-owned office has been shared by the ACTFL leadership since Ed's death.

Clifford then unveiled a special plaque dedicated to Scebold that would occupy a place of honor in the new headquarters building.

The perspectives of some of ACTFL's founding members, "In the Words of Our Founders," presented "those pillars of the language learning community who joined the newly formed American Council on the Teaching of Foreign Languages back in 1967," as they discussed their views of the language profession and gave their advice as we looked toward the future in 2008. Those luminaries include Leo Benardo, F. André Paquette, Lynn Sandstedt, and Helen Warriner-Burke (*The Language Educator*, Vol. 3, Issue 4, August 2008, pp. 30–33).

Clifford also reported another less auspicious but nonetheless significant initiative that would add to the association's status as a professional organization launched in 2007: an ACTFL Statement of Professional Responsibility was being drafted and revised after it had been shared with various stakeholders, especially the Assembly of Delegates.

At the end of June 2008, the International Research and Studies (IRS) grant competition results were announced. ACTFL was awarded a three-year grant for its program "A Decade of Foreign Language Standards: Influence, Impact and Future Directions." The national foreign language standards had evolved considerably from their original 1996 document to their 2000 document (*Standards for Foreign Language Learning in the 21st Century*), which now included language-specific standards for Chinese, Classical Languages, French, German, Italian, Japanese, Portuguese, Russian, and Spanish, to their third edition (2006), which contained standards for learning Arabic.

ACTFL's initiatives to ensure proper training for foreign language teachers continued. The ACTFL Mentoring Program was made permanent in May 2008. In collaboration with Weber State University, Ogden, UT, the organization developed an online teaching methods course that reflected current research and best practices in foreign language education. Organized around the national standards, the course taught students about current theoretical bases for second language acquisition.

ACTFL's publications were proving successful as well. Now that it was a recognized international foreign language journal, *FLA* published a much-needed position statement on co-authorship, since universities often did not accept co-authored articles for consideration for promotion and tenure (*FLA*, Vol. 41, No. 3, 400). Its Fall 2008 issue announced a search for a new *FLA* editor, whose term would begin in July 2009. *TLE* was increasing in popularity as it offered its readers a wealth of practical information for the classroom, consistent updates in legislative matters affecting foreign languages, and discussions on a variety of topics: heritage language speakers, advocacy, less commonly taught languages, technology.

On November 7, 2008, the National Board for Professional Teaching Standards (NBPTS) Board of Directors accepted newly revised world language instruction standards.

The ACTFL 2008 Annual Convention and World Languages Expo took place in Orlando on November 21–23. Its theme was *Opening Minds to the World through Languages*. More than 5,600 guests attended more than 500 sessions, meetings, and special events, as well as two ACTFL-sponsored special feature sessions, one focusing on what research showed about language teaching and learning, the other exploring assessment challenges and solutions. Toni Theisen, a French teacher from Loveland High School in Loveland, CO, was announced as the 2009 ACTFL National Language Teacher of the Year.

Janine Erickson
ACTFL President 2009

The year 2009 welcomed a new President of the U.S., Barack Obama, who promised change that would impact education across the country. In December 2008, Obama's transition team contacted ACTFL for information about foreign language priorities and initiatives for the incoming administration. With the January appointment of Arne Duncan as the U.S. Secretary of Education, the impact became more evident; Duncan had been a strong advocate of foreign language programs in the Chicago public schools. When President Obama posted his administration's education agenda on the White House website, however, it did not mention language education specifically. ACTFL responded by sending a message to both Obama and Duncan, reminding them of the importance of language education (*TLE*, Vol. 4, Issue 3, April 2009, p. 55).

This same year welcomed Janine Erickson, a 23-year teacher of Spanish at Horizon High School in Thornton, CO, as the 2009 ACTFL President. Erickson's goal was: "Every educational conversation in the nation embraces foreign language as a necessary component in the learning journey of all students" (*TLE*, Vol. 4, Issue 1, January 2009, p. 7).

ACTFL continued to grow. By January, its membership had climbed to over 12,000 (a 14% increase over 2007), the number of SIGs had increased—adding one for Arabic language educators and another for heritage languages—and the organization's website had been upgraded and improved.

In the fall of 2008, ACTFL had mailed a survey to high-school foreign language teachers across the nation and asked them to share the survey with their students. Results from 126,444 students and 2,208 teachers were collected. The 2009 report on this survey revealed that foreign language teachers believed that learning to effectively integrate technology into their classroom instruction was their most pressing professional need. Interestingly, teachers believed that their students were taking foreign language courses for college entrance and high-school graduation requirements, but students reported that they were also seeking to understand the language and its culture by taking these courses (*TLE,* Vol. 4, Issue 2, February 2009, p. 20).

The spring issue of *FLA*, co-edited by Dolly Jesusita Young and Richard Sparks, focused on language learning and disabilities, anxiety, and special needs. The April 2009 issue of *TLE* (Vol. 4, Issue 3, p. 19) announced that *FLA* was being published by Wiley-Blackwell, one of the world's foremost academic and professional publishers.

The 2009 Annual Convention and World Languages Expo was announced for November 20–22 in San Diego, with the theme *Speaking Up for Languages…The Power of Many Voices*. In her "President's Message" in *TLE* (Vol. 4, Issue 4, August 2009, p. 7), President Erickson said that ACTFL was working on two position statements—the *Statement of Professional Responsibility*, and a statement on the use of the target language in the classroom—for presentation to the Assembly of Delegates in 2009.

The August 2009 issue of *TLE* announced the new Editor of *FLA*: Leslie L. Schrier from the University of Iowa. Former Editor Long had completed a three-year contract and was moving to the editorship of *Hispania*, the official publication of the AATSP.

The year 2009 marked the 50th anniversary of Title VI, part of the National Defense Education Act (NDEA) signed into law by President Eisenhower in September, 1958. Title VI, called "Language Development," authorized centers, fellowships, research and studies, and language institutes. The new law aimed to ensure "trained expertise of sufficient quality and quantity to meet U.S. national security needs" (*TLE*, Vol. 4, Issue 4, August 2009, pp. 40–45).

President Erickson mentioned that technology had taken a front-row seat in ACTFL's activities and products. The organization's electronic information and communication technologies were aimed at informing members of professional development opportunities and ongoing advocacy efforts that promote quality foreign language education programs. New services had been added in 2009, including:

- Ava, the avatar who would lead people through the ACTFL Oral Proficiency Interview by Computer (OPIc©). This online test was available in Arabic, Chinese, Korean, Persian Farsi, French, Russian, and Bengali.
- ACTFL's news alert, *SmartBrief*, which became available to members in November, pulling together news stories of interest to language educators.
- ACTFL's presence on Facebook and LinkedIn, and the organization's own social network, the ACTFL Online Community, which was unveiled at the San Diego meeting.
- The availability of *The Language Educator* not only in print, but also as a virtual issue on the ACTFL website.
- ACTFL's *Talk Radio—Promoting Quality Language Education*, an Internet-based free radio show that gave members the opportunity to share their voices with the world and reach out to the profession. (*TLE*, Vol. 4, Issue 6, November 2009, p. 7).

The 2009 annual meeting in San Diego was very successful, despite the financial difficulties that threatened some language programs. Almost 6,000 attendees participated in the 700+ sessions and events. Two intertwined ideas in the conference theme, *Speaking Up for Languages: The Power of Many Voices*, were repeated throughout the convention: the importance of language

advocacy at that time more than ever, and the need for increasing and improving the connections made among the community of language educators (*TLE*, Vol. 5, Issue 1, January 2010, p. 32). The 2011 ACTFL National Language Teacher of the Year was Lisa Lilley, a Spanish teacher in the International Baccalaureate Program at Central High School, Springfield, MO.

Back in May 2007, the Modern Language Association had published a report of its Ad Hoc Committee on Foreign Languages, *Foreign Languages and Higher Education: New Structures for a Changed World* (New York: The Modern Language Association of America, retrieved from http://www.mla.org/flreport). This report was truly eye-opening: the MLA was supporting "a broad, intellectually driven approach to teaching language and culture in higher education…. The usefulness of studying languages other than English is no longer contested. The goals and means of language study, however, continue to be hotly debated" (pp. 1 & 2). The ACTFL Board of Directors was discussing whether the organization should publish a statement that would address the MLA report and give its own position on this ongoing debate of language vs. literature, humanists vs. language specialists, and the goals of foreign language study. The MLA report hoped to convince humanists that new models of language study had to be devised— and that meant change. National standards entered into the discussion, particularly strongly in *Principles and Practices of the* Standards *in College Foreign Language Education* (Virginia Scott, Ed. [2009], in *Issues in Language Program Direction*, AAUSC 2009. Carl S. Blythe, Ed. Boston: Heinle Cengage Learning). ACTFL was perfectly poised to lead this discussion.

At the close of the new millennium's first decade, ACTFL was in a very strong position both fiscally and professionally. It had its own office in a strategic location, a dynamic Executive Director and staff, a hard-working Board of Directors, its largest membership ever, and incredible momentum moving forward.

NEW VISIONS 2000

Below are selected summary highlights of the status of the New Visions effort as of the end of 2000, in terms of the main areas targeted for study and action. Priorities and action items shown are highlights only and do not represent an exhaustive description of the work being undertaken. Work on this major effort is continuing.

ARCHITECTURE OF THE PROFESSION

Subcommittees:
- Curriculum, Instruction, Articulation and Assessment
- Research
- Teacher Development
- Teacher Recruitment

Essential Question:

How can we, as members of the Foreign Language Profession, organize in the most efficient and effective way to accomplish the goals of the New Visions project in the 21st Century?
- Phase 1: What could we do? June 1999: (Aberdeen, Georgia)
- Phase 2: What should we do? June 2000: (Leesburg, Virginia)
- Phase 3: What will we do and who will do it? (Ongoing)

Architecture Subgroups:

National Agenda
- Develop mission statement
- Complete press release
- Solicit statements from presidential candidates
- Guidelines for talking about K-12 Foreign Language issues with national, state, and local candidates

Collaborations and Structures
- Develop survey for all language associations to deter mine a set of profiles of what these associations offer to their members

Technology
- Explore infrastructure of the profession in terms of connections and duplication of services
- Develop policy for integration of technology into language instruction and delivery

methods
- Connect language instruction with "real world" use of languages in business, industry, and government

CURRICULUM, INSTRUCTION, ARTICULATION AND ASSESSMENT

- Effectively link curriculum assessment and instruction to develop a seamless articulation in a pre K-16 sequence of language learning
- Identify, collect, evaluate and disseminate models of effective instruction that reflect both an articulated Pre-K-16+ sequence and sequences that consider multiple entry points
- Strategic direction: Redefine existing instructional levels in terms of performance
- Integrate language and culture content in meaningful contexts that are task-based
- Provide effective strategies and instructional models for diverse student learners
- Delivery of instruction-establish criteria for selection of effective instructional materials and resources
- Seek out and gather standards-based assessment models at various levels
- Establish a bridge (vertical and horizontal) between academic levels Pre-K-16+
- Support research on optimal learning and teaching environments
- Identify alternative actions
- Identify immediate priorities

TEACHER DEVELOPMENT

Mentoring
- Bibliography of articles and books
- List of successful mentoring programs

Professional Development
- Letter and survey to institutions of higher learning about oral proficiency guidelines

National Foreign Language Education Model Group
- Letter and survey regarding foreign language methods courses
- Survey of teacher education courses in the United States

Diverse Learners
- Knowledge bases for teaching a foreign language to diverse learners
- Rationale for the work of the diverse learners program
- Diverse learners working definition and best practices

TEACHER RECRUITMENT AND RETENTION

National Agenda
- Establish a collaborative, develop alliances, participate in related organizations

Retention
- Develop models for mentoring, support teacher compensation, seek other incentives

Alternate Certification
- Recruit those who possess the language and/or pedagogical training from other fields, establish and disseminate "best practices" model programs, maintain connections with New Visions Teacher Development initiatives

Incentives
- Recommend to schools, universities, and industries financial benefits; career opportunities; family assistance and educational opportunities
- Establish a clearinghouse to link district/State/ACTFL incentives
- Identify alternate funding sources Public relations
- Identify target audiences and messages relating to the value of FL learning
- Collaborate in joint ventures
- Organize publicity using prominent figures, etc., in conjunction with other New Visions initiatives

Redefine the Candidate Pool
- Include heritage speakers, native speakers from abroad, "early and late start" students, retired teachers, college apprentices, parents and paraprofessionals, bilingual teachers, Teach-for-America Clubs

K-16+ Collaboration
- Develop a "re-entry" volunteer program for returning study-abroad students
- Link high school students to elementary/middle school students

- Encourage retired and veteran teachers to mentor new teachers and interns
- Collaborate with Future Educators of America and others

Other Actions
- Minority hiring
- Continuing advocacy
- Programs to link with universities abroad
- Recruitment and initial training abroad
- Broadened definition of diversity to include race and gender

RESEARCH
National Research Agenda
- Gather database of what has been done
- Examine essential questions
- Prepare researchers to address issues
- Describe characteristics of a variety of paradigms
- Identify funding sources
- Communicate results

Expanded Vision of Research
- Develop program for all levels of educators
- Encourage collaborative projects/models
- Solicit questions from stakeholders
- Promote the value of a variety of approaches

National Clearing House for Foreign/Second Language Research
- Develop searchable dataset of research materials
- Encourage use of dataset within and beyond the profession
- Conduct surveys to find gaps
- Identify active researchers for a network

Collaboration in Research
- Create a mentoring system
- Establish incentives for interdisciplinary research
- Provide inservice opportunities
- Revisit academic alliances
- Investigate collaboration via technologies
- Create a research culture among undergraduates
- Disseminate results
- Pursue funding sources

Improve Dissemination of Access
- Create a community of inquiry
- Disseminate to wider audiences
- Make research accessible for foreign language educators at all levels
- Integrate research into professional development

from *FLA*, Vol. 34, No. 1, pp. 65, 76-78.

C. EDWARD SCEBOLD
NOVEMBER 21, 1939 – SEPTEMBER 16, 2001

IN MEMORIAM

C. Edward Scebold
1939-2001

C. Edward Scebold, Executive Director of the American Council on the Teaching of Foreign Languages for more than 30 years, died Sunday, September 16, 2001, at Sloan-Kettering Memorial Hospital in Manhattan. He was 61 years old.

A tireless advocate for language education at the national level, Mr. Scebold spearheaded the effort to shift the focus of language instruction in this country towards the development of proficiency. The ACTFL Proficiency Guidelines, a modification of the federal government's language scale, have become the recognized standard for measuring language abilities in the nation's academic and corporate sectors. Under his leadership, ACTFL formed a coalition with other language organizations to develop the National Standards for Foreign Language Education, a project funded under the Goals 2000 initiative. The standards have been widely accepted and implemented in almost every state. His service to the profession includes fifteen years in a variety of capacities on the Board of Directors of the Joint National Committee for Languages in Washington, DC, an organization he helped found, and as a representative to the Interagency Language Roundtable, a network of federal agencies responsible for ensuring that government and military services have the foreign language expertise necessary to support national interests.

When Mr. Scebold assumed leadership of ACTFL in 1970, the organization was three years old with several hundred members. Today, its membership numbers more than 8000 teachers of all languages, kindergarten through postsecondary, as well as government and business language educators. Its annual convention attracts more than 6500 attendees from across the nation and around the world.

Raised on his family's farm in Missouri Valley, IA, Mr. Scebold began his career in foreign language education as a junior high school Spanish teacher in Shawnee Mission, KS. He served as state foreign language consultant in the Nebraska Department of Education prior to coming to ACTFL as Executive Secretary in 1970. He was only the second person to hold that position, which was changed to Executive Director in 1977.

He is survived by his wife, Jamie; parents, Robert and Fern; a son, Brian, and daughter, Brenda Thompson, from his marriage to the former Janet Minnear, and daughter, Alexandra, from his marriage to the former JoAnn Tamaiuolo. He also leaves a brother, Richard; sister, Eleanor Buerstetta; and one grandson.

from *FLA*, November/December 2001 (Vol. 34, No. 6, pp. 609–611)

TRIBUTES TO C. EDWARD SCEBOLD

Leo Benardo,
ACTFL President, 1969

The three decades during which Ed Scebold served as Executive Director were the most productive and exciting in ACTFL's history. Ed spearheaded the move to develop oral proficiency tests, the planning and execution of a vast number of training workshops throughout the country and, more recently, the national standards for language instruction.

As President-Elect of ACTFL in 1968, I served with Kenneth Mildenberger of the MLA on the committee to select the successor to Andy Paquette, the larger-than-life and prodigiously-talented first Executive Director. Our choice was Ed, a young, soft-spoken but vigorous, high school teacher of Spanish from Nebraska. We hoped for the best but privately wondered if anybody could really fill Paquette's shoes.

History has proven that we had selected wisely. In his unique, quiet, unassuming way, Ed not only got the job done but, in the process, smoothed the ruffled feathers of a particularly fractious profession. Ed preferred to let others receive the applause, never sought the spotlight even at a time when celebrity was so sought after, and never demanded credit for his obvious achievements.

One had to like Ed, a kind man of uncommon sensitivity. He quickly rose from employee to colleague to friend. I yield to no-one in my admiration for him, and we shall all miss him.

❖

Dale L. Lange,
ACTFL President, 1980

In June, 1970, I was in New York for a meeting at ACTFL's then home at the Modern Language Association. Here for the first time, I met C. Edward Scebold or Ed, as he wanted to be called. He had just become ACTFL's Executive Secretary. We began collaboration on the Annual Bibliography and the Foreign Language Education Series. It was the beginning of a collegial relationship and 31-year friendship.

As a colleague, Ed's major concerns were always for ACTFL and for the Foreign Language Education Profession. One instance where these two interests came together was in 1981. We were representing ACTFL at a meeting at Georgetown University. The question was asked, "Which of the represented organizations is willing to take on the development of the oral interview in post-secondary education?" Ed asked for a recess. Outside, we walked sidewalks, recognizing the importance of the answer to the question for both ACTFL and the profession. Both have benefited from Ed's call.

How can I honor a best friend? He was best man at my wedding in 1981. We had long professional and personal conversations on the phone until he was too sick. We enjoyed each other's company enormously. And, we thought alike on many issues. In fact, a person said to us once, "You guys act just like brothers; if one of you doesn't think of something, the other one will!"

I write this tribute to honor a valuable colleague, a consummate professional, and a precious friend. Ed, I will miss you always!

❖

Kathleen M. Riordan,
ACTFL President, 1995

ACTFL and Ed Scebold: impossible to separate when Ed lived among us. It is difficult to do so now as we celebrate and honor Ed's life and his contributions to ACTFL and foreign language education.

As a member of the Executive Council and as President, I was impressed on a daily basis by Ed's work ethic, his energy, and his selfless commitment to his role as ACTFL's Executive Director. He did it all. He was the visionary and the big idea person. He was just as comfortable and willing to roll up his sleeves for the less glamorous and usually unnoticed tasks. He understood that leaders must be ready and willing to do it all.

Ed never placed himself in the forefront for ACTFL projects or accolades. He always put others in the limelight, on the stage, or before the cameras. He never sought the credit or praise.

Even as Ed often sacrificed his personal agenda for his work, he cared about foreign language professionals as persons. He cared deeply about us, and our families. I will always remember his many acts of kindness to my mother.

I miss Ed. I miss his sense of humor, his intelligence, his wit, and his ability to focus on the important issues in foreign language education. I know that I learned from working with him. I value having known Ed as a colleague and as a friend.

❖

Lynn A. Sandstedt,
ACTFL President, 1991

From the early 70's to the present, Ed Scebold successfully lead ACTFL from its fragile beginnings to become the vital and dynamic force that it is today. From the outset Ed was committed to carrying out the mission and goals of the organization and dedicated most of his professional life to helping improve Foreign Language Education throughout the country. He was deeply concerned not only about the status of foreign language teaching, but also about the welfare of teachers engaged in this endeavor.

Ed played a major role in introducing language proficiency and oral proficiency testing to the profession in the 80's which resulted in a significant change in classroom teaching practices and assessments.

His approach to the development of the Foreign Language Student Standards was exemplary in that he insisted upon having representatives from the various language associations be included on the task force which would be responsible for the development of the generic standards document. That task accomplished, he led in the formation of the Foreign Language Collaborative that subsequently wrote the language specific standards document.

Proficiency and the Student Standards more than any other recent developments have made the greatest impact on the improvement of foreign language education over the past several years. Through Ed's efforts ACTFL and the FL Collaborative are presently engaged in helping to write the Accomplished Teacher Standards of the NBPTS, the Entry Level Teacher Standards of INTASC and the Teacher Education Program Standards of NCATE. Ed has also expanded ACTFL's Professional Development programs to meet the needs of teachers currently in the field who need to be aware of current trends in FL teaching.

Ed was an articulate and effective spokesperson for the profession at the state, regional and national levels whether he was speaking to teachers, administrators or congressmen in Washington, D.C.. Over the years Ed became a highly valued and respected leader and colleague, but more importantly he was a caring and loyal friend. Ed will be greatly missed not only as the concerned individual that he was, but also as a role model of those in the field who are in a position of leadership. Ed's positive influence on the profession will be felt for many years to come.

❖

Helene Zimmer-Loew,
ACTFL President, 1984

My earliest memory of Ed was when he approached me after a session I presented on the teaching of culture at a New York State Association of Foreign Language Teachers meeting in 1972. He gave me his card and asked that I write up my presentation for publication in *Accent on ACTFL*. As a high school teacher, I had never given a thought to publishing what I did in the classroom until he encouraged me to do so. I still have the copy! This was Ed's way—to get the best ever so gently from those around him. His ready smile, his warm sense of humor, and his deep caring for others were characteristics we'll all remember and treasure. His ability to speak clearly, calmly, and cogently to any audience on almost any topic was also one of Ed's great strengths. He represented us well wherever he was.

Working closely with Ed as an ACTFL Executive Council member and President and then as a fellow Executive Director in the National Foreign Language Standards Collaborative and JNCL/NCLIS, I learned what a great and dedicated professional he was and how much he contributed to the progress we have made as a discipline nationally and internationally. What he accomplished will continue to inspire those of us who will carry on after him. ♦

ACTFL EXECUTIVE DIRECTOR JOB POSTING/DESCRIPTION

Executive Director

American Council on the Teaching of Foreign Languages

The American Council on the Teaching of Foreign Languages invites applications and nominations for its Executive Director. ACTFL, an 8,000-member organization located north of New York City in Yonkers, is dedicated to promoting and enhancing the study of languages and cultures in educational institutions at all levels.

Responsibilities of the Executive Director:
- Promote the interests of ACTFL at the national level; interpret the mission to the membership, public, and potential funders
- Provide leadership in the development and implementation of ACTFL professional services programs
- Manage a professional/administrative staff of 15
- Create and manage a budget of approximately 3 million dollars, consisting of hard and soft monies
- Negotiate and execute contracts for facilities, conferences, and technical support
- Report to an Executive Council elected by the membership

Qualifications
- Masters degree required/doctorate preferred in field related to languages, international studies, or education
- Total of 8 years combined experience in foreign language teaching, research, or administration and association, non-profit, education, governmental, or business management
- Demonstrated ability to work collaboratively with constituents, executive council, staff, professional organizations, and government entities
- Successful record of pursuing and managing grant and development activities
- Ability to create and implement projects/initiatives/policies important to the foreign language profession
- Demonstrated commitment to the role of languages and cultures in a diverse U.S. education system

Nominations and applications should be submitted to Search Committee, ACTFL Headquarters, 6 Executive Plaza, Yonkers, New York 10701-6801. Applicants should include a detailed letter describing their experience and qualifications as they relate to the position, a current Curriculum Vitae, and names and contact information for three professional references. All applications will be acknowledged and held in the strictest confidence. Review of applications will begin December 1, 2001 and continue until the position is filled. Starting date negotiable but available Spring 2002. ACTFL offers a competitive salary and benefits package. ACTFL is an equal opportunity employer. For further information about the organization, consult www.actfl.org.

TEN RECOMMENDATIONS FROM THE NASBE STUDY

The Study Group on the Lost Curriculum formulated ten (10) recommendations for state policymakers to ensure that the arts and foreign languages are not lost, and, above all, to position both as integral parts of the core curriculum.

1. Adopt high-quality licensure requirements for staff in the arts and foreign languages that are aligned with student standards in these subject areas.
2. Ensure adequate time for high-quality professional development for staff in the arts and foreign languages.
3. Ensure adequate staff expertise at the state education agency to work in the areas of the arts and foreign languages.
4. Incorporate both the arts and foreign languages into core graduation requirements, while simultaneously increasing the number of credits required for graduation.
5. Encourage higher education institutions to increase standards for admission and include arts and foreign language courses when calculating high school grade point averages.
6. Incorporate arts and foreign language learning in the early years into standards, curriculum frameworks, and course requirements. Also, encourage local school districts to incorporate the arts and foreign languages into instruction in the early years, whenever possible.
7. Advocate continued development of curriculum materials for the arts and foreign languages from the textbook publishing industry.
8. Incorporate all core subject areas, including the arts and foreign languages, into the improvement strategies promoted by the No Child Left Behind Act.
9. Urge the National Assessment Governing Board to increase the frequency in the administration of NAEP assessments for both the arts and foreign languages.
10. Urge Congress and legislatures to make a greater commitment to the arts and foreign languages.

ACTFL Events for 2005: The Year of Languages

As part of the national celebration of 2005 Year of Languages, ACTFL will identify an area of focus for each month of the yearlong endeavor. Events will be planned which will feature the monthly focus. Participating organizations are encouraged to plan events in their own communities that reflect the same focus. This is a tentative list that is subject to change.

November 2004 Focus: Kick-Off
Kickoff of the 2005 Year of Languages at the ACTFL Annual Convention in Chicago with announcements of the ACTFL-sponsored events and testimonials of support from noted people from the political, business, and entertainment arenas.

December 2004 Focus: Media
Press conference held at the National Press Club in Washington, D.C. with public statements of support from the President of the United States, the Secretary of State, the Secretary of Education, Secretary of Commerce, and the Secretary of Defense.

January 2005 Focus: Language Policy
The focus on language policy will encourage local, state, and national policy makers to examine the role of languages in their schools, and work and business environments.
ACTFL event: An interactive teleconference with chief policymakers broadcast from the University of North Carolina at Chapel Hill which will engage language educators, business leaders and policymakers in a discussion of national, state, and local initiatives that focus on language use and language learning.

February 2005 Focus: International Engagement
Activities that highlight the importance of international engagement will be encouraged by participating organizations. Building relationships with countries around the world will be featured as well as sister city initiatives and study abroad programs.
ACTFL event: A panel of Fulbright Exchange participants as well as representatives from other international programs will be featured at a symposium on the importance of study abroad programs and using language beyond the classroom.

March 2005 Focus: Connecting Languages to Other Areas
This focus will encourage activities that show the interrelationships between languages and other subject areas or professional fields.
ACTFL event: A panel discussion of languages and the connections to other fields will feature scientists, mathematicians, sociologists, and artists.

April 2005 Focus: Higher Education
This focus will provide a forum for discussion of enrollments, curricula, programs, and initiatives in the higher education institutions in the United States. Symposia that focus on higher education initiatives that promote advanced levels of languages will be featured.
ACTFL event: Students who have participated in the National Security Education Program (NSEP) will be featured along with programs that combine business with language, such as the University of Rhode Island. This program will be featured on CSPAN.

May 2005 Focus: Language Advocacy
This month participating organizations are encouraged to identify ways that language learning and multilingualism can be promoted in their own communities. Highlighting languages in the media will be a primary mechanism for promotion.
ACTFL event: In conjunction with the JNCL Delegate Assembly, events will be held on Capitol Hill to highlight the importance of languages at the federal level including building our language capacity as a nation through various programs and initiatives.

June 2005 Focus: Adult Learning and Language Use
During this month, language learning and language use by adults will be featured. Organizations that offer programs for adults to learn languages will be highlighted as well as ways that languages are used in work and leisure situations.
ACTFL event: A symposium on "Language Use in the Work World" will feature policies and practices found in the U.S. business world.

July 2005 Focus: Languages and Communities
This focus will encourage participants to feature the languages and cultures found in their own communities. Chambers of Commerce, Rotary Clubs and other service organizations, as well as libraries should be tapped for participation at the local level.
ACTFL event: The annual Folk Life Festival sponsored by the Smithsonian Museum will feature communities throughout the United States and their respective languages and cultures.

August 2005 Focus: Parents
The important role that parents play in providing language opportunities for their children will be highlighted. Information on the brain research and other important benefits for students will be emphasized as well as the important role that parents play in supporting language programs.
ACTFL event: The National Council of PTAs will cosponsor a forum that will provide parents with cogent benefits and rationales for beginning to learn languages at an early age. K-12 programs that highlight language learning will be featured.

September 2005 Focus: Heritage Languages
Emphasis will be on promoting the learning and maintenance of heritage languages including Native American as well as endangered languages and American Sign Language.
ACTFL event: A nationwide teleconference will feature heritage languages found in Texas, Louisiana, and Maine and efforts being made to preserve those languages.

October 2005 Focus: Early Language Learning
The benefits of early language learning will be emphasized as well as various program models that can be used at the elementary level. Participating organizations will be encouraged to make presentations at PTA meetings and to school boards highlighting the rationale for beginning language programs in elementary schools.
ACTFL event: A Saturday festival featuring elementary students who are studying languages will be organized with presentations of songs, skits, and artwork.

November 2005 Focus: Celebrating Accomplishments & Looking Ahead
Culmination of 2005 Year of Languages at the ACTFL Annual Convention in Baltimore.
The first National Language Teacher of the Year winner will be announced.

December 2005 Focus: Culture
Participating organizations are encouraged to highlight the learning of culture during this month.
ACTFL event: Culminating cultural program at the Kennedy Center in Washington, D.C. sponsored by ACTFL and various embassies.

from *FLA*, Vol. 37, No. 2, p. 321

As ACTFL looks to the future, it has begun to focus more energy on research priorities and advocacy, but continues in its official mission: providing vision, leadership, and support for quality teaching and learning of languages.

CHAPTER 6

THE 2010s

From 2010 to the Golden Anniversary

The 2009 Convention and World Languages Expo in San Diego set the stage for what promised to be an energizing year for the profession—beginning new endeavors, and continuing to build on the past year's accomplishments. Eileen Glisan (Indiana University of Pennsylvania, Indiana, PA) became President for 2010 at the end of the 2009 annual meeting. Her primary focus was to establish research priorities for language education. This was a time of increasing educational accountability, and foreign language professionals had to defend their classroom activities. High-stakes decisions were being made by politicians and administrators, often based on their perceptions of the benefits gained by foreign language classroom instruction. So, more than ever, language educators at all levels needed knowledge of the research findings that undergird classroom practices and ability to articulate the ways in which research informs our practices to those outside the profession. In the Fall 2009 issue of *FLA,* Editor Leslie Schrier said the profession must begin a productive conversation concerning the relationship between research and practice.

With the impetus for new areas of research in mind, ACTFL recognized the need to establish a set of research priorities as the profession charted a direction for language education. In the plenary session on research at the 2009 Convention, the panel members described the need for "widespread, organized, rigorously done longitudinal ethnographic research on world language communities across geographic regions and across K–20 levels, carried out in real classrooms." Research questions included:

- What kinds of understandings, knowledge, and skills are learners developing from participation in their classroom language communities?
- What are the communicative practices by which learners build and sustain their community? Into what kinds of practices are students being socialized?

Eileen Glisan
ACTFL President 2010

- How does language develop in long sequences of instruction?
- How can language programs be sustained over time and what are the outcomes of these programs?
- What teaching practices contribute to language learning and enable language and content to be integrated? How can we prepare teachers to engage in these practices? (*FLA*, Vol. 43, No. 1, pp. 1–2)

In the April issue of *TLE* (Vol. 5, Issue 3, April 2010, p. 47), the Statement of Professional Responsibility was released after extensive edits dating back to 2007 (see Appendix A). In the August 2009 issue (Vol. 5, Issue 4, p. 9) appeared a call for applications for research priorities grants for Phase I-Review of the Literature, a new initiative to develop a set of research priorities for foreign language education. In this initial phase, ACTFL was looking for projects in four categories: (1) high leverage teaching practices; (2) integration of content and language learning K–16; (3) learning outcomes and processes; and (4) foreign language teacher development (K–16).

The electronic National Standards Survey, completed in mid-2010, assessed the impact of the *Standards for Foreign Language Learning in the 21st Century* on the profession. Its analyzed data included information on how states, language organizations, and resource centers had included the National Standards in their initiatives. The survey examined how methods course instructors were integrating the standards into the development of new teachers and revealed the extent of professional development with a standards focus for inservice teachers. Results from the preliminary findings from teachers were: (1) the two goal areas (or "Cs") easiest to teach were Communication and Cultures, and (2) the "Cs" hardest to teach were Communities and Connections (*TLE*, Vol. 5, Issue 4, August 2010, p. 24).

Three new position statements from ACTFL were also announced in the August 2010 issue of *TLE*: "Language Learning for Heritage and Native Speakers," "Maximum Class Size," and "Use of the Target Language in the Classroom." This last position statement has had profound effects on the profession, especially the assertion that "ACTFL therefore recommends that language educators and their students use the target language as exclusively as possible (90% plus) at all levels of instruction during instructional time and, when feasible, beyond the classroom" (*TLE*, Vol. 5, Issue 4, August 2010, p. 29). (See Appendix B for these three position statements.) Simultaneously, discussions were continuing on the Board of Directors about three additional position statements: (1) Alternative and Add-On Certification, (2) the Role of Technology in Learning, and (3) Distance Learning and Technology-Mediated Learning. After the vote of the Board of Directors and acceptance by the Assembly of Delegates, ACTFL published its position statement on Alternative Teacher Certification and Add-on Certifications or Endorsements (see Appendix C).

Following several articles that had appeared in *The Language Educator* from October 2009 through February 2010, all based on the theme "Getting Connected in the 21st Century," ACTFL began to work with P21 (Partnership for 21st Century Skills) in advocating 21st century readiness for every student and creating a "21st Century Skills Map for World Languages." The latter would produce educator-created examples of how subjects in world languages could be fused with language skills to create engaging learning experiences that promote 21st century knowledge and skill acquisition. The final version was expected to be released in February 2011 in conjunction with *Discover Languages Month* (*TLE*, Vol. 5, No. 5, October 2010, pp. 25–29).

For the first time, the slate of candidates for the ACTFL presidency and diverse Board of Directors positions was printed in *TLE* in the October issue. Also appearing was the latest update from the National Standards Survey: while the effects of the standards on curriculum and instruction seemed to be significant, assessment lagged behind.

The 2010 Convention and World Languages Expo was announced for November 19–21 in Boston, on the theme of *Languages: Gateway to Global Communities*. Three exciting plenary sessions, arising from the 2010 events and discussions, were held during the convention: (1) The Lost "C": The Communities Goal Area; (2) Research Priorities: A Vision for Moving Language Education Forward; and (3) World Language Teacher Development: Urgent Issues. Attendance reached a new all-time high of 7,100+. For the second year, the Assembly of Delegates was co-sponsored by NADSFL and NCSSFL, and the Board of Directors received very positive feedback from the Assembly. The 2010 ACTFL National Language Teacher of the Year was Clarissa Adams Fletcher of Dunwoody High School in Dunwoody, GA.

In her speech at the Opening General Session, President Glisan offered her perspective on the state of the language education profession and reflected on how we might move forward:

Some might say that we are currently in a crisis in world language education, given the increasing number of language programs that have been closed at K–16 levels, and—in many cases, the use of technology to replace the face-to-face contact and support provided by a teacher.

How can our government and citizens continue to ignore the large body of research that clearly confirms the need to begin language study in the elementary grades and continue through the postsecondary level in an uninterrupted fashion? Our nation still seems to be not convinced that language study is critical to every student's education in the 21st century. This danger brings with it a wake-up call and an opportunity to reconsider what we must do to move forward as a profession.

She then mentioned the three main areas in which language educators had to put greater efforts:

- Do a better job of bridging research in the field with classroom practice, in order to prepare students who are equipped to communicate in target language communities.
- Foster greater professional unity and a collective voice so as to stand as a united front and send out one powerful message to our fellow citizens regarding the value of and need for language learning.
- Take personal responsibility as individual language professionals to advance and promote language study through efforts such as modeling up-to-date teaching practices that reflect current research in our field; engaging in at least one partnership with fellow educators at a different level of instruction or with professionals outside of our field; sharing and discussing new ideas with colleagues; mentoring teaching candidates and beginning teachers; educating our administrators about current language teaching practices and research about language learning; disseminating information about the value of language study to our colleagues in other subject areas; and advocating for language programs by communicating with legislators, school boards, and university boards of trustees. (*TLE*, Vol. 6, Issue 1, January 2011, pp. 33–34).

In fact, ACTFL began this forward push when it hired The Sheridan Group from Washington, D.C. This group's goal is "helping the good do better" by seeing that "the interests of the common good get the representation they deserve in the halls of government" (Retrieved from http://www.sheridangroupdc.com/index.php/about_us/). They were to assist with the legislative agenda set by ACTFL's Board of Directors.

According to Marty Abbott, The Sheridan Group helped ACTFL set and achieve its legislative goals, primarily with the congressional letters signed by members of Congress in November 2014, that resulted in the commissioning of the American Academy of the Arts and Sciences to write a report on U.S. language capabilities vis-à-vis our economic competitiveness, global security and other areas (see Appendix D).

The 2010 ACTFL Annual Convention and World Languages Expo was not only a record-breaker in participants, but also a great success in professional development experiences.

2011: Another Big Change

The year 2011 saw another big (but unexpected) change in ACTFL during the term of Barbara (Rupert) Mondloch. Rupert had been principal at Brookdale Elementary School in The Franklin Pierce Schools, Tacoma, WA, as well as a teacher of first-year through AP levels of high-school Spanish. She insisted that *all* students in the U.S., regardless of demographics, should have access to global and linguistic proficiency beginning at an early age. Her comments in her first "President's Message" in *FLA* (Vol. 44, No. 1, p. 1) reflect the MLA study of 2007 and the work of NCATE: "As language educators, we had to recognize our mutual inter-independence to accomplish the goal of languages for all…. Healthy PreK–12 programs feed Higher Education language, literature, and international programs. Strong teacher education programs are essential to a successful PreK–12 system" (p. 1). She thus announced the theme of the 2011 Annual Convention and the year as *Empowering Language Educators Through Collaboration* (*TLE*, Vol. 6, Issue 1, January 2011, p. 7). The 2011 Annual Convention was to be held in Denver on November 18–20.

The January 2011 issue of *TLE* was the magazine's 5th-anniversary issue. The introduction to the article *"It's the Fifth Anniversary of* The Language Educator: *Time to Celebrate!"* read:

> *Readers want to know what is happening with their colleagues, see what is happening in language education across the country, learn how their profession is growing and changing…and discover new ways that they can help foster better language programs for all students in all languages and at all levels of instruction* (TLE, *Vol. 6, Issue 1, January 2011, p. 18).*

The article included a retrospective of all 30 issues of *TLE*. In 2010, the magazine won the Silver Medal award for "Monthly Trade Association–Organization budget greater than $1 million" in the 2010 Association TRENDS All-Media Contest. A highlight of this anniversary issue was a conversation with Leo Benardo, the second President of ACTFL, who led the organization in 1969 in its infancy. (His interview can be found in Appendix E.)

In the April issue of *TLE*, President Mondloch announced the release of the World Languages 21st Century Skills Map, in which ACTFL had a leading role, in collaboration with the Partnership for 21st Century Skills (P21). The World Languages Skills Map took

Barbara (Rupert) Mondlach
ACTFL President 2011

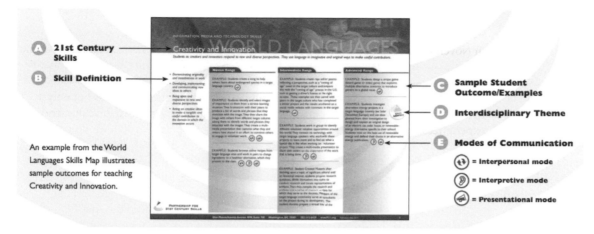

Figure 1. A sample of the World Languages 21ˢᵗ Century Skills Map

its place alongside skill maps for five other core subjects: arts, English, geography, social studies, and science (Fig. 1).

Past President Paul Sandrock (2006) took a new ACTFL position: Assistant Director of Professional Development. One of his main responsibilities was workshop presentation, along with his work on the ACTFL Webinars for Professionals (*TLE*, Vol. 6, Issue 3, April 2011), p. 25). The official Program Guide for the 2010 ACTFL Annual Convention and World Languages Expo won an Award of Excellence in the APEX 2011 23ʳᵈ Annual Awards for Publication Excellence Competition for Communications Professionals (*TLE*, Vol. 6, Issue 4, August 2011, p. 6).

Then...an unexpected event: Bret Lovejoy, Executive Director of ACTFL for eight years, left the organization. He told the Board of Directors the he was ready to move on to new challenges. During the search for a new Executive Director, several staff members stepped in and assured the organization's well-being: Marty Abbott, Elvira Swender, Julia Richardson, and Howie Berman, the new Director of Membership (*TLE*, Vol. 6, Issue 4, August 2011, p. 29). President Mondloch mentioned that transitions always present new opportunities to examine how to best achieve an organization's mission, which was certainly true for ACTFL.

In the November issue of *TLE* (Vol. 6, Issue 6, November 2011, p. 7), the new Executive Director of ACTFL was announced: Marty Abbott, former association President and Director of Education since 2004. A more complete announcement was published in *TLE*, Vol. 7, Issue 1, January 2012, p. 28). Abbott was chosen as the new Executive Director by the Board of Directors and stepped into the position shortly before the ACTFL Annual Convention in Denver. After the convention, the new Executive Director announced that ACTFL staffing would undergo restructuring to provide the organization with better checks and balances and to improve efficiency.

Marty Abbott
Executive Director, ACTFL
2011–Present

In this same November 2011 issue of *TLE*, there appeared an article, "Revisiting the National Standards: Highlighting the Connection with Major Initiatives" (Vol. 6, Issue 6, November 2011, p. 20). The national standards were released in 1996, and now, 15 years later, experiences of educators intending to implement the standards and other education initiatives suggested areas in which revise or "refresh" the standards so they could reflect more than a decade of progress (p. 20). Feedback from across the spectrum of language learning reinforced the strength and value of the original goal areas, the five "Cs."

Implementation of the standards, however, was inconsistent. Of importance in 2011 was the impact two additional initiatives were having on education in schools across the U.S.: (1) Common Core State Standards in English language and mathematics, and (2) the Partnership for 21st Century Skills. With this in mind, ACTFL received support from the Standards Collaborative Board to invite input on revisions for the standards. ACTFL convened a working group to revisit the standards in terms of these two new initiatives, and asked both NCSSFL and NADSFL to participate in this effort. An expert panel reviewed the draft document, which strongly linked national standards for language learning with the Common Core State Standards for English language arts (*TLE*, Vol. 6, Issue 6, November 2011, p. 20), for presentation to the Assembly of Delegates in November at the Annual Convention.

A bequest to ACTFL from the estate of Wilga Rivers prompted the Board of Directors to vote to rename the Florence Steiner Award for Leadership in Foreign Language Education, Post-Secondary, as the Wilga Rivers Award for Leadership in Foreign Language Education, Postsecondary. Also, part of the money from the bequest was to be used for a research initiative in honor of Rivers' work. In addition, another new award was created: the ACTFL Award for Excellence in K–12 Foreign Language Instruction Using Technology with IALLT.

The 2011 Annual Convention in Denver, ACTFL's 45th meeting, attracted more than 5,800 participants. For the first time, attendees used an ACTFL Convention mobile app to locate sessions and plan their personal schedules. In her speech at the Opening General Session, Mondloch announced that ACTFL had more than 12,300 members representing over 50 different languages from 57 different countries worldwide. Japanese teacher Yo Azama from North Salinas High School, Salinas, CA, received the ACTFL National Language Teacher of the Year for 2012.

Though successful, this meeting was but the beginning of a focus on the critical need for collaboration in foreign language instruction. The next convention, in Philadelphia on November 16–18, would further enable America's many languages to speak with "one united voice" to make language education a top priority (*TLE*, Vol. 7, Issue 1, January 2012, p. 35).

At the Board of Directors meeting in Denver in November 2011, the Professional Programs and Professional Development departments reported:

ACTFL first signed an OPI testing contract with the DLI in 2002, administering 70 OPI tests during the first fiscal year. Because of ongoing collaboration between DLI and ACTFL, in fiscal year 2011 there were 11,641 OPIs administered.

ACTFL's newest and most innovative teaching tool, the ACTFL Assessment of Performance Toward Proficiency in Languages (AAPPL) Suite—the result of a collaboration with STARTALK—was presented to the Board. This program assessed performance through three modes: (a) Interpersonal Listening/Speaking, (b) Presentational Writing, and (c) Interpretive Reading and Listening. This assessment tool could be used to engage the student in communicative activities and help teachers identify what was needed to build competence. It was anticipated that the cost of the assessment would be $20 per student and that the live assessment would be available by Spring 2012. (Visit the AAPPL site for a more complete discussion of the program: http://aappl.actfl.org/)

A new version of the *ACTFL Proficiency Guidelines for Speaking, Writing, Listening, and Reading* (2012) premiered at the 2011 Annual Convention. This version introduced a new major skill level—Distinguished—which was added to the Speaking and Writing guidelines. The Advanced level was divided into three sublevels of High, Mid, and Low for the Listening and Reading guidelines, and general-level descriptions at the Advanced, Intermediate, and Novice levels of all skills were added (*TLE*, Vol. 7, Issue 1, January 2012, p. 28). A more detailed explanation of the changes in the 2012 revisions appeared in *TLE* (Vol. 7, Issue 2, February 2012, pp. 46–48).

The new year 2012 brought in a new Executive Director and a new President—Dave McAlpine of the University of Arkansas at Little Rock. In his first "President's Message" in the January 2012 issue of *TLE* (Vol. 7, Issue 1, p. 7), McAlpine set the tone and theme for the year: *Many Languages, One United Voice*. He was not suggesting that ACTFL be that one voice, but that our profession could come together in the collaborative spirit of the 2011 Annual Convention and find more ways to collaborate…

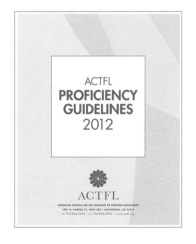

> …*so that when opportunities arise for language professionals to provide input at the local, state, regional, national, and international stages, we can speak with one voice for what we believe will move language forward in the 21st century. Each language organization has knowledge and experiences to share. We can certainly learn much from and support one another during these challenging times for language programs (p. 7).*

Then, in masterful strokes, McAlpine presented the various elements that willingly cooperate to give our professional the "one unified voice" he was seeking. In each of his messages in *FLA* throughout 2012, he gave insights into what each element had to offer to the unified profession (Fig. 2, p. 160).

For the January 2012 issue of *TLE*, in her article "More Than a Decade of Standards: A Look at How Far We've Come" (*TLE,* Vol. 7, Issue 1, pp. 42–47), Editor Sandy Cutshall indicated that *TLE* would run a five-part series focusing on the national standards for the rest of 2012. Each issue would examine one goal area and the standards contained within it, offering examples of some educators who were incorporating and integrating the 5 Cs in their instruction.

The 2012 Annual Convention and World Language Expo was announced for November 16–18, 2012, in Philadelphia. ACTFL members were urged: "Let's turn our collective voices into a unified message!" (*TLE*, Vol. 7, Issue 2, February 2012, inside front cover).

ACTFL had enjoyed a strong working relationship with NCATE since ACTFL's standards for teacher accreditation were accepted in 2002. The February 2012 issue of *TLE* (Vol. 7, Issue 2, February 2002, p. 8) announced that, late in 2011, NCATE had merged with the Teacher Education Accreditation Council (TEAC) to create the Council for Accreditation of Educator Preparation (CAEP), which was scheduled to begin accrediting programs in 2013, and was planning to require training programs to improve their processes for selecting candidates.

Dave McAlpine
ACTFL President 2012

More than 20 language organizations devoted to fostering the study of the languages, cultures, & literatures of the world language disciplines found in U.S. schools & universities.

ACTFL's relationship to language organizations: "ACTFL sees its role to promote and support organizational members and the AATS are the mainstay of that collaboration. Whether it's the student standards, NCATE representation, or revisions of the ETS PRAXIS II exams, ACTFL collaborates with the AATs to make sure that all languages are represented in national initiatives." Marty Abbott, ACTFL Executive Director

(*FLA*, Vol. 45, No. 3, p. 306)

ACTFL Board of Directors

Accomplishes its work through four standing committees who meet face-to-face twice a year and virtually throughout the year as needed. Each committee has representation from both K–12 and higher education; ACTFL staff members are divided among the committees:

1. Finance and Organization Committee
2. Convention and Professional Development Committee
3. Membership and Education Committee
4. Communications Committee

(*FLA*, Vol. 45, No. 1, pp. 1-2)

Modern Language Association (MLA) & Association of Departments of Foreign Languages (ADFL)

MLA—one of the largest academic organizations offering programs and services to both English & foreign language teachers numbering nearly 30,000 members. Offers four periodicals.

ADFL—offers foreign language educators a source of college & university teaching and administrative positions through its Job Information List. Serves all languages and every type of postsecondary institution, providing a forum for exchanges through a website, seminars, and a journal.

(*FLA*, Vol. 45, No. 2, pp. 165–166)

National Foreign Language Resource Centers (NFLCRs) & the Center for Applied Linguistics (CAL)

NFLCRs—their goal is to promote the learning and teaching of foreign languages in the U.S. Led by nationally & internationally recognized language professionals, NFLRCs create materials, offer professional development workshops, and conduct research on FL learning.

CAL—a private, non-profit organization dedicated to the study of language & culture & to the application of research on language & culture to educational & social concerns.

(*FLA*, Vol. 45, No. 4, pp. 465–466)

The Five Regional FL Organizations

Most of these organizations predate ACTFL and some were created as early as 1949 to provide professional development opportunities for teachers in their regions:

1. The Central States Conference on the Teaching of Foreign Languages (CSCTFL)
2. The Northeast Conference on the Teaching of Foreign Languages (NECTFL)
3. The Pacific Northwest Council for Languages (PNCFL)
4. The Southern Conference on Language Teaching (SCOLT)
5. The Southwest Conference on Language Teaching (SWCOLT)

(*TLE*, Vol. 7, Issue 3, p. 7)

State Language Associations, NADSFL, & NCSSFL

In 2012, there were 47 state language teacher associations including GWATFL (Greater Washington [DC] Association of Teachers of Foreign Languages).

National Association of District Supervisors of Foreign Languages (NADSFL)

National Council of State Supervisors for Languages (NCSSFL)

(*TLE*, Vol. 7, Issue 4, August 2012, p. 7)

TESOL, NABE, IALLT

Teachers of English to Speakers of Other Languages (TESOL), now officially called TESOL International Association

The National Association for Bilingual Education (NABE)—the only national professional organization devoted to representing bilingual learners & educational professionals

The International Association of Language Learning Technology (IALLT)—members provide leadership in the development, integration, evaluation, and management of instructional technology for the teaching and learning of language, literature, & culture.

(*TLE*, Vol. 7, Issue 5, p. 7)

Figure 2. President McAlpine's summary of contributions of foreign language organizations to a unified voice

In the summer of 2012, *FLA*'s special focus issue—*ACTFL Research Priorities in Foreign Language Education, Phase I*—appeared, co-edited by Eileen Glisan and Richard Donato. As 2009 President-elect of ACTFL, Glisan had asked for the organization to begin "Phase I of a long-term project to identify the key areas in which research in foreign language instruction and learning is currently needed to inform and improve classroom practice" (*FLA*, Vol. 45, No. S1, Summer 2012, p. S1). She had envisioned attracting researchers for this purpose, and ACTFL would sponsor this research through funding, publication, and dissemination of the research results to the field and to other stakeholders. Through this process, she reminded the Board of Directors that, without research-based information, "we can only have anecdotal evidence to support much of what we do as world language educators" (*FLA*, Vol. 45, No. S1, Summer 2012, p. S1). The second phase of ACTFL's research priorities initiative was announced in a plenary session at the 2012 Annual Convention in Philadelphia.

Protase E. "Woody" Woodford

On March 25, 2012, one of ACTFL's long-time friends and advocates, Protase E. "Woody" Woodford, died. Woody had worked with the Educational Testing Service (ETS) for 25 years before retiring, and had been a major contributor to the proficiency movement.

In April 2012, ACTFL presented the language education community a document that provided an explicit "crosswalk" showing the strong link between the National Standards for Learning Languages and the Common Core State Standards for English Language Arts and Literacy in History/Social Studies, Science, and Technical Subjects. The 17-page PDF file showed explicitly how each aspect of the Common Core aligned with the national standards at the Novice, Intermediate, and Advanced levels (*TLE*, Vol. 7, Issue 4, August 2012, p. 24).

Beginning in the fall of 2012, new and renewing members of ACTFL would receive free membership in one of the Special Interest Groups (SIGs) as part of their annual membership. The number of SIGs had grown and now included:

J. David Edwards

- African-American Students
- Arabic
- Community Colleges
- Distance Learning
- Film (Cinema)
- Heritage Languages
- Immersion
- Korean
- Language Learning for Children
- Less Commonly Taught Languages
- Modern Greek
- Portuguese
- Research
- Small German Programs
- Spanish for Native Speakers
- Teacher Development
- Teaching and Learning of Culture

J. David Edwards retired from his position as JNCL-NCLIS Executive Director after 31 years of service. Edwards, who always claimed he was not "one of us," was told by President McAlpine in a letter on his retirement, "...you are indeed 'one of us' as you have been able to represent us so expertly over these many years" (*TLE*, Vol. 7, Issue 4, August 2012, p. 55). Edwards was replaced by William P. Rivers.

In the November 2012 issue of *TLE*, readers were invited to explore ACTFL.org, the new website that launched earlier in the fall of 2012. The new website was more user-friendly and offered a pleasant experience for all visitors, along with better organized information and increased services for members (Vol. 7, Issue 6, pp. 20–22). (Just imagine—in the early 1990s, ACTFL was debating whether to have a website at all, what it should look like, and what it should contain!)

In the same November 2012 issue of *TLE*, Douglass Crouse wrote an article, "Professional Collaboration at the State Level—What 'One United Voice' Looks Like" (*TLE*, Vol. 7, Issue 6, pp. 24–26). Clearly, President McAlpine's message to ACTFL members about unity was coming through very clearly.

In August 2012, ACTFL had conducted a comprehensive membership survey to gain extensive feedback from its members. While the numbers were still being crunched, some interesting statistics emerged about ACTFL members:

- They embraced technology: 42% used an iPhone regularly; another 36% used an iPad regularly.
- They integrated technology into instruction: 90% used computers/laptops in their classrooms.
- They embraced professional development: Most (53%) preferred in-person workshops for professional development; webinars came in second at 18%.
- They wanted to be connected to one another: 89% said that they were members of ACTFL "to be part of the greater language education community."
- They cared about research: 39% wanted project-based education to be the next phase of ACTFL's research agenda; 22% preferred immersion education.
- They strongly valued the Annual Convention: 1 in 5—20% of respondents—said they attended the ACTFL Annual Convention & World Languages Expo every year. (*TLE*, Vol. 7, Issue 6, November 2012, p. 27)

The winter issue of *FLA* (Vol. 45, No. 4, p. 464), announced a search for a new editor. Leslie Schrier, editor for the past four years, would step down after the publication of the winter 2012 issue. Anne Nerenz became Interim Editor for the 2013 Spring and Summer issues.

At the 2012 Annual Convention in November in Philadelphia, more than 6,900 attendees packed 788 sessions and workshops. Noah Geisel, a Spanish teacher at East High School in Denver, was named 2013 ACTFL National Language Teacher of the Year. A special event was held to mark the 30th anniversary of the ACTFL Oral Proficiency Interview (OPI). Again, ACTFL sponsored and presented special plenary sessions to present key topics facing the education community, such as "Language Education in the United States—Current Status and Future Vision." In another plenary, Phase II of ACTFL's research priorities was introduced, promoting research in the five priority areas emanating from Phase I: (1) Foreign Language Teacher Preparation Model Programs: Documentation, Implementation, and Outcomes; (2) Profiles of High-Performing Foreign Language Teachers in K–12 Settings; (3) Language Use in the Community; (4) Mentoring K–16 Foreign Language Teachers and Classroom Discourse; and (5) High-Leverage Teaching Practices (*TLE*, Vol. 8, Issue 1, January 2013, p. 36).

Toni Theisen
ACTFL President 2013

Toni Theisen, a French teacher from Loveland High School and 2009 ACTFL National Language Teacher of the Year, was elected President for 2013. Her theme for the year and the Annual Convention in Orlando was *New Spaces New Realities: Learning Any Time, Any Place*, which highlighted changes in the learning landscapes—not only schools and classrooms, but also the many virtual spaces that connect learners worldwide. As former chair of the ACTFL 21st Century Skills Map Committee, she said:

In order for 21st-century learners to be 'world-ready' for postsecondary college and career opportunities, they must be able to master content from a wide variety of subjects, sources, and perspectives with an understanding of and respect for diverse cultures. These essentials of learning will require that students have not only the basic skills of reading, writing, mathematics, and the ability to communicate in more than one language, but also the ability to research, analyze, synthesize and evaluate (TLE, Vol. 8, Issue 1, January 2013, p. 7).

Therefore, throughout the year connections would be made to the 21st Century Skills Map for World Languages. Articles in three of *TLE's* 2013 issues (January, February, April) highlighted and expanded on the Framework for 21st Century Learning and demonstrated how it might look in the classroom. They addressed a routine topic of discussion among teachers: *Our students need to master 21st century skills to compete successfully in the global economy.*

In the January 2013 issue of *TLE*, more results of the ACTFL Membership Survey were published, revealing the following about members:

- They found their membership valuable: 89% of respondents said they were members to be part of the greater language education community; 72% cited professional development opportunities as their motives for membership.
- They belonged so they could stay informed.
- They were eager for language news and information about current events.

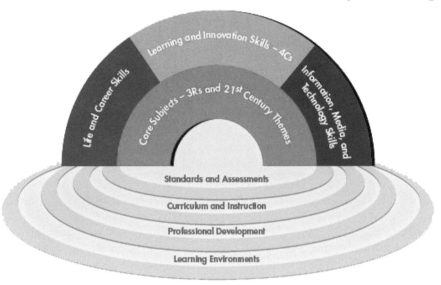

A Framework for
21st Century Learning

They enjoyed ACTFL's publications and professional development: 79% identified *The Language Educator* as very or extremely useful; 75% identified the convention as very or extremely useful; 69% identified *FLA* as very or extremely useful.

They wanted research to enrich their instruction. (*TLE*, Vol. 8, Issue 1, January 2013, p. 17)

ACTFL announced its 2013–2014 Mentoring Program, designed to help early career language teachers succeed in their current assignments and learn the skills necessary for long-term success. Also announced was the release of the *Performance Descriptors for Language Learners*, designed to reflect how language learners perform whether learning in classrooms, online, through independent project-based learning, or in blended environments.

The *Standards for Foreign Language Learning* (1996, 1999, 2006) described what students needed to know and be able to do as they learned another language, defining the "what" of language education. The *ACTFL Performance Guidelines for K–12 Learners* (1998) had described "how well" language learners were expected to do the "what" from the content standards. The new *ACTFL Performance Descriptors for Language Learners* updated and revised the earlier 1998 *Performance Guidelines* (*TLE*, Vol. 8, Issue 1, January 2013, p. 29).

The new *ACTFL Performance Descriptors for Language Learners*

The year 2013 brought changes to *TLE*. As the ACTFL Board of Directors had proposed, the magazine would present a year of six themed issues:

- **August 2013**—How do we personalize the language learning experience?
Focus on: The Learner
- **October 2013**—How do today's learners shape a new learning environment?
Focus on: Technology
- **November 2013**—How are our practices helping students learn?
Focus on: Instruction
- **January 2014**—How do encounters with cultures change our learners' views of the world?
Focus on: Cultural Proficiency
- **February 2014**—What kinds of assessments improve learning and teaching?
Focus on: Assessment and Feedback
- **April 2014**—How can educators improve their effectiveness?
Focus on: Professional Development

In the Spring 2013 issue of *FLA* (Vol. 46, No. 1, p. 3), Interim Editor Anne Nerenz addressed the purpose of the journal: "It is dedicated to the dissemination of research on the teaching and learning of languages and places particular value on studies that have clear implications for curriculum design, instructional practice, and assessment." She then discussed the overarching framework to help guide future research initiatives set in motion by the 2010 President Glisan, and the three-part framework that focused researchers' attention on:

1. **the participants:**
   a. *students:* their interests, special needs, attitudes, motivations, concerns, and beliefs about language learning
   b. *teachers:* how they achieve and maintain

certification, what they know and can do, their beliefs about teaching and learning, their proficiency in the language, and their knowledge of the cultures where the language is used
2. **the teaching-learning process:** curricular content, classroom materials, and instructional practices; specifically the extent to which the target language is used and the ways in which the standards guide instructional design and assessment
3. **the outcomes:** how student learning outcomes are defined and assessed, with particular emphasis on how and to what extent students develop advanced levels of language proficiency.

Nerenz used these three components to help her select the articles/studies for the Fall 2013 issue of *FLA* (*FLA*, Vol. 46, No. 1, Spring 2013, p. 3), in which she also wrote that it is "Only by translating into action the research findings in these critical domains that meaningful change could occur. To that end, in addition to posing important questions and reporting carefully collected quantitative and qualitative data," the authors of the articles/studies had thought deeply about the translational power of their findings and had provided rich and significant implications designed to transform the teaching and learning of languages (*FLA,* Vol. 46, No. 3, Fall 2013, p. 327).

The ACTFL Board of Directors, with leadership of the National Association of District Supervisors of Foreign Languages (NADSFL) and the National Council of State Supervisors for Languages (NCSSFL), released a position statement to describe how four major initiatives in the U.S. linked with language learning: Common Core, the 21st Century Skills Map, STEM (Science, Technology, Engineering, Mathematics), and the national foreign language standards. Local, state, regional, and national perspectives were

ACTFL Digital Badge

represented in this position statement, as an additional 70 organizations provided input and comment. This statement is called "Languages as a Core Component of Education for All Students" (see Appendix F).

In 2013, ACTFL introduced a sixth 'C' to accompany the 5Cs of the national standards—Compassion—on the premise that helping students to develop compassion and social consciousness builds on all goal areas of the standards and brings in the human component to language education and learning. This sixth 'C' was to be introduced at the 2013 Annual Convention in Orlando under the theme of *ACTFL Global Giving*. This global giving would "not only offer compassionate connection with those in need across the globe but [would] also give language educators the opportunity to better foster empathy and cultural understanding in their students" (*TLE*, Vol. 8, Issue 4, August 2013, p. 20). For the first year, ACTFL supported the Bon Samaritain School in Port-au-Prince, Haiti. In one gesture of compassion, language teachers were asked to donate items from a list ACTFL had provided to the school.

In her fifth "President's Message" in *TLE* (Vol. 8, Issue 5, October 2013, p. 7), President Theisen focused on "Technology and the Ever-Changing Learning Ecosystem." She commented on the myriad changes that had occurred in the past few years. Google was only 15 years old; the Minitel, first introduced in France in 1982, provided access to phone numbers and train reservations. The tech journey had taken the world from simple searches to smartphones and cloud computing. Students could now Skype with people in other countries, virtually walk around a city with a street view, create and share their own movies, and publish their own online books. She said:

> *The impact of technology is reimagining how, where, why, and with whom we learn and more particularly how students can access, use, and experience language learning in more authentic real-world contexts. The 21st Century Skills Map for World Languages [tinyurl.com/languages-skillsmap] guides our thinking around information literacy, media literacy, and technology literacy.*

In this same technological vein, ACTFL introduced the Digital Badge at ACTFL 2013, which *TLE* defined as "online representations of earned knowledge and skills and a new way to showcase professional development achievements" (*TLE*, Vol. 8, Issue 5, October 2013, p. 17).

New ACTFL publications were appearing very rapidly:

- *NCSSFL/ACTFL Can-Do Statements*. This publication connected NCSSFL's LinguaFolio® with ACTFL's Proficiency Guidelines. The combination of these two documents into a single, cohesive set of statements makes clear how the performance that language learners demonstrate in the familiar context of the instructional setting points toward a targeted proficiency level.
- *Implementing Integrated Performance Assessment*. A follow-up to the *ACTFL Integrated Performance Assessment Manual* (2003), this book by Bonnie Adair-Hauck, Eileen W. Glisan, and Francis J. Troyan explores the IPA, which was designed to

address the national need for assessing learner progress in meeting the content areas of the national standards, in demonstrating performance depicted in the *ACTFL Performance Descriptors*, and in illustrating progress toward specific proficiency levels in the *ACTFL Proficiency Guidelines*. The IPA enables learners to demonstrate their ability to communicate within specific goal areas of the national standards across the interpersonal, interpretive, and presentational modes of communication.

- *The Keys to Planning for Learning: Effective Curriculum, Unit, and Lesson Design*. This book, written by Donna Clementi and Laura Terrill, joined ACTFL's *Keys* series of books: *The Keys to the Classroom* (Paula Patrick) and *The Keys to Assessing Language Performance* (Paul Sandrock).

Anne Nerenz, outgoing member of the ACTFL Board of Directors and Interim Editor of *FLA*, was named the new Editor of the journal. Her term would begin January 1, 2014 (*TLE*, Vol. 8, Issue 6, November 2013, p. 16). Furthermore, *TLE* now offered an online version of the acclaimed magazine that could be accessed from any device. Readers could virtually turn the pages and easily navigate through the issue with hyperlinks, zoom, and other special features. Keywords could be searched. The magazine could be shared via e-mail or social media. Readers could link directly to the discussion group on the ACTFL Online Community (*TLE*, Vol. 8, Issue 6, November 2013, p. 33). At their Orlando meeting in November, the Board of Directors decided that beginning with the August/September 2014 issue, the magazine would reduce the number of print issues from six to four, in part because more people were accessing *TLE* digitally.

The 2013 Annual Convention and World Languages Expo, held in Orlando on November 22–24, attracted more than 5,700 attendees, a drop from the past few years. It had three plenary sessions:

1. Authentic Student Voice—Let's Listen to Our Learners!
2. The Tipping Point—Language Learning for a Changed World
3. Current Studies in Research Priorities Areas

Linda Egnatz, a Spanish teacher from Lincoln-Way Community High School in Frankfort, IL, was named 2014 ACTFL National Language Teacher of the Year.

For those who could not attend ACTFL 2013 or who could not afford to benefit from its many sessions, the organization offered Access ACTFL 2013, which let them sign up online and catch up on some major features of the meeting. Those who signed up could receive 12 hours of professional development units or CEU credits and view a package of 10 learning sessions along with the handout materials from those videotaped sessions, the keynote address, the welcome address from the ACTFL President, and one plenary session.

At the end of 2013, ACTFL revised the 2002 ACTFL/CAEP Program Standards for the Preparation of Foreign Language Teachers, which CAEP approved. By 2016, programs seeking national recognition had to use the 2013 revision.

Mary Lynn Redmond
ACTFL President 2014

The 5Cs goal areas

At the final Board of Directors meeting at the Annual Convention, President Theisen passed the gavel to Mary Lynn Redmond, a Professor of Education at Wake Forest University, Winston-Salem, NC.

The January 2014 issue of *TLE* (Vol. 9, Issue 1, p. 6) was announced that the National Standards for Learning Languages had been recently revised based on what language educators had learned from more than 15 years of implementing the standards. "The guiding principle in revision was to clarify what language learners would do to demonstrate progress on each standard" (p. 6). The revision is: *World-Readiness Standards for Learning Languages.*

The 2011 report, *A Decade of Foreign Language Standards: Impact, Influence, and Future Directions,* guided the revisions. Many state frameworks and local curricula were now aligned with the 5Cs goal areas and the details of the 11 standards. The new wording was guided by the Standards Collaborative Board with input from language organizations and educators across the country; the five goal areas and the 11 standards were maintained. These revised standards are applicable to learners at all levels from PreK through postsecondary, native speakers, and heritage language speakers, including ESL students, American Sign Language, and Classical Languages (Greek and Latin) (*TLE*, Vol. 9, Issue 1, January 2014, p. 6). (See Appendix G)

In her first "President's Message" in *TLE* (Vol. 9, Issue 1, January 2014, p. 7), President Redmond announced that ACTFL's focus for the year was *Reaching Global Competence,* examining the role that world language educators play in helping our students gain the ability needed to live and thrive in our global society. In fact, the newly revised World-Readiness Standards reflected the shift in the way the profession was looking at language expectations for students in PreK–16—preparation for life in our globalized world and consideration of current education reform initiatives including the Common Core standards, 21st Century Skills, and College and Career Readiness to guide development and implementation of curriculum, instruction, and assessment. In particular, the "Communities" standards were "refreshed" to illustrate more specifically what it means to be able to function in multilingual communities (p. 7). The focal theme was also the theme of the 2014 Annual Convention and World Expo that was to be held in San Antonio, TX, on November 21–23, and also the theme of the January 2014 issue of *TLE.*

In her second "President's Message," Redmond wrote about the passion that language teachers have for their work and pointed out that these educators have a global mindset. She cautions, however, that "we unfortunately live in a society that does not yet value languages as a core subject and expectation of education in this country" (*TLE*, Vol. 9, Issue 2, February 2014, p. 7). So, we have to reach out to stakeholders and share with them what our students can do in languages as a result of their experience in our classrooms, and help them develop a global mindset. One such effort was a new book available through the ACTFL Online Store, *Raising Global Children*, by Stacie Nevadomski Berdan.

ACTFL announced that it was entering Phase III of the Research Priorities Project that was begun in 2010. This phase would support empirical research on five priority areas that are critical to improving language education:

- Research Priority Area #1: Integration of Language, Culture, and Content
  - Immersion and other innovative programs
  - Heritage language programs
- Research Priority Area #2: Foreign Language Teacher Development
  - Model teacher preparation programs
  - Mentoring
  - Preparing foreign language teachers for urban/rural settings
- Research Priority Area #3: Classroom Discourse
  - Use of L1 vs. L2
  - Interactional practices
  - Dialogic inquiry
- Research Priority Area #4: High-Performing Language Programs
  - Profiles of effective PreK–16 teachers
  - Profiles of effective PreK–16 classrooms
  - High-leverage pedagogical practices and/or assessment
- Research Priority Area #5: Language Use in the Community
  - Service Learning
  - Study abroad

(*TLE*, Vol. 9, Issue 3, April 2014, p. 17; *TLE*, Vol. 9, Issue 4, August 2014, p. 23)

TLE announced a new theme series for 2014–2015:

- August/September 2014—Taking Language Beyond the Classroom
- October/November 2014—Creating Comprehensible Input and Output
- January/February 2015—Moving Along the Proficiency Continuum
- March/April 2015—Designing Learner-Centered Language Instruction (*TLE*, Vol. 9, Issue 3, April 2014, p. 25).

At the May 2014 Board of Directors meeting in Alexandria, VA, the Board approved of a shift in focus of the Global Giving Program away from activities designed to encourage philanthropy among ACTFL members to a focus on publicizing outstanding efforts in the area of social action originating in world language programs in schools and colleges in which students are learning about language and culture through activities such as service learning and volunteerism. With that the initiative's name was changed from ACTFL Global Giving to ACTFL Global Engagement.

FLA, under the editorship of Anne Nerenz, announced that it had begun using the ScholarOne Manuscripts™ platform for online submission and review of articles (*FLA*, Vol. 47, No. 2, Summer 2014, p. 205). In this same issue of *FLA*, President Redmond discussed preparing global professionals, which fit in with her theme for the year and annual meeting, *Reaching Global Competence*. She mentioned that, over the past few years, many reports in the fields of education, business and government had highlighted the urgency of world-readiness in preparing global professionals, giving several common themes as recommendations for global education:

1. To gain the levels of language proficiency and intercultural competence now required for many jobs, U.S. schools should provide longer sequences of study, beginning in lower grades and continuing through the postsecondary level.

ACTFL 2014 (from L to R): Pete Swanson, ACTFL President-Elect 2016; Jacque Bott Van Houten, ACTFL President Elect 2015; Mary Lynn Redmond, ACTFL President 2014; Marty Abbott, ACTFL Executive DIrector

2. PreK–16 schools should provide leading-edge language instruction that focuses on 21st century communication and provides students with opportunities to demonstrate language usage in real-world contexts.
3. Partnerships should be created among PreK–12, community colleges and higher education, business, and government to sustain ways for students to gain intercultural competence. (*FLA*, Vol. 47, No. 2, Summer 2014, p. 205)

In the fall of 2014, President Redmond discussed professional learning communities (PLCs) in which language educators should share experiences and learn from one another. One of the primary PLCs is ACTFL, which began to offer a new "Invite a Colleague" feature on the registration form for the 2014 Annual Convention, which would help encourage

participants to involve their fellow educators so that they could benefit from these experiences, and would then hopefully become active participants (*TLE*, Vol. 9, Issue 4, August 2014, p. 9).

The same issue of *TLE* announced that the National Federation of Modern Language Teachers' Associations (NFMLTA) had joined ACTFL to play a larger role in supporting research in the field of foreign language education. NFMLTA became a major supporter of the ACTFL Research Priorities Project and authorized $10,000 in dissertation support grants for its Phase III. In the "President's Message" in the Fall 2014 issue of *FLA*, both President Redmond and Executive Director Marty Abbott announced a new campaign that would be launched in 2015—*Lead with Languages*:

...a landmark national advocacy campaign to promote language learning in the United States. An unprecedented initiative, the campaign will mark the start of a sustained movement to make languages a national priority and to create a new generation of Americans competent in other languages and cultures. Lead with Languages is a clarion call for the American public and the country's leadership to recognize the essential role of languages in the 21st century in shaping citizens who can compete and cooperate in a global age. Deploying a wide range of media channels, partners, and public personalities, the campaign intends to create a cultural shift in awareness and attitudes on languages and to galvanize Americans to become a nation of multilingual speakers. (FLA, Vol. 47, No. 3, Fall 2014, p. 373)

ACTFL released its position statement on global competence in the October/November issue of *TLE* (Vol. 9, Issue 5, p. 16) (see Appendix H). This was indeed a fitting component of the push toward global competence, leading to the *Lead with Languages* campaign in 2015.

Additionally, more and more states were recognizing students' mastery of two or more languages with an initiative awarding students with a Seal of Biliteracy on high school diplomas and academic transcripts, if a high level of proficiency in one or more languages besides English is met. In late 2014, eight states had officially approved the seal: California, Washington, Minnesota, New Mexico, Texas, Louisiana, Illinois, and New York. Listed as "under consideration" were Utah, Virginia, New Jersey, Massachusetts, and Rhode Island. Listed in "early stages" were Oregon, Wisconsin, Indiana, Michigan, Ohio, Maryland, and Florida (*TLE*, Vol. 9, Issue 5, October/November 2014, p. 58).

On August 13, 2015, a press release announced that ACTFL, along with the National Association of Bilingual Education (NABE), NCSSFL and TESOL International Association, had officially drafted recommendations for implementing the Seal of Biliteracy (retrieved from http://www.actfl. org/news/press-releases/seal-biliteracy-guidelines-released): "The Seal serves to certify attainment of biliteracy [proficiency in English and one or more other world languages by high school graduation] for students, employers, and universities" (*TLE*, August-September 2015, p. 14). These guidelines were developed for state departments of education and local school districts to ensure consistency of meaning of this recognition.

The Fall 2014 Member Survey results were summarized in the January/February 2015 issue of *TLE* (Vol. 10. Issue 1, p. 6). The survey asked respondents their opinions on key issues relating to the organization and gathered general information about the members:

- A great majority (87%) believed the current ACTFL mission accurately reflected the organization's current priorities.
- There was no clear consensus on ACTFL's name. A small plurality (31%) wanted to keep the full name, while 26% preferred using the acronym ACTFL alone. Only 15% wanted to see a name change. Apparently, the discussion about changing the name of the association was, and will continue to be, a topic of discussion and debate.
- Most respondents said they were members of ACTFL to be "part of the greater language education community;" 71% were looking for professional development opportunities.
- Almost as many respondents claimed they had never attended the convention (24%) as those who attended every year or almost every year (27%). Of the former group, budget reasons were the primary cause for not attending.

The Annual Convention in San Antonio attracted 6,486 attendees who participated in more than 835 different sessions, events, and meetings, including three plenary sessions: (1) *Framing Language Learning Within the International Context of Global Competence: What Does It Take to Prepare Our Students for International Engagement?* (2) *Reframing World Language Learning Within Global Competence Models,* and (3) *Research Priorities—Phase II: Using Research to Move Language Education Forward.* The 2015 ACTFL National Language Teacher of the Year was Nicole Naditz, a French teacher from Bella Vista High School in Fair Oaks, CA.

Jacque Bott Van Houten
ACTFL President 2015

Jacque Bott Van Houten from the Jefferson County (KY) Public Schools, a former World Language & International Education consultant at the Kentucky Department of Education, was ACTFL President for 2015. Her first "President's Message" (*TLE*, January-February 2015, p. 7) began with a title indicating new things happening: "A New Year—A New Focus." Van Houten was eager to connect with members "as we collaborate to move language and intercultural competence into a place of higher priority in our teaching practices, in the public mindset, and in our nation's educational policies." She said:

Our shared goal of making language a national priority is the result of a decade of preparation during which scholarly, as well as action, research shored up the framework for proposing new, long-overdue language learning policies. Ten years of 'discovering languages' have resulted in significant advances in how we perceive, provide, and recognize learning opportunities, and how we access language proficiency and intercultural competency. This ongoing growth within our profession needs to be manifested in learner outcomes and shared with the public at large in order to drive national policy changes (TLE, January-February 2015, p. 7).

The Assembly of Delegates drew up its 2015 "New Year's Resolutions: Top Ten Advocacy Goals Defined by States"(Fig. 3). President Van Houten announced that the theme of the 2015 ACTFL Annual Convention and World Languages Expo was "Inspire. Engage. Transform;" she hoped the convention experience would *inspire* attendees to think creatively and stimulate new knowledge as they *engaged* in networking and

Figure 3: The Assembly of Delegates drew up these 2015 Advocacy Goals.

TOP TEN ADVOCACY GOALS DEFINIED BY STATES

1. Proclamation from an Elected Official in Support of Language Education

2. Arrange for a meeting with State Legislative or Congressional Representatives

3. Advocate for a State Supervisor for Languages

4. Lobby State Legislature/Board to Support National Board Certification with Stipends or Licensure Renewal

5. Encourage Statewide Promotion of Early Language Learning

6. Develop PK–16 Agreements to Establish Policies for Secondary to Postsecondary Transition

7. Develop a Teacher of the Year Program

8. Work to Educate Candidates Running for Office Regarding the Importance of Language Education

9. Work to Legislate a High School Language Graduation Requirement

10. Develop a Biliteracy Seal Program for the High School Diploma

(*TLE*, January-February 2015, p. 59)

sharing with presenters and colleagues, so that they could return to their classrooms with new strategies that would *transform* learning.

The January-February 2015 issue of *TLE* offered the first of a series of valuable focus topics, "Moving Along the Proficiency Continuum," with an introduction by Chantal Thompson of Brigham Young University, who mentioned that it had been thirty years since the publication of the seminal issue of *Teaching For Proficiency, The Organizing Principle* in the ACTFL Foreign Language Education Series (Higgs, 1984). The endless search for the Holy Grail of language teaching had still not been fruitful; so much was on the methodological menu that the "eclectic approach" had become the *plat du jour*. Instead of searching for one definitive approach to language teaching, the profession now realized the need to identify an organizing principle by which various methods, approaches, materials, and curricula might begin to make collective sense (Alice C. Omaggio, [1984]. The proficiency-oriented classroom, in *Teaching for Proficiency, The Organizing Principle. The ACTFL Foreign Language Education Series, 15,* 44). That organizing principle was the ACTFL Proficiency Guidelines, which "describe and measure [the] continuum [of real-world tasks and contexts] in terms of actual linguistic and communicative development" (*TLE,* January-February 2015, p. 24). The Proficiency Guidelines have since given rise to national world-readiness standards, performance descriptors for language learners, and such performance assessment measures as the OPI, the IPA, and the AAPPL.

One of ACTFL's top policy and advocacy goals for 2014 was to ask the American Academy of Arts & Sciences (AAAS) to conduct a study on "how language learning influences economic growth, cultural diplomacy, the productivity of future generations, and fulfillment of all Americans" (*TLE,* January-February 2015, p. 58). On November 20, 2014, a bipartisan group of four

U.S. senators wrote that request (see Appendix D) which was signed by Senators Mark Kirk (R-IL), Brian Schatz (D-HI), Orrin Hatch (R-UT), and Tammy Baldwin (D-WI). Reps. Leonard Lance (R-NJ), Rush Holt (D-NJ), Don Young (R-AK), and David E. Price (D-NC) sent a very similar letter the following day.

As a result, a July 30 ACTFL press release announced that Marty Abbott was invited to participate in a newly formed AAAS Commission on Language Learning:

> *…a national effort to examine the current state of U.S. language education, to project what the nation's education needs will be in the future, and to offer recommendations for ways to meet those needs…. The Commission will work with scholarly and professional organizations around the country to gather available research about the benefits of language instruction at every educational level, from pre-school through lifelong learning, and will help to initiate a nationwide conversation about languages and international education. It will study all the ways in which Americans receive language education, from classes in traditional academic settings to government programs to workplace enrichment, in order to identify best practices and opportunities for improvement. The last major, national report on language learning was* Strength Through Wisdom: A Critique of U.S. Capability, *published in 1979 by the President's Commission on Foreign Languages and International Studies. (Retrieved from http://www.actfl.org/news/press-releases/actfl-executive-director-appointed-aaas-commission-conduct-national-study-language-learning).*

President Van Houten said:

> *Much like how the report 'Rising Above the Gathering Storm' created the political will for the America COMPETES Act, ACTFL believes the results of the AAAS study will help*

lawmakers understand language learning in an economic context and lead them to take transformative legislative action to expand support for language learning. We look forward to working with the American Academy of Arts and Sciences over the course of their study.

ACTFL was also to work with AAAS to coordinate the report's release with the launch of a public awareness campaign, *Lead with Languages* (see http://www. leadwithlanguages.org/), which would initiate a sustained movement to make language instruction a national priority and to create a new generation of Americans competent in other languages and cultures.

Founded in 1780, the AAAS is one of the country's oldest learned societies and independent policy research centers, convening leaders from the academic, business, and government sectors to respond to the challenges facing the national and the world. AAAS dates from the period when Latin and French were integral parts of most schools' curricula.

In 2015, ACTFL was undertaking an important study to determine what listening and reading proficiency levels may be attained after several years of college language study. As a result of the 2012 revision of the ACTFL Proficiency Guidelines and the development of the ACTFL Interpretive Listening and Reading Proficiency Tests (LPTs and RPTs) in a number of languages, measurement of interpretive listening and reading proficiency levels of U.S. college students was now possible. The study appeared at a key time when many language educators were rediscovering interpretive skills and their role in higher education. In addition, since receptive skills develop faster than productive ones, the productive skills were poised to move beyond the Intermediate-Mid threshold. As the *TLE* article on this subject (March-April 2015, p. 11) concluded:

If, in fact, it is the case that professional (Advanced) levels of proficiency may be achieved in interpretive skills and can be documented, this may give a boost to foreign language departments and their students by documenting these professional skills for students completing a language minor, or perhaps even after a 2-year foreign language requirement. This is particularly important with respect to the global workplace in the 21ˢᵗ century, in which high levels of interpretive listening and reading proficiency are crucial.

The August-September 2015 issue of *TLE* (pp. 10-12) ran an article on John B. Carroll's landmark study analyzing the oral proficiency of students in language programs in the U.S., which was first profiled in the first issue of *FLA* in 1967. This new 2014–2015 study promised to be the "next major milestone in our professional understanding of how students acquire language—this time focusing on interpretive reading and listening" (*TLE*, August-September 2015, p. 10). ACTFL partnered with LTI in conducting the *ACTFL Listening and Reading Proficiency Benchmark Study*, gathering data from close to 4,000 assessments of college students in two modalities (reading and listening), yielding approximately 8,000 tests. These students came from 22 colleges and universities with data from seven world languages: Spanish, French, German, Russian,

Italian, Portuguese, and Japanese. The study explored three research questions:

1. Are professional (advanced) levels of proficiency in the interpretive modes possible in college foreign language programs?
2. What is the relationship between the interpretive and productive modes in second-language acquisition?
3. What role does language distance play (i.e., similarity of the language to one's native language; for example, for native English speakers, Spanish is a Category I language, and Korean is a Category IV)? (*TLE*, August-September 2015, p. 11)

The complete benchmark study appeared in the fall of 2015.

Following up on the 2013 position statement "Languages as a Core Component of Education for All Students [Appendix F]" and continuing ACTFL's ongoing emphasis on proficiency, the organization published a poster, "Oral Proficiency Levels in the Workplace," emphasizing the main language functions a learner can do with full control at each of the major levels of proficiency. The poster was also included in the October/November 2015 issue of *TLE*. Through sharing the poster's information with language learners, parents, administrators, and other stakeholders, the vital role of the importance of functional language ability in the workplace, in the global economy, and in economic competitiveness would be stressed (Fig. 4, p. 176).

In August 2015, ACTFL also announced a new initiative: the Languages and Literacy Collaboration Center (LLCC), to investigate changes in literacy and their effects on learning a second language. This initiative was funded through a grant from the Bill and Melinda Gates Foundation to create a virtual resource center and meeting place for educators and their colleagues from across the U.S. As Donna Clementi

Languages and Literacy Collaboration Center Offerings

mentioned in her article, "Building Literacies in the 21st Century," the ongoing technological revolution had resulted in an expanded definition of what it means to be 'literate' in today's world (*TLE*, August-September 2015, pp. 20–21). Formerly, literacy was defined as the ability to read and write, but by now it had evolved into multiple, multimodal, and multifaceted literacies—"new literacies." "Literacy in the 21st century requires learners to develop new skills and competencies in order to successfully communicate with people locally and globally." Through participation in the LLCC, teams had access to:

- up-to-date articles and resources focused on literacy;
- a library of model units and lessons created by participating literacy teams;
- online discussions related to the development and assessment of the six literacy competencies;
- webinar series on literacy development through the teaching of world languages; and

Figure 4. Oral Proficiency Levels in the Workplace
(Retrieved from http://www.actfl.org/sites/default/files/pdfs/TLE_pdf/OralProficiencyWorkplacePoster.pdf)

ORAL PROFICIENCY LEVELS IN THE WORKPLACE

ACTFL Level	ILR	Language Functions	Corresponding Professions/Positions*	Examples of Who Is Likely to Function at This Level
Distinguished	5 / 4	Ability to tailor language to specific audience, persuade, negotiate. Deal with nuance and subtlety.	Foreign Service: Diplomat, Contract Negotiator, International Specialist, Intelligence Specialist	• Highly articulate, professionally specialized native speakers • Language learners with extended (17 years) and current professional and/or educational experience in the target culture
Superior	3	Discuss topics extensively, support opinions, hypothesize. Deal with linguistically unfamiliar situations.	University Language Professor, Financial Services Marketing Consultant, Foreign Area Officer, Lawyer, Judge, Court Interpreter	• Well-educated native speakers • Educated language learners with extended professional and/or educational experience in the target language environment
Advanced High	2+	Narrate and describe in past, present, and future. Deal effectively with an unanticipated complication.	Physician, Human Resources Communications Consultant, Financial Services Senior Consultant, Quality Assurance Specialist, Marketing Manager, Financial Advisor, Broker, Military Linguist, Translation Officer	• Language learners with graduate degrees in language or a related area and extended educational experience in target environment
Advanced Mid			Banking and Investment Services Customer Service Representative, Fraud Specialist, Account Executive, Medical Interpreter, Patient Advocate, Court Stenographer, Court Interpreter, Human Resources Benefits Specialist, Technical Service Agent, Collections Representative, Estimating Coordinator	• Heritage speakers, informal learners, non-academic learners who have significant contact with language • Undergraduate majors with year-long study in the target language culture
Advanced Low	2		K–12 Language Teacher, Nurse, Social Worker, Claims Processor, Police Officer, Maintenance Administrator, Billing Clerk, Legal Secretary, Legal Receptionist, 911 Dispatcher, Consumer Products Customer Services Representative, Retail Services Personnel	• Undergraduate language majors
Intermediate High	1+	Create with language, initiate, maintain, and bring to a close simple conversations by asking and responding to simple questions.	Fire Fighter, Utilities Installer, Auto Inspector, Aviation Personnel, Missionary, Tour Guide	• Language learners following 6–8 year sequences of study (e.g., AP) or 4–6 semester college sequences
Intermediate Mid			Cashier, Sales Clerk (highly predictable contexts), Receptionist	
Intermediate Low	1			• Language learners following 4-year high school sequence or 2-semester college sequence • Language learners following an immersion language program in Grades K–6
Novice High	0+	Communicate minimally with formulaic and rote utterances, lists, and phrases.		• Language learners following content-based language program in Grades K–6
Novice Mid	0			• Language learners following 2 years of high school language study
Novice Low				

*The levels of proficiency associated with each of the positions above are minimal levels of oral proficiency based on task analyses. The minimal levels were determined by subject matter experts from companies and agencies who use ACTFL proficiency tests.

Note: The important messages reinforced by this chart include (1) Two years of studying a language is NOT sufficient; (2) The professions or positions that correspond to each proficiency level are based on analysis of the minimal language requirements for each job, determined by experts who use ACTFL proficiency tests; and (3) Studying a language may get a person to the Advanced levels, but experiences immersed in the environment of the target language and culture are needed to reach the highest levels (*TLE*, October/November 2015, p. 9)

- webinar series on determining the effectiveness of new instructional strategies through exploratory practice. (*TLE*, August-September 2015, p. 21)

The LLCC was fully operational by the 2015 ACTFL annual meeting in San Diego, CA. *TLE* announced the focus topics for its 2016 issues:

- January/February — Implementing the World-Readiness Standards
- March/April — Creating Standards-Based Assessment, Evaluation, and Grading
- August/September — Empowering Educators
- October/November — Connecting Literacy and Language Learning

Jacque Bott Van Houten opened the 2015 annual meeting in San Diego at the general session by engaging in a conversation with former CNN correspondent Susan Candiotti, a dedicated supporter of language education. They discussed the importance of connectivity in today's global workplace. Rick Steves, the famous author and television personality who focuses on European travel, delivered the inspiring keynote address.

At that meeting, nearly 7,000 attendees took part "in the largest annual professional development opportunity for language educators" (*TLE*, January/February 2016, Vol. 11, Issue 1, p. 18), which held 879 different educational sessions, events, and meetings, including pre-convention workshops, educational and exhibitor sessions, in addition to roundtable and poster sessions, Teacher of the Year (TOY) talks, and three plenary sessions: "The Inspiration Behind the Science of Language Learning," Global Engagement: Stories from Around the World," "Research Profiles—Phase III: Using Research to Transform Professional Practice." More than 43% of the attendees were first-timers, and 95% were teachers at all levels: 53% K–12, 43% postsecondary. Edward Zarrow, a Latin teacher at Westwood High School, Westwood, MA, was named 2016 National Language Teacher of the Year.

In early December, President Obama signed into law the new version of the Elementary and Secondary Education Act. This replaced No Child Left Behind (NCLB), which was passed in 2002 and expired in 2007. Now called the Every Student Succeeds Act (ESSA), this overarching law defines federal involvement in K–12 education. It was supported by large majorities of both Republicans and Democrats in a joint House-Senate panel. The ESSA will:

- put more control of education back into the hands of states and school districts;
- end the one-size-fits-all scoring system known as "Adequate Yearly Progress;"
- give more flexibility to school districts in how they use federal dollars to educate students and enable states to determine how to measure student achievement and school performance;
- allow states and districts to determine which assessments and curricula work best for students and their teachers;
- prohibit the federal government from requiring states to adopt Common Core; and

"When we travel, we humanize 'them' and they get to humanize us. And it makes it tougher for their propaganda to dehumanize us and demonize us, and it makes it tougher for our propaganda to dehumanize and demonize them."

—Rick Steves

Pete Swanson
ACTFL President 2016

Achievements Through Collaboration in **2015**

World-Readiness Standards for Learning Languages released

Leadership Initiative for Language Learning—where more than **100** language professionals gathered to develop their leadership skills

Seal of Biliteracy now adopted in **14** states, *International Skills Diploma Seal* approved in **3** others to recognize students' global competencies

Executive Director Marty Abbott appointed to serve with other prominent individuals on the *American Academy of Arts and Sciences Commission on Language Learning*, a national effort to examine the current state of U.S. language capacity

Certifications for *National Board Certified Teachers* expanded to more languages beginning in 2017-2018

Figure 5. Achievements Through Collaboration in 2015

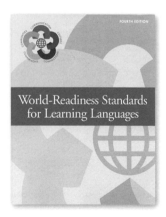

The World-Readiness Standards for Learning Languages was 'refreshed' in 2014.

- help identify schools that are underperforming and determine what needs to be done to get them back on track. (*TLE,* January/February 2016, p. 56)

Pete Swanson from Georgia State University in Atlanta assumed the presidency of ACTFL for 2016. In his first "President's Message" (*TLE,* January/February, 2016, p. 7), he pointed out ACTFL's achievements through collaboration in his predecessor's year as President (Fig. 5). Swanson also pointed out that, by integrating a standards-based communication approach to language teaching with the Proficiency Guidelines and the (NCSSFL-ACTFL) Can-Do Statements, educators can build a strong sense of efficacy—the belief that we can impact student learning—which is critical for effective teachers. He indicated that his goal was to identify, recruit, and prepare the next generation of teachers, as well as to support veteran teachers to become effective language educators—"an endeavor which is crucial to laying the foundation for building our nation's language capacity."

The January/February 2016 issue of *TLE* was focused on "Implementing the World-Readiness Standards" that were "refreshed," in President Swanson's words, in 2014. This fourth edition of the national standards was available in 14 different languages, now including Scandinavian ones. This issue could be purchased as an eBook or in a print version.

In the March/April 2016 issue of *TLE* (p. 14), ACTFL announced a change in its membership structure. On July 1, 2016, a new-tiered membership structure was unveiled, retiring the 50-year-long membership based on the career stage of the individual—Regular, New Teacher, Student. The new categories will be benefit-driven, with members having more control over the benefits they receive, as well as the format of those benefits:

- Basic: an online-only package;
- Plus: a package that closely mirrors members' current membership;
- Preferred: a package that bundles professional development with some of ACTFL's books.

Current membership would not be affected until the next renewal period.

Plus ça change, plus c'est la même chose
[The more things change, the more they stay the same]

In his second "President's Message" in *TLE* (March/April 2016, Vol. 11, Issue 2, p. 7), "Looking for the Next Generation of Language Teachers," Swanson continued his push for teacher efficacy, which led to positive outcomes for teachers and students alike, as well as in the identification, recruitment, and preparation of the next generation of language teachers, "an issue which ACTFL takes seriously." He said:

Since the end of World War II, there has been a shortage of language educators in many parts of the world. In the 1950s, President Dwight D. Eisenhower and Canadian Prime Minister Lester Pearson called international attention to the shortage of language teachers at all levels. The US Congress responded by passing the National Defense Education Act of 1958 to help alleviate the shortage. Researchers and various organizations continued to note the need for more language teachers for decades afterward. Despite efforts to raise public awareness, a shortage of language educators still exists in many parts of the United States and Canada. In fact, during his final State of the Union Address in January [2016], President Obama noted the shortage and called for the recruitment of more teachers.

The value of functional ability in another language is essential to our globalization efforts. Companies are noting the need for employees with global competence—those able to understand and affect issues of global significance—for employers rate bilingualism or multilingualism as skills required for high-growth and high-wage occupations. "They found that more than 60% of employers rated knowledge of foreign languages as increasingly important for high school and college graduates—more so than for any other basic knowledge area or skill" (*TLE*, March/April 2016, Vol. 11, Issue 2, p. 7).

In fact, at the November 2015 ACTFL Board of Directors meeting in San Diego, the organization released a new position statement that spells out the various ways educator effectiveness and student growth are best measured: "Demonstrating Educator Effectiveness and Documenting Student Growth" (*TLE*, March/April 2016, Vol. 11, Issue 2, pp. 16-17). Its concluding paragraph truly sets the stage for teachers, for students, for ACTFL:

The purpose for documenting student growth is to measure progress toward developing learners' global competence, which contributes to building a multilingual and multicultural work force that can successfully compete and collaborate in the world. Learning languages is an integral part of being college-, career-, and world-ready, and being able to participate effectively in diverse communities at home and around the world. Motivation and engagement are enhanced as language learners reflect on their own progress and see language as a tool to help better achieve their learning goals and a professional proficiency. The evidence that can be captured during a period of learning is only one indicator to demonstrate educator effectiveness. Lifelong learning is the enduring measure. (*TLE*, March/April 2016, Vol. 11, Issue 2, p. 17)

Desiann Dawson, Director of World Language Education at the Oklahoma State Department of Education and 2017 President of ACTFL, will be at the helm of our ship as we move toward the future.

Desu Dawson
ACTFL President 2017

Il faut lever les yeux
[We must lift our vision]

In 1999, F. André Paquette, past Executive Director of ACTFL, gave his own retrospective of ACTFL (*FLA,* Vol. 33, No. 1, pp. 133-34). He concluded his remarks by making a very historical yet prophetic summary/prediction:

In the 1960, the Internet did not exist, except for a handful of people; today, the opposite is true.

Yet in the U.S. the debate over internationalism versus isolationism continues.

In the "new world order," many national identities are giving way to ethnic identities—with the attendant issues of language and culture. Ironically, at the same time, English is becoming more universal as a second language.

In the "new world order," the leadership role of the U.S. (including its armed forces) has been redefined, not reduced or eliminated. The violence that marked the '60s has become the terrorism— domestic and international—that marks the beginning of the new millennium.

In our country, family has been redefined at the same time that the role of the schools acting in loco parentis is virtually passé.

And schools are no longer just schools; they are total social institutions.

At the same time, we are facing educator shortages that will make all previous ones pale in comparison.

The birth of the global village makes competence in more than one language more compelling than ever.

Finally, the need for vision and leadership in the language-teaching field is as great as it was thirty years ago.

These and other factors in today's world make ACTFL more necessary than it was three decades ago.

But we must remember to lift our vision. [...] I am in awe of what ACTFL has become and has achieved in thirty years. [...] We must lift our eyes and create a new vision for the future.

This is Paquette's charge to all of us involved and engaged in the teaching of world languages. This has been and will remain the charge to all of us, both past and future: individual members of ACTFL, presidents of ACTFL, members of the organization's Executive Council/Board of Directors, Executive Directors of ACTFL— *Il faut lever les yeux* [We must lift our vision].

ACTFL STATEMENT OF PROFESSIONAL RESPONSIBILITY

Purpose of and Need for the Statement

This Statement of Professional Responsibility is intended to reflect the standard of professionalism to which individuals involved in the teaching of languages hold themselves. The Statement is needed to demonstrate to the public, parents, students, school administrators, policymakers and media that ACTFL members hold themselves to a high standard of professional conduct. Such statements are the hallmark of many esteemed professional societies in the world and provide guidance to language educators about what is expected of them as professional educators.

Preamble

Members of ACTFL and the language teaching profession are dedicated to the promotion of language learning, multilingualism, cultural understanding, and international competence, and are guided by the following principles of professional conduct and ethical practice:

Commitment to the Student

ACTFL members are committed to developing the linguistic and communicative competence and unbiased cultural understanding of every student. Members are responsible for establishing and maintaining appropriate and positive relationships with students that respect the personal integrity and privacy of students at all times. Members advocate for open access to language programs for all students and support and encourage appropriate assessments for each student. Members establish learning environments in which student diversity in all its forms is recognized and respected and all students are treated fairly and with sensitivity.

Professional Expertise

Members are committed to achieving and maintaining high levels of appropriate linguistic and communicative competence, and cultural knowledge and understanding by participating in ongoing professional development related to world languages, including experiences in the target cultures. Members are committed to pedagogical practices that incorporate national and state standards, the best current research in language learning, and assessment programs that effectively and appropriately measure student progress in language learning and cultural understanding.

Professional Community

Members maintain a professional attitude and act with integrity when interacting with colleagues, students, parents, and the public. They exchange and share information and successful ideas, strategies and activities to enhance language learning. Members adhere to high ethical standards and practices when teaching, conducting research, publishing, mentoring, and when providing and participating in professional development. Members serve the profession by promoting language education and cultural understanding.

Public Responsibility

Members maintain the highest standards of professional conduct in their communities, classrooms, and professional affiliations, and exhibit the highest standards of expertise by maintaining their professional skills in the field of language teaching. They model the advantages of having linguistic competence in the community. ACTFL members support and advocate for effective language programs at all levels by promoting the benefits of language learning and cultural awareness and by providing accurate and applicable information to the public on this topic.

from *The Language Educator*, Vol. 5, Issue 3, April 2010, p. 47.

THREE NEW POSITION STATEMENTS

The ACTFL Board of Directors recently approved the following three position statements:

Language Learning for Heritage and Native Speakers

The American Council on the Teaching of Foreign Languages (ACTFL) and its members encourage learning environments that support heritage and native speakers of languages other than English. It is critical that these students be able to continue to develop their heritage linguistic and cultural skills in order to become fully bilingual and biliterate in today's global environment. By doing so, they will be well-positioned to live and work in an increasingly multilingual environment in the U.S. Native speakers (those raised in an environment using mainly a language other than English) and heritage speakers (those raised in an environment where the language was most likely spoken in the home) benefit from instruction that draws on and enhances their native or heritage language skills and cultural knowledge. In addition, research has shown that continuing to learn their native and heritage language benefits them in their acquisition of English language proficiency.

In keeping with the goal of an educated citizenry that reflects the rich multicultural and multilingual nature of U.S. society, ACTFL encourages the active recruitment, training, and retention of heritage and native speakers as teachers. ACTFL further supports pre-service training and ongoing professional development for all language teachers to help them address the unique learning needs of heritage and native speakers.

Successful language programs ensure the academic success of heritage and native speakers by providing:

- curriculum design that reflects the fact that the needs of native speakers and heritage students are often significantly different from non-native and non-heritage speakers;
- challenging curriculum that builds upon the existing linguistic skills and the cultural heritage and knowledge of the students;
- assessments that integrate language, culture and literature for all students Pre-K through 16;
- opportunities for heritage and native speakers to become involved in their language communities beyond the classroom; and
- systems to award credit or appropriate placement for oral and written proficiency and prior learning for native and heritage speakers.

Maximum Class Size

Since the goal of a standards-based language program is to develop students' ability to communicate, there must be opportunities for frequent and meaningful student-to-teacher and student-to-student interaction, monitored practice, and individual feedback during instructional time.

Therefore, while ACTFL recognizes the fiscal realities faced by schools and institutions of higher education, ACTFL supports the recommended class size of no more than 15 students, made by both the National Education Association (NEA) and the Association of Departments of Foreign Languages (ADFL). Since the most important consideration in determining class size should be pedagogical efficacy, ACTFL's position applies to both traditional and online classroom settings. Where larger class sizes exist, teachers must be provided with additional support in order to maintain sound pedagogical practices.

Use of the Target Language in the Classroom

Research indicates that effective language instruction must provide significant levels of meaningful communication* and interactive feedback in the target language in order for students to develop language and cultural proficiency. The pivotal role of target-language interaction in language learning is emphasized in the K–16 *Standards for Foreign Language Learning in the 21ˢᵗ Century*. ACTFL therefore recommends that language educators and their students use the target language as exclusively as possible (90% plus) at all levels of instruction during instructional time and, when feasible, beyond the classroom. In classrooms that feature maximum target-language use, instructors use a variety of strategies to facilitate comprehension and support meaning making. For example, they:

1. provide comprehensible input that is directed toward communicative goals;
2. make meaning clear through body language, gestures, and visual support;
3. conduct comprehension checks to ensure understanding;
4. negotiate meaning with students and encourage negotiation among students;
5. elicit talk that increases in fluency, accuracy, and complexity over time;
6. encourage self-expression and spontaneous use of language;
7. teach students strategies for requesting clarification and assistance when faced with comprehension difficulties; and
8. offer feedback to assist and improve students' ability to interact orally in the target language.

*Communication for a classical language refers to an emphasis on reading ability and for American Sign Language (ASL) to signed communicative ability.

These position statements were developed with the broad input of ACTFL members and can be used in advocacy efforts and when talking with administrators. All of ACTFL's position statements may be viewed in the **Newsroom** area of *www.actfl.org*.

from *The Language Educator*, Vol. 5, Issue 4, August 2010, p. 26.

NEW POSITION STATEMENT ON ALTERNATIVE TEACHER CERTIFICATION AND ADD-ON CERTIFICATION OR ENDORSEMENTS

To ensure the quality of new world language teachers, it is the position of the American Council on the Teaching of Foreign Languages (ACTFL) that programs offering alternative certification or add-on certifications/endorsements should include at least the following components:

1. A requirement that teacher candidates pass a screening process to ensure that they have the requisite knowledge and skills for teaching a world language, as outlined in the ACTFL/NCATE Program Standards for the Preparation of Foreign Language Teachers. The six content standards describe knowledge and skills in: Language Proficiency—Interpersonal, Interpretive, and Presentational Communication; Cultures, Linguistics, Literatures, and Concepts from Other Disciplines; Integration of Standards in Planning, Classroom Practice, and Use of Instructional Resources; Assessment of Languages and Cultures—Impact on Student Learning; Language Acquisition Theories and Knowledge of Students and Their Needs; Professional Development and Ethics.

2. Verification that teacher candidates demonstrate proficiency in speaking and in writing in the language at a minimum level of Advanced Low (Intermediate High for Arabic, Chinese, Japanese, Korean) according to the ACTFL Proficiency Guidelines for Speaking and Writing.

3. A requirement that teacher candidates successfully complete a methods course that deals specifically with the teaching of languages, and that is taught by a qualified language educator whose expertise is language education and who is knowledgeable about current instructional approaches and issues at K–12 levels.

4. Verification that teacher candidates demonstrate knowledge of how to teach in the U.S. educational system.

5. A required mentored induction program, through which teacher candidates are supervised throughout the first year or longer by a qualified world language educator who is knowledgeable about current instructional approaches and issues in the field of language education at K–12 levels.

from *TLE*, Vol. 7, Issue 2, February 2012, p. 27.

CONGRESSIONAL LETTER OF NOVEMBER 20, 2014

United States Senate
WASHINGTON, DC 20510

November 20, 2014

Dr. Don M. Randel
Chair of the Board
American Academy of Arts and Sciences
Norton's Woods
136 Irving Street
Cambridge, MA 02138

Dr. Jonathan F. Fanton
President
American Academy of Arts and Sciences
Norton's Woods
136 Irving Street
Cambridge, MA 02138

Dear Dr. Randel and Dr. Fanton:

We write to request that the American Academy undertake a new study, proceeding from the excellent work presented in *the Heart of the Matter*, to examine the nation's current capacity in languages, how a greater attention to language training can improve the education of a citizenry prepared to thrive in a multicultural society and a global economy, and how such preparation influences international cooperation and diplomacy, trade and foreign investment, national security, and the ability of all Americans to enjoy a rich and meaningful life.

English is no longer sufficient as a *lingua franca*—neither at home nor abroad. The percentage of the world's population that speaks English as a first language is declining rapidly; if current demographic trends continue, only 5% will be native English speakers by 2050. At the same time, the ability to communicate in languages other than English has never been more important, as:

- American jobs and exports are more dependent than ever on foreign markets;
- The American population is increasingly multilingual;
- Americans are more engaged diplomatically and militarily around the globe than ever before; and
- Challenges like poverty and disease, and opportunities in scientific research and technological innovation, all require greater international understanding and cooperation.

The American Academy of Arts & Sciences has the ability to provide critical assistance in this effort by assembling education, business, and policy leaders to examine the relationship between language learning and the nation's strength, competitiveness, and well-being.

In order to assess the national impact of language learning, we request that the American Academy examine the following questions:

How does language learning influence economic growth, cultural diplomacy, the productivity of future generations, and the fulfillment of all Americans? What actions should the nation take to ensure excellence in all languages as well as international education and research, including how we may more effectively use current resources to advance language learning?

Your answers to these questions will help Congress, the states, and local communities design effective programs to ensure that America remains competitive and strong. We look forward to reviewing the results of your efforts.

Sincerely,

Mark Kirk
United States Senator

Brian Schatz
United States Senator

Orrin G. Hatch
United States Senator

Tammy Baldwin
United States Senator

INTERVIEW WITH LEO BENARDO

Q&A INTERVIEW

with
Leo Benardo
charter member and
early president of ACTFL

Q: Much has changed in the years since the American Council on the Teaching of Foreign Languages was formed in 1967 as an outgrowth of the Modern Language Association. What would you say is the most important contribution that ACTFL has made in its history? What are the greatest challenges we face?

A: From the beginning, ACTFL was focused on how to actually teach languages in the classroom. Before ACTFL, we had no national umbrella organization to bring foreign language teachers together for this purpose. Most principals at the time stayed away from languages, many school superintendents had no interest in languages, and guidance counselors often gave poor advice about what languages students should take—so teachers often felt they were on their own.

After all these years, I'm delighted that ACTFL is doing as well as it is doing and I'd like to live longer to see it continue to thrive. We do, however, face several challenges. Unfortunately, in these economic times, foreign languages seem to be easy to drop when budget cuts are made, when money is short, and schools are being rated on reading and math skills. That is the pain of the moment, some programs that were building in the 1990s and early 2000s are being dismantled. One weakness we have is articulation—students may move from FLES programs into middle school, but they often start over in the language. The idea of an articulated program Pre-K–12 is essential; the lack of this is an enormous challenge to our success.

Another thing is that as a professional community, we really need to communicate with one another. The whole issue of communication—exactly the basis of what we teach when we teach languages—is also so important within our profession. We need to borrow and lend more than we do, to share our ideas and best practices with our colleagues.

from *The Language Educator*, Vol. 6, Issue 1, January 2011, pp. 28–29

Q: You were the second ACTFL president (in 1969) and one of the key people involved in the birth of the organization. When ACTFL was created, it brought together some of the most well-known and respected leaders in foreign language education of that or any time. The first president, Emma Birkmaier—or "the mother of ACTFL" as you have called her—was an organizer in her own right, both for women and for women in education. Many other individuals worked alongside of you both to get the organization off to a strong start. What should we know about them and what do you see as their legacy?

A: Emma Birkmaier was wonderful and really ahead of her time. She came from a higher education background and both she and the first Executive Director Andy Paquette felt that the second president should come from the K–12 sector. And that turned out to be me. So, from the beginning the idea was there that ACTFL was meant to bring together all levels. Paquette was another great leader who helped really set the tone for what ACTFL could be. Many of the other charter members were actually Emma's students—and some later became ACTFL presidents themselves. So, she had a huge impact on many people. Following her was an enormous challenge and I was young—only 41. It was quite an experience for me at that time because I was learning from greats like Wilga Rivers and Nelson Brooks. Once, when I was teaching in an NDEA Institute at the University of Maryland in the summer of 1962, Brooks (who was considered **the** authority at the time), came in and just told me: Leo, keep doing what you are doing (i.e., pushing for changes in teaching methods). It was very meaningful to me.

C. Edward Scebold, who was executive director for many years, served ACTFL well and made a great contribution over his tenure. Today, with Bret Lovejoy as executive director, I think the organization is in great hands. I think that Bret must be given much of the credit for the explosion of ACTFL in the last seven years—and I mean explosion in the best possible terms, in terms of the positive impact on the profession, the excellent publications, the ongoing quality of *Foreign Language Annals*, and the introduction of *The Language Educator*.

Q: What advice would you give to a new language teacher just starting out in the profession? Is there anything in particular that you wish someone had told you early in your career? Today—with all the new technologies and opportunities that these advances can offer the language classroom—what do you think are the enduring principles that we should all remember?

A: Number one: Keep improving your own language skills. That's where travel comes in (and in *TLE* you always have such great items focused on travel!) Teachers must continue to improve their own language and one of the best ways is to spend time in an area with native speakers as much as you possibly can. These days, Spanish is everywhere. In New York City, I can go through a number of neighborhoods and not use a word of English.

Secondly, watch good teachers. Find out—either in your school or a neighboring school or even in your state organization—who are the great teachers, and then beg, borrow, or steal time to watch them in action. For the rest of us in the profession, we need to keep producing videos of great teachers and put them out there for new teachers to see.

We also all have different personalities, so different methods may work for one teacher or another. But, look to the students as a guide. If what you are doing captures your students' imaginations, stay with it. Stay with what works.

Q: How do you think ACTFL can best serve its members going forward? What do you think current and future leaders of ACTFL can do to tune into what classroom teachers need from their professional organization?

A: We can do this by highlighting the best teachers. Using video is one way—and another is giving awards to best teachers, as many as we can possibly give. We have to find the people who are really good so that they can become models. The only way to improve is to have a model to follow. You can't do it in a university classroom where the professor says this is the best way to teach and organize your lesson. You learn by watching a master teacher do it.

Focusing on technology is important and it can be a great assistance. The outgrowth of ACTFL offering the webinar series, for example, is a marvelous development! But, of course, we still need the teacher to orchestrate online teaching and we cannot lose the face-to-face component of our profession. In the end, you need human interaction to learn language, so it is important that ACTFL take a stand on the efforts to replace good teachers with technology and software programs. You need the face-to-face, the eye contact, the direct communication of having a teacher. Technology should be used, but it should not replace teachers.

Finally, ACTFL needs to have meetings with administrators and perhaps feature convention sessions for them specifically, so they can understand what language learning is like today. We need to educate them, too.

NEW POSITION STATEMENT ON LANGUAGES AS A CORE COMPONENT OF EDUCATION FOR ALL STUDENTS

Languages as a Core Component of Education for All Students

In the 21st century, language learning meets real world needs:

- Rewards learners with a resume differentiator—the ability to communicate and collaborate in another language across cultures and time zones
- Provides access to information and collaboration in any field—including science, technology, engineering, mathematics; business; and health care
- Develops critical literacies by practicing skills to understand, exchange opinions, and present ideas
- Develops flexible and adaptable thinking, plus an ability to function in new and unfamiliar situations
- Prepares learners to think and interact in a global community

Language learning develops these 21st century skills as learners:

- Participate in face-to-face interactions via technology, internships and volunteer opportunities in the community.
- Apply their competence in a new language to their career and personal goals, broadening their thinking beyond self-serving goals.
- Become more adept in understanding diverse cultural perspectives and their own identity.

These benefits are essential for and are within reach of all learners. An early start to learning a second language, programs of immersion or dual language immersion, and long learning sequences show strong results in helping all learners achieve these results. More states are setting up processes to verify second language competency (whether learned through classroom experiences or not) and provide academic credit.

The five goal areas (5 Cs) of the National Standards become a rationale for learning languages and provide a roadmap for effective and motivating teaching and learning.

Standards-based language learning develops literacy and numeracy. By learning communication strategies to use language for interpersonal, interpretive, and presentational purposes, learners expand their repertoire to elicit information and exchange ideas, to comprehend and interpret, and to create effective oral and written messages. As learners compare the new language with their native language, they gain a deeper awareness of how language functions. As learners collect and interpret data, they practice numeracy. This process builds literacy and numeracy skills as described in the Common Core State Standards for English Language Arts and Mathematics.

Through language learning, learners:

- Develop literacy with a balance of informational and literary text
- Use their second language to access, discuss, and create content across all disciplines
- Access increasingly complex text
- Provide text-based answers
- Write from sources to explain, persuade, and convey experience
- Build academic language

Standards-based language learning prepares learners in the STEM areas. The goal area of connections broadens the content for learning languages to any area where learners might use language. Project- or Problem-based language learning with STEM (Science, Technology, Engineering and Math) content develops problem solving, critical thinking, and inquiry skills when activities are at a level of cognitive challenge that is age/developmentally-appropriate. Examples include:

- Reading informational text on STEM topics
- Using technology to access information not available in English
- Creating surveys for learners to conduct, interpret, and share the results with non-English speaking audiences
- Participating in projects underway throughout the world

Standards-based language learning engages learners through practical applications for special purposes. By interacting with new information and acquiring new perspectives that are only available through the target language, learners expand their knowledge beyond what they are learning through their native or heritage language. Learners identify local and global communities in which they can apply their new skills, perspectives and language skill in purposeful ways. Service learning, business environments, the arts, and technology provide opportunities for students to demonstrate their ability to communicate in culturally appropriate ways. In these contexts, learners build a disposition for lifelong learning while they acquire technical skills.

Standards-based language learning strengthens college and career readiness. Learners heighten their essential 21st century skills of communication, critical thinking and problem solving, collaboration, and creativity. Strengthening their performance in each of the modes of communication, learners become ready for post-secondary education and careers as described in the Common Core State Standards: responding to the varying demands of audience, task and purpose; developing collaboration skills; presenting or conversing with clarity and precision; comprehending as well as critiquing; valuing evidence; and using technology and digital media strategically and capably. These skills are also identified as essential for all high school graduates by state employability standards and postsecondary initiatives (such as Project LEAP). By using their new language to explore interests and any subject areas, learners build strong content knowledge.

Language learning is real world education; the knowledge and skills are applied lifelong.

from *The Language Educator*, Vol. 8, Issue 4, August 2013, p. 6.

GOAL AREAS AND STANDARDS IN THE 2014 REVISION WORLD-READINESS STANDARDS FOR LEARNING LANGUAGES

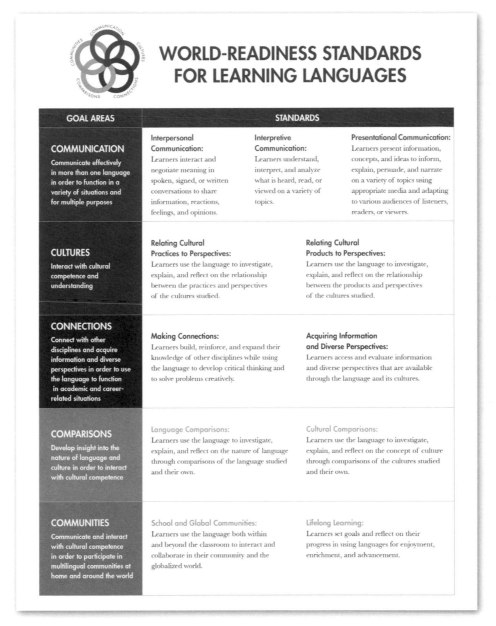

WORLD-READINESS STANDARDS FOR LEARNING LANGUAGES

GOAL AREAS	STANDARDS		
COMMUNICATION Communicate effectively in more than one language in order to function in a variety of situations and for multiple purposes	**Interpersonal Communication:** Learners interact and negotiate meaning in spoken, signed, or written conversations to share information, reactions, feelings, and opinions.	**Interpretive Communication:** Learners understand, interpret, and analyze what is heard, read, or viewed on a variety of topics.	**Presentational Communication:** Learners present information, concepts, and ideas to inform, explain, persuade, and narrate on a variety of topics using appropriate media and adapting to various audiences of listeners, readers, or viewers.
CULTURES Interact with cultural competence and understanding	**Relating Cultural Practices to Perspectives:** Learners use the language to investigate, explain, and reflect on the relationship between the practices and perspectives of the cultures studied.	**Relating Cultural Products to Perspectives:** Learners use the language to investigate, explain, and reflect on the relationship between the products and perspectives of the cultures studied.	
CONNECTIONS Connect with other disciplines and acquire information and diverse perspectives in order to use the language to function in academic and career-related situations	**Making Connections:** Learners build, reinforce, and expand their knowledge of other disciplines while using the language to develop critical thinking and to solve problems creatively.	**Acquiring Information and Diverse Perspectives:** Learners access and evaluate information and diverse perspectives that are available through the language and its cultures.	
COMPARISONS Develop insight into the nature of language and culture in order to interact with cultural competence	**Language Comparisons:** Learners use the language to investigate, explain, and reflect on the nature of language through comparisons of the language studied and their own.	**Cultural Comparisons:** Learners use the language to investigate, explain, and reflect on the concept of culture through comparisons of the cultures studied and their own.	
COMMUNITIES Communicate and interact with cultural competence in order to participate in multilingual communities at home and around the world	**School and Global Communities:** Learners use the language both within and beyond the classroom to interact and collaborate in their community and the globalized world.	**Lifelong Learning:** Learners set goals and reflect on their progress in using languages for enjoyment, enrichment, and advancement.	

ACTFL Position Statement on Global Competence

In August 2014, the ACTFL Board of Directors approved a new Position Statement on Global Competence. Below is the complete statement:

The ability to communicate with respect and cultural understanding in more than one language is an essential element of global competence.* This competence is developed and demonstrated by investigating the world, recognizing and weighing perspectives, acquiring and applying disciplinary and interdisciplinary knowledge, communicating ideas, and taking action. Global competence is fundamental to the experience of learning languages whether in classrooms, through virtual connections, or via everyday experiences. Language learning contributes an important means to communicate and interact in order to participate in multilingual communities at home and around the world. This interaction develops the disposition to explore the perspectives behind the products and practices of a culture and to value such intercultural experiences.

The Need for Global Competence:
Global competence is vital to successful interactions among diverse groups of people locally, nationally, and internationally. This diversity continues to grow as people move from city to city and country to country. The need to communicate with someone of a different language or culture may arise at any time; knowing more than one language prepares one to know how, when, and why to say what to whom.

Need in the Global Economy: Import and export data demonstrate the interconnectedness of the economies of countries across the globe; jobs increasingly depend on collaborating with clients/customers who speak other languages and contribute diverse perspectives and ideas; employers identify cultural knowledge and understanding plus communication skills in more than one language as increasingly important in their hiring.

Need in Diplomacy/Defense: The military identifies its mission balanced between defense/peace-keeping around the world and building connections with citizens in areas facing unrest or war; training of service personnel includes cultural sensitivity, understanding of diverse perspectives, and strategies for communicating with local populations speaking other languages.

Need in Global Problem-Solving: Issues related to the environment, health, and innovation require collaboration across borders; creative solutions are more likely to occur when knowledge and unique perspectives and insights are shared.

Need in Diverse Communities: Opportunities to interact with people who speak other languages and who have different cultural practices, products, and perspectives are increasing in each community; heritage communities are supported when their languages and cultures are valued rather than eliminated.

Need in Personal Growth and Development: Global competence—the ability to interact and communicate with people from other cultures—opens doors to new relationships, knowledge, and experiences.

Describing Global Competence:
Global competence is the ability to:
1. Communicate in the language of the people with whom one is interacting.
2. Interact with awareness, sensitivity, empathy, and knowledge of the perspectives of others.
3. Withhold judgment, examining one's own perspectives as similar to or different from the perspectives of people with whom one is interacting.
4. Be alert to cultural differences in situations outside of one's culture, including noticing cues indicating miscommunication or causing an inappropriate action or response in a situation.
5. Act respectfully according to what is appropriate in the culture and the situation where everyone is not of the same culture or language background, including gestures, expressions, and behaviors.
6. Increase knowledge about the products, practices, and perspectives of other cultures.

Means to Achieve Global Competence:
Individuals will follow different pathways to reach global competence. Developing global competence is a process that needs to be embedded in learning experiences in languages and all subject areas from prekindergarten through postsecondary. Identified by the various initiatives around this common goal, effective practices include the following actions:
1. Recognize the multiplicity of factors that influence who people are and how they communicate.
2. Investigate and explain cultural differences as well as similarities, looking beneath the surface of stereotypes.
3. Examine events through the lens of media from different countries and cultures.
4. Collaborate to share ideas, discuss topics of common interest, and solve mutual problems.
5. Reflect on one's personal experiences across cultures to evaluate personal feelings, thoughts, perceptions, and reactions.

* Global competence is a critical component of education in the 21st century, as reflected in national initiatives focused on literacy and STEM at the PK–12 level and included in the essential learning outcomes of the Liberal Education and America's Promise (LEAP) program of the Association of American Colleges and Universities (AAC&U).

Appendices

Appendix A — Presidents of ACTFL

Throughout its history, ACTFL has benefited from the outstanding and unselfish leadership of the top professionals in language education. This list of ACTFL Past Presidents is truly a Hall of Fame of the outstanding teachers and administrators who have made this organization a dynamic, respected voice for languages. Their vision and dedication should be an inspiration for all those who will follow in their footsteps.

Emma Marie Birkmaier†

Leo Benardo†
(1968-1970)

Lester McKim†
(1969-1971)

Lowell Dunham†
(1970-1973)

Gail Hutchinson Eubanks†
(1971-1973)

Jermaine Arendt†
(1972-1974)

Carl Dellaccio†
(1973-1975)

Frank M. Grittner†
(1974-1976)

Note: ACTFL Presidents serve for three years—the first year as President-elect, the second as President, and the third as Past President. The dates in parentheses indicate the full term of each President. The year of the presidency is the middle of the three years, i.e., 1993-1995 = 1993 President-elect, 1994 President, 1995 Past President.
† - Deceased

Helen P. Warriner-Burke
(1975-1977)

Howard B. Altman†
(1976-1978)

Lorraine A. Strasheim†
(1977-1979)

Jane M. Bourque†
(1978-1980)

Dale L. Lange
(1979-1981)

Thomas H. Geno
(1980-1982)

Charles R. Hancock†
(1981-1983)

Robert Gilman
(1982-1984)

Helene Zimmer-Loew
(1983-1985)

William N. Hatfield
(1984-1986)

Alice C. Omaggio
(1985-1987)

Jacqueline Benevento
(1986-1988)

Toby Tamarkin
(1987-1989)

Robert J. Ludwig†
(1988-1990)

Diane Birckbichler
(1989-1991)

Lynn Sandstedt†
(1990-1992)

Gerard L. Ervin
(1991-1993)

Ray T. Clifford
(1992-1994)

Robert M. Terry
(1993-1995)

Kathleen M. Riordan
(1994-1996)

Valorie S. Babb†
(1995-1997)

Ann Tollefson
(1996-1998)

Elizabeth Hoffman
(1997-1999)

Emily Spinelli
(1998-2000)

Paul A. Garcia
(1999-2001)

June K. Phillips
(2000-2002)

Christine L. Brown
(2001-2003)

Martha Abbott
(2002-2004)

Thomas Keith Cothrun
(2003-2005)

Audrey Heining-Boynton
(2004-2006)

Paul Sandrock
(2005-2007)

Rita A. Oleksak
(2006-2008)

Ray T. Clifford
(2007-2009)

Janine Erickson
(2008-2010)

Eileen Glisan
(2009-2011)

Barbara (Rupert) Mondloch
(2010-2012)

David McAlpine
(2011-2013)

Toni Theisen
(2012-2014)

Mary Lynn Redmond
(2013-2015)

Jacque Van Houten
(2014-2016)

Peter Swanson
(2015-2017)

Desa Dawson
(2017-2019)

Executive Directors

André Paquette
1967–1970

C. Edward Scebold
1970–2001

Linda M. Wallinger
2001

Bret Lovejoy
2002–2011

Martha G. Abbott
2011–Present

Appendix B — Members of the Executive Council/ Board of Directors 1967–2016

1968
Clara Ashley (1968–1971)
Kai-Yu Hsu (1968–1971)
Gail Hutchinson (1968–1971)
Jack Stein (1968–1971)
Elizabeth Keesee (1968–1971)
Joe Malik, Jr. (1968–1971)
Barbara Ort (1968–1971)

1969
Jean Carduner (1969–1972)
Frank Grittner (1969–1972)

1970
Edward H. Bourque (1970–1973)
Mari–Luci Ulibarri (1970–1973)

1971
Lois Ellsworth (1971–1974)
Henry W. Hoge (1971–1974)

1972
Joanna Breedlove Crane
(1971– 1973)
Helen Warriner (1972–1975)

1973
Richard Scanlan (1973–1976)
William De Lorenzo (1973–1976)

1974
Charles R. Hancock (1974–1977)
Lorraine A. Strasheim (1974–1977)
John B. Tsu (1974–1977)

1975
Samuel Lieberman (1975–1978)
Gladys M. Simpson (1975–1978)

1976
Harold B. Wingard (1976–1979)
Helen H. Jorstad (1976–1979)

1977
Frederick L. Jenks (1977–1980)
Genelle Morain (1977–1980)
Anthony Gardisnik (1977–1980)

1978
Helene Zimmer-Loew (1978–1981)
Lynn A. Sandstedt (1978–1981)

1979
Renate A. Schulz (1979–1982)
Toby Tamarkin (1979–1982)

1980
Anne A. Beusch (1980–1983)
Carol L. Sparks (1980–1983)
Joseph A. Tursi (1980–1983)

1981
Jacqueline Benevento (1981–1984)
Robert C. Lafayette (1981–1984)

1982
John L. D. Clark (1982–1985)
Rosanne Royer (1982–1985)

1983
Sr. Eloise Therese Mescall (1983–1986)
Alice Omaggio (1983–1986)
Robert M. Terry (1983–1986)

1984
Gail Guntermann (1984–1987)
Judy Rodgers (1984–1987)

1985
Luz Maria N. Berd (1984–1986)
Robert Ludwig (1985–1988)
Philip J. Campana, CSCTFL
 (1985– 1986)
Barbara Gonzalez-Pino, SWCOLT
(1985–1988)
Frank Medley, Jr., SCOLT (1985–1987)
Ray Verzasconi, PNCFL (1985)
Rebecca Stracener, NECTFL
(1985– 1986)

1986
John Darcey (1986–1989)
Mary Hayes (1986–1989)
Joan Manley (1986–1989)
Hyde Flippo, PNCFL (1986–1989)

1987
James E. Becker (1987–1990)
Katherine R. Olson-Studler
(1987– 1990)
Suzanne Jebe, CSCTFL (1987–1990)
Dora Kennedy, NECTFL (1987–1990)

1988

James Becker (1988–1991)
Helena Curtain (1988–1991)
John Darcey (1988–1991)
Hyde Flippo (1988–1991)
Paula Fordham, SCOLT (1988–1991)
Barbara Gonzalez–Pino (1988–1991)
Mary Hayes (1988–1991)
Jan Herrera (1988–1991)
Robert Ludwig (1988–1991)
Katherine Olson–Studler (1988–1991)
Joy Renjilian-Burgy, NECTFL (1988–1991)
Joan Manley, (1988–1991)

1989

Manuel C. Rodriguez, SWCOLT (1989–1992)

1990

Gregory W. Duncan (1990–1993)
June K. Phillips (1990–1993)
Kathleen M. Riordan (1990–1993)
Ann Tollefson, PNCFL (1990–1993)

1991

Valorie S. Babb (1991–1994)
Stephen L. Levy (1991–1994)
Phillip J. Campana, CSCTFL (1991–1994)
Nancy Anderson, NECTFL (1991–1994)

1992

Constance Knop (1992–1995)
Donald H. Reutershan (1992–1995)
Wayne Figart, SCOLT (1992–1995)

1993

Mary De Lopez, SWCOLT (1993–1996)

1994

Marilyn Barrueta (1994–1996)
Gale Crouse (1994–1996)
Emily Spinelli (1994–1997)
Susan (Suki) Vance, PNCFL (1994–1996)

1995

Celeste Carr, NECTFL (1995–1998)
Paul A. Garcia (1995–1998)
Shirley G. Lowe (1995–1998)
Patrick T. Raven, CSCTFL (1995–1999)

1996

Christine Brown (1996–1999)
Anne Fountain, SCOLT (1996–1999)
Robert Robison (1996–1999)

1997

Gordon S. Hale, SWCOLT (1997–2000)

1998

Virginia Gramer (1998–2001)
Audrey Heining–Boynton (1998–2001)
Deborah Parks, PNCFL (1998–2001)
Alfred N. Smith (1998–2001)

1999

Martha Abbott, NECTFL (1999–2002)
Harry L. Rosser (1999–2002)
Paul Sandrock, CSCTFL (1999–2002)
Jody Thrush (1999–2002)

2000

Carl Falsgraf (2000–2003)
Rita A. Oleksak (2000–2003)
Robert M. Terry (2000–2003)

2001

Janine Erickson, SWCOLT (2001–2004)

2002

John Grandin, NECTFL (2002–2006)
John Lalande, II (2002–2006)
Myriam Met (2002–2005)
Toni Theisen (2002–2005)

2003

Stephen Flesher, PNCFL (2003–2006)
John Grandin, NECTFL (2003–2006)
Richard Kalfus (2003–2006)
Sheri Spaine Long (2003–2006)
Laura Terrill, CSCTFL (2003–2006)

2004

C. Maurice Cherry, SCOLT (2004–2007)
Guadalupe Valdés (2004–2007)
Beverly Harris-Schenz (2004–2007)

2005

Mara Sukholutskaya, SWCOLT (2005–2008)

2006

Joyce Szewczynski (2006–2009)
Carol S. Orringer (2006–2009)
Yu–Lan Lin (2006–2009)
Barbara Rupert, PNCFL (2006–2009)
Frank Mulhern, NECTFL (2006–2009)

2007

Desa Dawson (2007–2010)
Vickie Scow, CSCTFL (2007–2010)
Martie Semmer (2007–2010)

2008

James Chesnut, SCOLT (2008–2011)
Donna Clementi (2008–2011)
David McAlpine (2008–2011)

2009

Carol Wilkerson, SCOLT (2008–2011)
James Yoder, SWCOLT (2009–2011)

2010

Lynn Fulton-Archer (2010–2012)
Mary Lynn Redmond (2010–2012)
Anronia Schleicher (2010–2012)
Bridget Yaden, PNCFL (2010–2013)

2011

Patricia Carlin, SCOLT (2011–2013)
Janine Erickson (2011)
Laura Franklin, NECTFL (2010–2012)
Anne Nerenz, CSCTFL (2011–2013)
Duarte M. Silva (2011–2013)
Ken Stewart (2011–2013)

2012

Joyce Danielson Raught, SWCOLT
(2012–2014)
Marjorie Hall Haley (2012–2014)
Thomas Sauer (2012–2014)

2013

Todd Bowen (2013–2015)
Ben Rifkin (2013–2015)
Deborah Robinson (2013–2015)

2014

Aleidine Moeller (2014–2016)
Juan Carlos Morales (2014–2016)
Lori Winne, CSCTFL (2014–2016)
Laurel Derksen, PNCFL (2014–2016)

2015

Lisa Lilley (2015–2018)
Fernando Rubio (2015–2018)
Caroline Switzer Kelly, SCOLT
(2015–2018)
Lynette Fujimori, SWCOLT (2015–2018)

2016

Susann Davis (2016–2019)
Helga Fasciano (2016–2019)
Erin Kearney (2016–2019)
William Anderson, NECTFL
(2016–2019)

Appendix C — ACTFL Conferences 1967–2017

1967

Sheraton-Blackstone Hotel
Chicago, IL
Dec. 27–29, 1967

General Session:

1. Prolegomena to ACTFL—Kenneth W. Mildenberger
2. ACTFL Can Serve the Foreign Language Classroom Teacher
3. Report to the Profession: The MLA-CAL-TFC Films on Principles and Methods of Teaching a Second Language
4. Flexible Scheduling: The Potential for Liberating Foreign Language Curricula
5. Foreign Language Learning in the Year 2000
6. State Organizations and the Progress of the Profession

1968

Park-Sheraton Hotel
New York, NY
Dec. 27–29, 1969

Opening General Session:

A Measure of Hope—F. André Paquette

A Report and Panel Discussion of the National Symposium on FLES

President: Emma-Marie Birkmaier

1969

Roosevelt Hotel
New Orleans, LA
Nov. 27–29, 1970

Pre-Conference Workshops:

- FLES Symposium II-"Managing Change"
- Secondary Symposium II-"Individualizing Instruction"

Opening General Session:

1. The Teacher as an Architect of Learning
2. A guide to the Third Annual Meeting
3. Announcement of Hearings on the MLA New Study Commission

President: Leo Benardo

1970

Biltmore Hotel
Los Angeles, CA
Nov. 26–29, 1970

Pre-Conference Workshops:

- The Supervisor's Role in Foreign Language Teacher Training
- Developing Performance Criteria

First General Session: Teachers as Students

Second General Session: Students as Teachers

Third General Session: Language—and the Intellectual Crisis

Keynote Speaker: John W. Snyder

President: Lester McKim

1971

Conrad Hilton Hotel
Chicago, IL
Nov. 25–28, 1971

Pluralism in Foreign Language Education: Opportunities and Innovations

Pre-Conference Workshops:

- Behavioral Objectives
- Teaching Culture

Conference on Child Language

General Session I: Pluralism in Foreign Language Education: Opportunities and Innovations

General Session II: The Place of Foreign Languages in American Education

General Session III: In the Beginning, A Word — or An Image — Contemporary Visual Culture

Keynote Speaker: Edward T. Hall

President: Lowell Dunham

1972

Regency Hyatt House
Atlanta, GA
Nov. 23–26, 1972

Pre-Conference Workshops:

- Is the old way good enough?—Alternatives in Foreign Language Programs
- Teaching Culture
- Black Literature of French Expression

Opening General Session: Foreign Language Education: Reappraisal and Projections for the Future
Second General Session: Foreign Languages and the International Interest

Third General Session: A Look at Foreign Language Education in the Future

Keynote Speakers:
F. André Paquette
Wallace Lambert

President: Gale Hutchinson

1973

Sheraton Boston Hotel
Boston, MA
Nov. 22–25, 1973

Many Goals — Many Roles

Pre-Conference Workshops:

- Bilingual Education
- The Francophone World in the French Classroom
- Relevant Teacher Training for the 1970's
- Humanizing Foreign Language Instruction Opening General Session: A School for Tomorrow General Session: Alternative Schools for Tomorrow

Keynote Speaker: Jack Frymier

President: Jermaine D. Arendt

1974

The Denver Hilton Hotel
Denver, CO
Nov. 28–Dec. 1, 1974

Future Shock—New Dimensions in Foreign Language Education

Pre-Conference Workshops:

- An International Workshop on the Francophone World: Year III
- Humanizing Foreign Language Instruction
- Changing Community Attitudes to Increase Foreign Language Enrollment: Ideas, Plans, and Procedures
- The Non-Language Major: Designing and Implementing a More Practical Curriculum
- How to Produce Inexpensive Visuals
- Careers and Career Education in Foreign Languages
- Extramural Funding: Preparing and Submitting Proposals
- Workshop for Foreign Language Consultants and Supervisors

Keynote Speaker: Gilbert A. Jarvis

President: Carl Dellaccio

1975

Washington Hilton Hotel
Washington, DC
Nov. 27–30, 1975

Teaching Foreign Languages—Why? A New Look at an Old Question

Pre-Conference Workshops:

- Career Education and FLs
- The Here, The Now, The Beyond— Language Learning from Within
- Teaching the Children of Immigrants
- The Teaching of German Culture in High School
- Teaching Foreign Languages for Use in Industry and Commerce
- Learner-Oriented Syllabus Development in Adult Education
- The Bicentennial and the Teaching of Foreign Languages
- Human Dynamics in the Foreign

Language Classroom
- Dramatization of Fables and Skits in French
- Workshop for Secondary School FL Supervisors
- Latin: 1975
- Extramural Funding: Preparing and Submitting Proposals

Keynote Speaker: James E. Alatis

President: Frank Grittner

1976

Fairmont Hotel
New Orleans, LA
10th Anniversary Meeting
Nov. 25–27, 1976

Choosing Among the Options to Strengthen Foreign Language Study

Pre-Conference Workshops:

- Enhancing Cultural Sensitivity: From Lifestyles to Culture
- Developing and Implementing Strategies for Career Education
- Emphasizing Communication Skills in Foreign Language Study
- Identifying and Adapting Materials for Bilingual/Bicultural Education
- Games for Second Language Learning
- Refining Skills in Supervision
- Creating Slide/Sound Culture Units
- Adapting Instruction to Students' Learning Styles
- Using Language to Communicate from Within: A Confluent Approach to Language Teaching and Learning
- Developing Skills for Intercultural Awareness and Identifying Relationships between Language and Culture
- Testing Speaking Proficiency

- Promoting Foreign Languages

General Session: The Issue: ACTFL

General Session: The Googol-plexity of American Education: Some Implications for Foreign Language Teachers

General Session: Educating Youth for Life in the New Millennium

General Session: Let's Get Moving Again

Keynote Speaker: Harold G. Shane

President: Helen P. Warriner

1977

Hyatt Regency, Embarcadero Center
San Francisco, CA
Nov. 24–26,1977

The Language Connection—From the Classroom to the World

Pre-Conference Workshops:

- Teaching and Testing Communicative Skills: Considerations and Techniques
- Developing Skills in Supervision
- Counseling Skills for Language Teachers
- Reading and the Affective Domain: Toward a Confluent Approach for Teaching Reading
- The Systems Approach to Language Learning
- The German Cultural Reader in the Classroom: From Theory to Praxis
- Piecing It Together: A Patchwork of Ideas for Foreign Language Teaching
- Ripley's Believe It or Not—English Is a Foreign Language Too! Common Concerns of ESL and FL Teaching
- Bring It on Home: Planning Short-Term Language Immersion Experiences
- How to Conduct a Successful

Workshop or Will They Come Back after Lunch?
- Career Education and Mini-Courses in the German Classroom

General Session: ACTFL's Connection to the Language Connection

General Session: From the Classroom to the World: From Student to Citizen—from Teacher to Educator

Keynote Speaker: Peter D. Strevens

President: Howard B. Altman

1978

Conrad Hilton Hotel
Chicago, IL
Nov. 24–27, 1978

The Issues: Curricula, Learning Styles, Teaching Strategies

Pre-conference Workshops:

- Proven Techniques for Enlivening Foreign Language Teaching
- Using Art as a Vehicle for Communication in the Foreign Language Classroom
- Interdisciplinary French Courses, or Let's Talk about Something Other Than Literature
- Through the Looking Glass: Modifying Programs and Providing for Change
- The Self-Actualized Teacher: Handling Your Ho-Hums and Hearing Your Own Hurrahs
- Un Niveau Seuil
- Career Education in the German Classroom
- Forward to Basics, or How to Cover the Material and Still Offer Options
- Finding a Solution to a Curricular Dilemma: High School Foreign Language Textbooks—Too Much

Between the Covers to Cover
- Basic Classroom Strategies for Improving Teacher Effectiveness
- Flexible Learning-Style Language Programs in and out of the Classroom
- Developing Skills in the Teaching of French Culture
- Teaching German Culture and Civilization

General Opening Session: Foreign Language Interdependence: The Teacher, the Learner, the Curriculum

General Session: Teaching, Talking, and Testing Tongues on the Outside

Keynote Speaker: Lorraine A. Strasheim

President: Lorraine Strasheim

1979

Hyatt Regency Hotel
Atlanta, GA
Nov. 22–24, 1979

Unity in Diversity

- National Policy Seminar for Language Leaders
- Writer's Workshop
- Public Awareness Workshop for Language Leaders
- Bringing the Community to the Classroom and the Classroom to the Community
- What's Going on in My Class? I'd Really Like to Know!
- Un Tour de France
- The Teaching of Grammar and the Development of Commu-nication Skills: Compatible Means to a Productive End
- Teaching Reading Skills in the Second Language

- UFO's—They Can Be Identified
- The Text Unifies—The Teacher Diversifies
- The Notional/Functional Syllabus: Can It Be Used in American Foreign Language Programs
- Limited Language Training for Non-Specialists: How to Achieve Micro-Communicative Competence
- A Demonstration and Discussion of Microcomputer Applications to Foreign Language Learning
- Folklore as Culture: Linking Life to Language
- German for Business and Business for German
- Instructional Fun Activities for the High School German Class

Keynote Speaker:
Nicholas T. Goncharoff

President: Jane M. Bourque

1980

Boston Sheraton Hotel
Boston, MA
Nov. 21–23, 1980

Foreign Language Priorities for the 1980s: From Theory to Reality

Pre-Conference Workshops:

- Policy Decisions—Societal Issues—Our Response
- Motivational Devices on the Secondary Level
- Unterrichtsthema: Deutsche Jugend
- Die Deutsche Novelle: Die "Unerhörte Begebenheit" in Theorie und Praxis
- Functional/Notional Materials Development and Teacher Awareness
- The Production and Utilization of Slides for Foreign Language Teaching

- Publish or Perish? Writing for Professional Publications
- The Role of Foreign Languages in International Education
- Theater in the Classroom
- Models for Curriculum-based Study Abroad and International Exchange Programs
- The Oral Proficiency Interview: Theory and Practice
- Acting Out the Nonverbal Dimension in French
- Communicative Foreign Language Teaching in the German Classroom

Keynote Speaker:
Senator Paul Tsongas

President: Dale L. Lange

1981

Denver Hilton Hotel
Denver, CO
Nov. 26–28, 1981

National Imperatives for an International Vision: Implementing the ACTFL Priorities

Pre-Conference Workshops [tentative]:

- Building and Maintaining a Successful Foreign Language Program
- Function/Notional Syllabus Design and Communicative Language Teaching
- Québec Culture, Language, and Literature
- State of the Art Computer Technology in Foreign Language Education
- Teaching and Promoting Cross-Cultural Understanding: Content and Context Treasures for the Language

Class: Teacher- and Student-Made Materials

Keynote Speaker: Jay Sommer

President: Thomas H. Geno

1982

Grand Hyatt Hotel
New York, NY
Nov. 25–27, 1982

People to People: Building Commitment and Involvement

Pre-Conference Workshops [only ACTFL workshops listed]:

- Language and Culture Immersion Workshop
- Designing and Implementing Foreign Language Exploratory Courses in Middle and Junior High Schools
- Microcomputers in the Foreign Language Program
- Oral Proficiency Interviewing and Rating
- Integrating Total Physical Response Strategy in the Second Language Classroom
- Creative and Communicative Activities: Meaningful Student Involvement in the Foreign Language Classroom
- Authentic Materials in the Foreign Language Classroom
- Involvement in the Foreign Language Classroom
- Authentic Materials in the Foreign Language Classroom
- Influence, Effectiveness, and Language Policy: A Political Action Workshop
- Public Awareness through Language Month: The Development of a Model

Keynote Speakers:
J. David Edwards & Rose Lee Hayden

President: Charles Hancock

1983

Hyatt Regency, Embarcadero Center
San Francisco, CA
Nov. 24–26, 1982

*Schools in the Community:
Bridges to the World*

Pre-Conference Workshops:

- Introduction to Microcomputers
- Advancing in CAI: A Workshop for Experienced Users of Computers in Language Teaching—Apple Computers
- Advancing in CAI: A Workshop for Experienced Users of Computers in Language Teaching—Radio Shack Computers
- Oral Proficiency Testing: A Familiarization Workshop
- La vie française d'aujourd'hui par la chanson
- Spanish Language and Culture Immersion
- Language Teaching at the Defense Language Institute, Monterey, CA
- A Functional Approach Toward Achieving Proficiency in the Four Skills
- Beyond the Classroom: Cross-Cultural Experiences for Second Language Learners
- Communicating in a Cultural Context: Discovery and Experience
- Building Language Programs for the Elementary and Middle School: Locating and Using Available Models and Resources

- Leadership Consortium

Keynote Speaker: Sheila Innes

President: Robert Gilman

1984

Chicago Marriott Hotel
Chicago, IL
Nov. 16–18, 1984

Making Foreign Language Study Count

Keynote Speaker: Richard D. Lambert

President: Helene Zimmer-Loew

1985

Marriott Marquis Hotel
New York, NY
Nov. 26–30, 1985

Citizens of the World Through Language Study

Keynote Speaker: Edward M. Batley

President: William N. Hatfield

1986

Loews Anatole Hotel
Dallas, TX
Nov. 21–23, 1986

20th Anniversary Celebration

Achieving Professional Responsibility

Workshops:

- An Apple for the Teacher: Now, Let's Review the Software
- Oral Proficiency Activities that Work
- Integrating Culture into the Everyday Classroom
- Oral Proficiency Testing Workshop
- Communicative FL Teaching at the Elementary School Level: The Realities
- Proficiency-based Materials & Techniques for Improving Students'

Discourse Skills

- Proficiency-Oriented Curriculum Development
- Teaching & Testing of Reading & Listening in L2 Learning: Immediate Recall Protocol
- Making the Connection from L2 Acquisition Research to Excellence in the Elementary School Classroom
- Developing Students' Oral Proficiency
- Reading Proficiency: Foundations & Prospects
- Culture & Language on the Brain: Adaptations for Meaningful Proficiency
- OPI Refresher Workshop

President: Alice C. Omaggio

1987

The Westin Peachtree Plaza
Atlanta, GA
Nov. 20–23, 1987

New Challenges and Opportunities

Keynote Speaker: Humphrey Tonkin

President: Jacqueline Benevento

1988

Doubletree Inn/Monterey Sheraton Hotel/Monterey Conference Center
Monterey, CA
Nov. 18–20, 1988

Issues and Challenges for the 90's

Keynote Speaker: Hank Dekker

President: Toby Tamarkin

1989

Marriott Copley Place Hotel
Boston, MA
Nov. 17–19, 1989

*Foreign Language Teachers:
A Powerful National Resource*

Keynote Speaker: Ruth B. Love

President: Robert J. Ludwig

1990

Opryland Hotel
Nashville, TN
Nov. 17–19, 1990

*Acting on Priorities: A Commitment
to Excellence*

Keynote Speaker: Maya Angelou

President: Diane W. Birckbichler

1991

The Grand Hyatt Hotel
Washington Convention Center
Washington, DC
(Silver Anniversary)
Nov. 23–25, 1991

*Promoting the Study of World Languages
and Cultures: A National Priority*

Keynote Speaker:
William H. Hopkins

President: Lynn Sandstedt

1992

Hyatt Regency O'Hare
Chicago/Rosemont, IL
Nov. 20–22, 1992

*Foreign Languages: New Visions,
New Worlds*

Keynote Speaker: Charles Osgood

President: Gerard L. Ervin

1993

Hilton Palacio Del Río & Hyatt Regency
Riverwalk
San Antonio, TX
Nov. 20–22, 1993

Enhancing Your Professional Status

Keynote Speaker:
Protase E. (Woody) Woodford

President: Ray T. Clifford

1994

Atlanta Hilton & Towers Hotel
Hyatt Regency Atlanta
Atlanta, GA
Nov. 18–20, 1994

*Languages: Key to the Past and
Passport to the Future*

Keynote Speaker:
Marcia A. Gillespie

President: Robert M. Terry

1995

Anaheim Hilton & Towers
Anaheim, CA
Nov. 18–20, 1995

*Standards and Assessment:
Implementing the Vision*

Keynote Speakers:
Protase E. Woodford &
A. Graham Downs

President: Kathleen M. Riordan

1996

Philadelphia Marriott
Philadelphia, PA
Nov. 22–24, 1996

One Profession— Working Together

Keynote Speaker: Peter Negroni

President: Valorie S. Babb

1997

Opryland Hotel
Nashville, TN
Nov. 20–23, 1997

*National Challenges—
Professional Priorities*

Keynote Speaker: Maya Angelou

President: Ann Tollefson

1998

Chicago (IL) Hilton
Chicago, IL
Nov. 20–22, 1998

Winds of Change

Keynote Speaker: Jerry Linenger

President: Elizabeth H. Hoffman

1999

Wyndham Anatole
Dallas, TX
Nov. 19–21, 1999

*Reflecting on the Past to Shape
the Future*

Keynote Speaker: Anna Deavere
Smith

President: Emily Spinelli

2000

Marriott Copley Place & Sheraton
Boston, MA
Nov. 16–19, 2000

*Language Learners in the 21st Century:
Every One, Every Day, Every Where*

Keynote Speaker:
Esmeralda Santiago

President: Paul A. García

2001

Grand Hyatt & Renaissance
Washington, DC
Nov. 17–18, 2001

*A Professional Odyssey:
Exploring New Spaces*

Keynote Speaker: Ronan Tynan

President: June K. Phillips

2002

Marriott & Wyndham Salt Palace
Convention Center
Salt Lake City, UT
Nov. 22–24, 2002

*Beyond our Customary Borders:
Language and Culture in Context*

Keynote Speaker: Corey Flintoff

President: Christine L. Brown

2003

Marriott & Pennsylvania Convention
Center
Philadelphia, PA
Nov. 20–23, 2003

*Building Our Strength through
Language: A National Priority*

Keynote Speaker: US Secretary
of Education Rod Paige

President: Martha Abbott

2004

Chicago Hilton & Towers
Chicago, IL
Nov. 18–21, 2004

Celebrating our International Spirit

Keynote Speaker: Chief Red Hawk

President: Thomas Keith Cothrun

2005

Hotel Regency & Baltimore Convention
Center
Baltimore, MD
Nov. 18–20, 2005

*2005–2015: Realizing Our Vision
of Languages for All*

Keynote Speaker: Nido Qubein

President: Audrey Heining-Boynton

2006

Renaissance Hotel & Nashville
Convention Center
Nashville, TN
Nov. 16–19, 2006

*Discover the Future...
Discover Languages*

Keynote Speaker: Forrest Sawyer

President: Paul Sandrock

2007

Henry B. González Convention Center
San Antonio, TX
Nov. 15–18, 2007

*Bridging Cultures
Through Languages*

Keynote Speaker: Tony Plana

President: Rita A. Oleksak

2008

Walt Disney World Swan & Dolphin
Resort
Orlando, FL
Nov. 20–23, 2008

*Opening Minds to the World
Through Languages*

Keynote Speaker: Neil Howe

President: Ray T. Clifford

2009

San Diego Convention Center
San Diego, CA
Nov. 20–22, 2009

*Speaking Up for Languages:
The Power of Many Voices*

Keynote Speaker: Steve Hildebrand

President: Janine Erickson

2010

Hynes Convention Center
Boston, MA
Nov. 19–21, 2010

*Languages: Gateway to Global
Communities*

Keynote Speaker: Richard Haas

President: Eileen Glisan

2011

Colorado Convention Center
& Hyatt Regency Denver Hotel
Denver, CO
Nov. 18–29, 2011

*Empowering Language Educators
Through Collaboration*

Keynote Speaker: Milton Chen

President: Barbara (Rupert) Mondloch

2012

Pennsylvania Convention Center
& Philadelphia Marriott Hotel
Philadelphia, PA
Nov. 16–18, 2012

Many Languages: One United Voice

Keynote Speaker:
K. David Harrison

President: David McAlpine

2013

Orange County Convention
Center & Rosen Center Hotel
Orlando, FL
Nov. 15–17, 2013

*New Spaces New Realities:
Learning Any Time, Any Place*

Keynote Speaker: Tony Wagner

President: Toni Theisen

2014

Henry B. González Convention Center
& Grad Hyatt San Antonio Hotel
San Antonio, TX
Nov. 21–23, 2014

Reaching Global Competence

Keynote Speaker: Annie Griffiths

President: Mary Lynn Redmond

2015

San Diego Convention Center
San Diego, CA
Nov. 20–22, 2015

Inspire, Engage, Transform

Keynote Speaker: Rick Steves

President: Jacque Van Houten

2016

Boston Convention & Exposition Center
Boston, MA
Nov. 18–20, 2015

ImpACTFL

Keynote Speaker: Mike Walsh

President: Peter Swanson

2017

Music City Convention Center
Nashville, TN
Nov. 17–19, 2017

President: Desa Dawson

Appendix D — Editors of *Foreign Language Annals* 1967–2016

Dates	Editor Name	Editor Affiliation
1967	Kenneth Mildenberger	Modern Language Association
1968 - 1971	Andre Paquette	ACTFL Executive Director and Editor
1972 - 1976	C. Edward Scebold	ACTFL Executive Director and Editor
1977 - 1979	Warren C. Born (Acting Editor)	MLA/ERIC
1980 - 1982	Cathy Linder	ACTFL
1983 - 1985	Patricia Cummins	West Virginia University
1986 - 1991	Vicki Galloway	Georgia Institute of Technology
1992 - 1999	Frank Grittner	Wisconsin Department of Education
2000 - 2005	Emily Spinelli	University of Michigan–Dearborn
2006 - 2009	Sheri Spaine Long	University of Alabama, Birmingham
2009 - 2012	Leslie Schrier	University of Iowa
2013	Anne Nerenz (Interim Editor)	Eastern Michigan University
2014 - present	Anne Nerenz	Eastern Michigan University

INDEX